CLUTTERING

CURRENT VIEWS ON ITS NATURE, DIAGNOSIS, AND TREATMENT

YVONNE VAN ZAALEN & ISABELLA K. REICHEL

CLUTTERING
CURRENT VIEWS ON ITS NATURE, DIAGNOSIS, AND TREATMENT

iUniverse books may be ordered through booksellers or by contacting:

iUniverse
1663 Liberty Drive
Bloomington, IN 47403
www.iuniverse.com
1-800-Authors (1-800-288-4677)

Because of the dynamic nature of the Internet, any web addresses or links contained in this book may have changed since publication and may no longer be valid. The views expressed in this work are solely those of the authors and do not necessarily reflect the views of the publisher, and the publisher hereby disclaims any responsibility for them.

Any people depicted in stock imagery provided by Thinkstock are models, and such images are being used for illustrative purposes only.
Certain stock imagery © Thinkstock.

In appreciation of Valerii Mamedov for beautifully recreating the cover and most of the images that appear in this book.

ISBN: 978-1-4917-4326-3 (sc)
ISBN: 978-1-4917-4327-0 (hc)
ISBN: 978-1-4917-4328-7 (e)

Library of Congress Control Number: 2014914258

Print information available on the last page.

iUniverse rev. date: 03/13/2015

With deep appreciation of the contributions of the modern pioneers in the field of cluttering research and treatment: Drs. Kenneth St. Louis, Florence Myers, and Coen Winkelman.

To people who clutter who strive to improve their communication skills and to the clinicians who choose to guide them in this challenging quest.

To my beloved husband Bertram, and children Desirée, Anouschka, Lloyd, Giorgio, Edwin and Eli.

Yvonne van Zaalen

To my devoted husband Aaron and children Raphael and Ariella, and in memory of my dear father, Abram Kanevsky.

Isabella K. Reichel

Contents

ILLUSTRATIONS

Foreword

Compared to other communication disorders, cluttering is a disorder that only recently gained interest. A review in the *Journal of Fluency Disorders* in 1996 (Myers, 1996) showed that between 1964, the year that Deso Weiss published his landmark text, *Cluttering*, and 1996, hardly 36 articles appeared on cluttering in the international literature. Actually, it is only in the last two decades, with the publication of some literature in North America, that the disorder became more widely recognized. No wonder then, that cluttering is often presented as "the orphan" of speech language pathology. It would seem, however, that cluttering is gradually finding its place within the family of communication disorders. This book certainly is a step forward.

The authors, Dr. Yvonne van Zaalen and Dr. Isabella K. Reichel, have dedicated themselves to cluttering for many years. Both have ample clinical experience with fluency disorders and cluttering, they are both actively involved in research and teaching on cluttering and take a leading role in the International Cluttering Association, as president and as chair of the Committee of International Representatives, respectively. By this book they contribute to realizing the goals of the International Cluttering Association: to increase public and professional awareness about this communication disorder. Interestingly, both authors originate from countries (The Netherlands and Russia) where cluttering was recognized and studied long before it was considered a disorder in its own right in other parts of the world. Their familiarity with some of the original sources on cluttering no doubt enriched their perspective.

There are not so many books on cluttering, and texts on cluttering are usually fraught with references to the many controversies that still surround the disorder. For the practicing clinician this may be confusing if not baffling. Van Zaalen and Reichel had the courage to take stances.

Based on their reading of the literature and their extensive clinical experience, they conclude that cluttering is a language-based fluency disorder and come up with clear suggestions, ideas and recommendations for both assessment and treatment. The practical orientation and amount of detail provided are really unique for a disorder like cluttering. For clinicians this book is a rich source of inspiration that can give guidance in their interventions for people who clutter. Some of the suggestions and recommendations included are supported by research; others, however, are practice-based and are still awaiting research evidence. As such this book also invites discussion on how to best proceed and may be inspiring for researchers in the field as well. The assimilation of knowledge acquired in the past, the personal perspective of the authors and the questions raised for future research make this book a publication that anyone in the general field of fluency disorders, and especially those with an interest in cluttering, will find compelling reading.

John Van Borsel

Ghent University, Ghent, Belgium
Veiga de Almeida University, Rio de Janeiro, Brazil

References
Myers, F. (1996). Annotations of research and clinical perspectives on cluttering since 1964.
Journal of Fluency Disorders, 21, 187-200.
Weiss, D. A. (1964). *Cluttering.* Englewood Cliffs, NJ: Prentice-Hall.

Authors' Preface

Cluttering was long considered the orphan or stepchild in the field of speech-language pathology (Weiss, 1964, 1968). The Swiss physician, David Bazin, may have been among the first in modern times to describe cluttering in 1717 (Luchsinger, 1963). However, it was not until the publications of the Austrian-born physician, Deso Weiss (1964), that cluttering began to gain widespread recognition. Cluttering did not fit into any other defined area until then and remained not widely understood until the end of the twentieth century. Beginning at that time, a variety of symptoms that were difficult to categorize began to be increasingly attributed to cluttering. There was no clear universally accepted understanding of the nature of cluttering. Since some literature about cluttering has been published in North America in the last two decades, the disorder has become more widely recognized. With this book, we will attempt to clarify the disorder of cluttering, in light of recent scientific research (evidence-based practice) and clinical reports (practical-based evidence). In addition, we will discuss its diagnosis and practical step-by-step approaches to its treatment.

Pure cluttering is rare; however, poor speech intelligibility due to mild cluttering symptoms, or a cluttering-like speech pattern, is rather common. This book describes all the forms of cluttering on this continuum. The theoretical basis, diagnostic instruments, intervention planning, and the many therapeutic suggestions that will be made in this book are based on frontiers of scientific research as well as extensive clinical experience.

Although cluttering has been mentioned along with stuttering for nearly two centuries now, this book will demonstrate that it is possible that cluttering is more widely associated with the speech of people with learning disabilities than was previously believed. During the past few decades, stuttering has been seen as a timing or motor disorder. Cluttering is a disorder in which, it appears, motor programming is intact, but planning at the sentence level (grammatical encoding) or word level (phonological encoding) is impaired due to a rate regulation and adjustment problem. This book will substantiate a theoretical paradigm explaining cluttering as a language-based fluency disorder, and will comprehensively describe the clinical aspects of cluttering management, such as differential diagnosis and treatment.

Minimal professional training in cluttering is offered in most schools of higher education around the world, according to recent studies (Ward & Scaler Scott, 2011; Reichel & Bakker, 2009). The topic of cluttering, however, deserves to be included in fluency disorders courses (Tetnowski & Douglass, 2011), and in the speech-language pathology curricula of courses in universities in developed and developing countries (Reichel, Myers, & Bakker, 2010). We believe that the time has come to recognize the importance of a deeper understanding of this communication disorder by widely institutionalizing the offer of independent courses in cluttering as has already been done in a number of universities in Europe and in the United States (Reichel & Bakker, 2009)

Chapter 1 describes the theoretical background of cluttering. The core characteristics of cluttering are clearly presented. New developments in the field of fluency disorders are also discussed, regarding the prevalence and development of cluttering, in relation to other disorders. The chapter also introduces the descriptive and explanatory models of Deso Weiss (1964, 1968) and Willem Levelt (1989), among others. The chapter concludes with discussions about negative stigma toward people with cluttering (PWC) as well as recent research on cluttering awareness and attitudes toward cluttering in various countries.

Chapter 2 starts with a discussion of the diagnostic criteria of cluttering and describes the symptomatic and theoretical bases of co-occurring symptoms of cluttering.

In Chapter 3, attention is given to the differential diagnostics of cluttering, stuttering and other fluency disorders. Firstly, the clinician can ascertain the likelihood of cluttering, by taking a comprehensive case history and using Daly's Predictive Cluttering Inventory (PCI), as revised by van Zaalen, Wijnen, and Dejonckere (PCI-r, 2009). There is an emphasis on the assessment instruments for the evaluation of the speech characteristics in various communicative contexts, and on the importance of a thorough assessment during the therapy process (diagnostic therapy). In addition, an explanation is provided regarding cluttering symptoms and differential diagnostic criteria of cluttering and other learning and communication disorders, such as stuttering, learning disabilities and autism spectrum disorder. Practical applications of the diagnostic findings are discussed. The assessment forms and norms can be found, in different languages, at http://www.NYCSA-Center.org.

Chapters 4, 5 and 6 describe the treatment of cluttering. PWC generally have poor monitoring skills and minimal symptom awareness. Recognition and understanding of cluttering symptoms form the first step of treatment. Cluttering therapy means a lot more than doing some simple "exercises." It means systematically changing speech behavior and overall communication. The modification and transfer of the new speech behaviors need special attention when it comes to cluttering. The methods of facilitating changes in speech behavior are described in various ways, such as by reducing the speech rate and improving the sequencing and formulation of thoughts.

Significant attention is given to the development of word retrieval skills during homework exercises and the transfer of newly acquired skills to daily communication. Suggestions are also offered as to how to overcome the specific challenges and difficulties that PWC experience.

Chapter 4 discusses the impact of cluttering therapy on clients and explains the benefits of integrating the three levels of monitoring (feedback loop) as proposed by Levelt (1983, 1987, 1989) into the treatment of cluttering. The interaction between the cognitive, emotional, verbal-motor and communicative aspects of cluttering is explained.

Chapter 5 focuses on the assessment and intervention planning. Diagnostic therapy is also thoroughly discussed. Guidelines for determining the intensity of the treatment and describing therapeutic goals are thoroughly set forth.

In Chapter 6, symptom-focused exercises are provided for speakers who are aware of the characteristics of cluttering. Treatment steps and exercises are detailed depending on which type of cluttering has been diagnosed. Material for therapy exercises and evaluation of therapy effectiveness are also available on the web site that has been created to supplement this book, at www.NYCSA-Center.org. Throughout this book, case examples are presented to illustrate therapeutic approaches.

In summary, this book does not merely provide clinicians with a theoretical framework for understanding the multifaceted phenomenon of cluttering; it also, and more importantly, assists PWC, their families, speech-language pathologists and other professionals by providing clinical insights into the nature, diagnosis, and treatment of this frequently overlooked, and often misdiagnosed communication disorder.

Yvonne van Zaalen, Ph.D.
Fontys University, Netherlands

Isabella K. Reichel, Ed.D.
Touro College, New York City, U.S.A.

THEORY

Chapter 1

Theoretical background

1.1 What is cluttering?

While most people around the world have an idea of what stuttering is all about, most are not familiar with the fluency disorder of cluttering. Cluttering is a disorder of speech fluency in which people are not able to adjust their speech rate to the syntactic (grammar) or phonological (word structure) demands of the moment (van Zaalen, 2009). PWC often say: "I think I stutter, but actually it is not real stuttering." Or they say "Others always complain that I am not intelligible and speak too fast, and I want to get rid of these complaints."

No one speaks absolutely fluently (Ward, 2006). Even the most articulate speaker makes errors every once in a while. Most people probably produce more errors than they realize. Different speech errors may occur. People can add sounds or words to gain some time, such as "uh" or "well." People can also repair the sentence structure during speech production when they notice that the sentences or words they just used do not have the expected or desired results. Repeating words or stumbling over words are other well known speech errors. Professional comedians sometimes intentionally employ these errors in exaggerated form to be funny.

In response to speech errors, people can say: "Oh, what am I stuttering again?" Merely repeating words is not necessarily an indication of stuttering. We call this "cluttering-like speech." If a person has a lot of misarticulations or hesitations at different times and in more than one speech situation, there is a possibility that the person has manifested cluttering.

Figure 1.1: Cluttering

Cluttering can undoubtedly be diagnosed in children of 10 years of age and older (van Zaalen, 2009). Does this mean that cluttering cannot be diagnosed before the age of 10? The answer to this question is no. Cluttering can be diagnosed earlier, but careful differential diagnostics is needed. In younger children, it is difficult to distinguish the errors and repetitions in speech production from other speech and/or language disorders. Around the time children reach the age of 10, their rate tends to accelerate. As a result of this natural rate increase, the rate control of adolescents is no longer strong, so in some cases, cluttering characteristics may emerge.

There is evidence that language planning disturbances are a causal factor of disfluencies and misarticulations in cluttering. To explain this, we use a diagram (Figure 1.7) of the mental processes underlying spoken language production, proposed by Levelt (1989) and presented in 1.6.3 and again in 5.6, as to how this model can contribute to a better understanding of cluttering. We also seek to provide an answer to the question of why some PWC exhibit disfluencies and others manifest less intelligible speech. Finally the question of why cluttering is present in some situations and absent in others will be answered.

Cluttering becomes stuttering
Cluttering can be considered a hidden disorder (Winkelman, 1993). Because cluttering and stuttering can co-exist in one person, it is very difficult to differentiate cluttering from stuttering in scientific studies. St. Louis, Hinzman, and Hull (1985) and St. Louis (1996) distinguished the fluency disorders of disfluent speakers based on their clinical knowledge. They concluded that PWC exhibit a high frequency of nonstuttering-like disfluencies (revisions, interjections, phrase- and multisyllabic word repetitions) and a low frequency of stuttering-like disfluencies. The focus of PWC on blocks and prolongations negatively impacts on their ability to pay attention to their poor speech intelligibility or normal disfluencies. Many experts in fluency disorders in the past century, and especially in the past few decades, have noted that the differential diagnosis between cluttering and stuttering is difficult because these two disorders share similar characteristics, and often co-occur simultaneously (Blood & Tellis, 2000; Freund, 1952; Mensink-Ypma, 1990; Preus, 1992; Scripture, 1912; Ward, 2006; van Zaalen, 2009). In some persons it is believed that cluttering turns into stuttering as a result of the development of speech fear. Speech fear and tension can develop based on negative experiences with speech or communication, as, for instance, by negative responses from the environment ("What did you say?", "I don 't understand you!" or "I don't get what you mean", "Slow down!"). Because the speech symptoms of cluttering are not mentioned specifically, they can make the speaker very insecure (Winkelman, 1990). From listeners' responses, PWC understand when they are doing something wrong, but they often do not know specifically what they are doing wrong.

In order to differentiate between cluttering and stuttering, the clinician should test communication skills in different speaking conditions, such as reading out loud, conversational speech, retelling a story, as well as testing of speech motor skills (Sick, 2004; St. Louis, Myers, Bakker, & Raphael, 2007; St. Louis, Raphael, Myers, & Bakker, 2003; Ward, 2006; van Zaalen, Wijnen, & Dejonckere, 2009a). The Fluency Assessment Battery (see 3.2) was developed to evaluate clients' speech and language in all of these communicative conditions.

1.2 History of cluttering research

Some of the earliest literature about cluttering was written in Europe. According to Godfrey Arnold (1970), the first European researchers and specialists in cluttering were physicians in various medical fields (neurology, paediatrics or otolaryngology). The above-referenced Bazin might be the first author to relate cluttering to a disturbance in the thinking process, when he stated, in 1717, that cluttering "depends more upon the mind than upon the tongue" (Weiss, 1964, p. 2). The French Mark Colombat de l'Isere (1849) is considered the person who first described the symptoms of cluttering most accurately, as extremely fast speech resulting in abnormal articulation and hesitation leading to difficulties in finding appropriate words or phrases (Weiss, 1964). The British James Hunt (1861) might be the person who coined the term "cluttering," in English. He found some additional differentiating criteria between stuttering and cluttering. In addition, he stated that cluttering and stuttering can occur simultaneously in the same person. In 1877, the German Adolf Kussmaul, whose work was known throughout Europe, included tachylalia (see 3.4.5) in the category of disorders called dysphrasia (see below). The European countries in which cluttering was first explored were Belgium, Bulgaria, Czechoslovakia, Denmark, England, France, Germany, Hungary, Netherlands, Norway, Russia and Switzerland. Throughout the first decades of the 20th century, many clinicians in countries of Eastern Europe followed the lead of Russian researchers in attempting to understand the disorder of cluttering. In 1934, the Russian psychologist Julia Florenskaya identified dysphrasia as an independent disorder characterized by an increased rate of speech as the main symptom. She observed that an abnormally fast rate can result in other lexical-grammatic and phonetic deficits. In 1937, Michael Khvatsev, a famous Russian expert in stuttering, "vividly described how sounds and words rumble from clutterers' lips, madly chasing one another, mixed and confused, swallowed and unfinished" (Reichel & Draguns, 2011, p.265). Another Russian, Vera Kotchergina (1969), described battarism and poltern as subtypes of tachylalia. Based on her theory, pure tachylalia reflects only a problem with speech rate, whereas battarism and poltern include morphological, lexical, and syntactic disorders.

In 1964, the Austrian phoniatrician Deso Weiss described cluttering as the result of a Central Language Imbalance (CLI). Weiss gave the following explanation of CLI: It is central (C), not only considering the central nervous system, but also considering all disorders of which language seems to be the basis. Language (L) is the common denominator of all communication channels (and not only speech). The imbalance (I) points to the deficit in language skills compared to cognitive skills, which can be overcome if speakers increase their attention to the process of speaking (Weiss, 1968).

Various other authors also discussed the presence of language problems in fluency disorders (Damsté, 1984; Freund, 1952; Luchsinger, 1963; St. Louis, 1992; St. Louis, Raphael, Myers & Bakker, 2003; Scripture, 1912; Voelker, 1935; Ward, 2004, 2006; Weiss, 1968; van Zaalen, Wijnen, & Dejonckere, 2009a). Freund (1952) and Luchsinger (1955) saw cluttering as a dysphrasia-like disorder, contrary to de Hirsch (1961), who described cluttering as a disruption of motor integration, resembling dyspraxia. The linguistic difficulties of PWC were described by van Riper (1982) as part of his track II stuttering classification (stuttering with a severe cluttering component). In 1984, Damsté distinguished between three types of cluttering: dysrhythmic (rhythm), dysarthric (phonology) and dysphasic (syntax) cluttering. The linguistic component in cluttering was further confirmed by St. Louis (1992) when he defined cluttering as a speech-language disorder. This was still further supported by Daly (1992), who defined cluttering as a speech and language processing disorder resulting in a fast, dysrhythmic, sometimes disorganized and often unintelligible speech, although Daly also pointed out that the speech of PWC is almost always characterized by difficulties in language formulation, but is not necessarily always fast.

In 1965, Luchsinger and Arnold found that 85-90% of all clients diagnosed with cluttering had another family member with speech or language problems, including cluttering (St. Louis et al., 2007). These numbers are not necessarily precise because cluttering in young children is hard to differentiate from developmental language problems (van Zaalen & Winkelman, 2009).

Mensink-Ypma (1990), Ward (2006), Daly (2008) and van Zaalen (2009) all concluded that cluttering manifests itself when language development is in a mature state and a person has a strong inner urge to speak. Reading and writing are other expressions of speech and language development. Problems in reading and handwriting are common in the cluttering population, especially in people who speak with a fast rate or in an inattentive manner (van Zaalen & Winkelman, 2009). Van Zaalen (2009) proposed a language automatization deficit model, based on rate control difficulties.

A few years later, a handbook was published, entitled *Cluttering: A handbook of research, intervention and education* (Ward & Scaler Scott, 2011). It consists of chapters written by authors of renown in the field. The handbook provides comprehensive coverage of major research on cluttering, and introduces diagnostic and intervention approaches highlighting collaboration and sharing of ideas by experts from various parts of the world. This handbook was followed by a book written by the same authors, entitled, *Managing Cluttering: A Comprehensive Guidebook of Activities* (Scaler Scott & Ward, 2013).

Cluttering in North America
About two centuries ago, interest in cluttering began to surface in several places in Europe, and then started to spread very slowly to other countries and continents, gradually becoming more attractive to physicians and scientists around the world (Reichel, 2010). American literature, however, has been less focused on cluttering than the literature of some European countries (Weiss, 1964), and most of the European publications that have addressed cluttering have not been translated into English (Simkins, 1973). European specialists in related fields paid more attention to cluttering than their counterparts in North America did due to the fact that the field of speech pathology in North America was influenced by behavioral psychology and empiricism, disciplines generally dominated by researchers reluctant to consider any condition without clear and easily recognized symptoms (St. Louis, et al., 2007). In North America, cluttering began to attract the attention of an increasing number of experts in Canada and the United States after the 1930s.

During World War II, Deso Weiss immigrated to the United States from Austria, so his monumental book on cluttering (1964) was actually published in English, and made many American professionals aware of the speech disorder of cluttering for the first time. Weiss described cluttering as a problem in the fluency of communication. In 1996 the *Journal of Fluency Disorders*, under the editorship of Kenneth St. Louis, devoted a full issue to cluttering. A research group in the United States, consisting of Kenneth St. Louis, Florence Myers, Klaas Bakker and Lawrence Raphael, have devoted much of their professional lives to educating colleagues about the intriguing disorder of cluttering. Most notable in this regard is their work on narrowing down the total number of symptoms that characterize cluttering (see 1.3). A groundbreaking book, *Cluttering: A Clinical Perspective*, edited by two members of this research group, Myers and St. Louis (1992) has had a tremendous impact in bringing awareness and disseminating knowledge about cluttering, not only in the United States, but around the world. This book has an interesting history, which is summarized by its first author as follows:

> *It was at one of the early Oxford Dysfluency Conferences that Dave Rowley and Chris Code asked me to write that little volume on cluttering after inviting me to give a talk on cluttering in 1988. I said I'd think about it. Dave and Chris had just founded a modest publishing company called FAR. I asked him what FAR stands for--he said Famous and Rich! Of course, I doubt that any of us got that FAR. In fact, FAR sold the rights of the book to a second publisher; then Singular (now Plural) stepped in the picture as the third publisher. Few copies of the book were sold, so it went out of print. The publisher contacted us to say that a bunch of those books were stored in a God-forsaken warehouse somewhere in the Southeast (Tennessee?) and Ken and I could buy them for $2 apiece. We did and gave them to our friends and students, anyone who might be interested in the disorder. Truly, during those early years, even a book about cluttering became homeless and orphaned.*
>
> (Florence Myers, personal communication,
> November 27, 2012)

In 2007, Myers and St. Louis produced a DVD, which was sponsored by the Stuttering Foundation of America, explaining the theoretical background of the disorder, providing valuable clinical insights and featuring PWC relating their experiences with cluttering. In 2011, Myers and Bakker created The Cluttering Severity Instrument (CSI) (see 3.3.9), which is designed to assess cluttering and its severity, and to measure the clinical efficacy of cluttering treatment.

International Cluttering Association (ICA)
The advances in the understanding of cluttering that had been sporadic over the centuries began to gain momentum at the turn of the 20th century. The upsurge in the awareness and knowledge of cluttering

paved the way for contemporary experts to get together in Bulgaria for the historic First World Conference on Cluttering in 2007, at which the International Cluttering Association (ICA) was founded.

With the Internet and increased globalization, a new sense of international interconnectedness has united scholarly, clinical, and consumer notables from many countries under the aegis of the ICA. They have generated a collaborative network through committees, seminars, brochures, a newsletter, and a creative and comprehensive web site. The web site serves as a valuable resource for PWC, their families, SLPs, and researchers. The ICA's multinational and multicultural efforts serve as a springboard for future research and bring all who are interested in the field closer to a full consensus as to the nature of cluttering, its diagnosis and treatment across continents, countries, and regions where PWC are searching for help (Reichel, Scaler Scott, & van Zaalen, 2012; Reichel & Draguns, 2011; Reichel, 2010).

1.3 Cluttering and definitions

"Cluttering is one of the most important disorders, not only of speech, but of language and communication in general"(Weiss, 1964, p. xi). Cluttering has been defined in many ways, due to the heterogeneous nature of this condition (Op't Hof & Uys, 1974). Many of these definitions are actually descriptions of the symptoms of the disorder. St. Louis (1992) and Bakker (1996) observed that the absence of a universal consensus on the definition of cluttering has interfered with research and with the development of effective clinical procedures. More recently, Ward (2006) advocated using the term "cluttering spectrum behavior" (CSB) to refer to the behaviors of people who suffer from the symptoms of cluttering, but who do not present a strong enough case to be diagnosed with cluttering. The internationally accepted working definition was formulated by St. Louis et al.:

> Cluttering is a fluency disorder wherein segments of conversation in the speaker's native language typically are perceived as too fast overall, too irregular, or both. The segments of rapid and/or irregular speech rate must further be accompanied by one or more of the following: (a) excessive 'normal' disfluencies; (b) excessive collapsing or deletion of

syllables; and/or (c) abnormal pauses, syllable stress, or speech rhythm (2007, p. 299).

While St. Louis et al. (2003, 2007) used a descriptive definition of cluttering, van Zaalen (2009) uses a causal definition of cluttering. Van Zaalen (2009) defines cluttering as a fluency disorder in which a person is not capable (enough) to adjust his/her speech rate to the linguistic and motor demands of the moment. She identifies a possible problem in the basal ganglia circuits which is in line with the findings of Per Alm (2011), who also suggests that the problem in speed regulation is located in the basal ganglia system (Alm, 2011).

Cluttering has been referred to in various ways in different languages over the years. Some of the terms for this disorder have been in use for some time, but new words for cluttering continue to be coined in different languages as awareness of the disorder is growing in various countries of the world. See Table 1.1 for an overview on names for cluttering in various languages.

Table 1.1: Words for cluttering in different languages

Language	Word for Cluttering	Language	Word for Cluttering
Arabic	إعتلاج الكلام	Indonesian	Groyok
Chinese	Yu shu zhang ai	Italian	Tartagliare
Dutch	Broddelen	Latin	Tumultus sermonis, agitophasia, tachyphemia, and paraphasia praeceps
English	Cluttering	Norwegian	Løpsk tale
Estonian	Cluttering	Polish	Geitkot or Mova bezladna.
Finnish	Sokkelus	Portuguese in Brazil	Taquifemia
French	Bredouillement, balbutiement, bafouillement, anonnement	Russian	Battarism, poltern, cluttering
German	Gaxen, Poltern, Bruddeln	Spanish	Tartajeo
Hebrew	דיבור חטוף	Swedish	Skenande tal
Hungarian	Hadards	Turkish	Hızlı konuşma

1.4 Key characteristics of cluttering

Op't Hof (1974) and Langova Moravek (1970) agree that identifying cluttering has always been a challenge, since most PWC do not consider its characteristics to be pathological, nor do they consider professional assistance. Wolk (1986) described frequent disagreement among professionals about the symptoms of cluttering, which further complicated the diagnosis of cluttering. St. Louis (1992) highlighted the importance of being specific in identifying the symptoms of cluttering in order to diagnose and differentiate it from other conditions.

According to the evidence-based practice and practice-based evidence, PWC have an articulatory rate that is perceived to be too fast and/or too irregular combined with one or more of the three main characteristics:

(a) Reduced speech intelligibility based on telescoping or word structure errors;
(b) A high frequency of normal disfluencies;
(c) Errors in pausing (St. Louis et al., 2007).

After discussing a fast or irregular articulatory rate, the above three main characteristics will be explained.

A fast and or irregular articulatory rate
When talking about an articulatory rate that is too fast or irregular, the key issue is not the number of syllables per second, but whether speakers adjust their rate to the time needed for language formulation. Normally, fluent speakers speak slower in more complex language contexts and challenging situations. Speakers tend to speak a little faster within easier language contexts and when emotionally attached to the subject. Speech of PWC is considered to be fast and/or irregular, although Bakker, Raphael, Myers and St. Louis (2000) postulated that if the count of syllables actually produced, as determined by using spectograms, was used as the basis for calculation, then the rate of the PWC fell within the normal range of syllables per second even though the individuals' speaking rate was perceived as very fast (St. Louis et al., 2007). We believe that this difference between objective measurements and listeners' subjective judgement is caused mainly by the high frequency of disfluencies, abnormal prosody,

and the errors in pausing and word structure. Speech production of PWC is disturbed so much that the listeners' processing time is affected, giving the impression that the speech goes even faster than measured. The problems in intelligibility are mainly caused by intra-verbal rushes. Intra-verbal rushes or speeding is characterized by reducing the number of syllables in multisyllabic words. This phenomenon of overcoarticulation is called telescoping (when syllables are omitted) or coalescence (when syllables are collapsed). The problems in misunderstanding are mainly caused by the formulation while thinking, resulting in a high frequency of normal disfluencies and errors in pausing.

(a) Reduced speech intelligibility based on telescoping or word structure errors. The articulatory rate (AR) is determined by the duration of speech sounds. The initiation of the next sound must be delayed in order to produce a long sound (with stress and emphasis). In case of an insufficient delay, the speech rate will be excessive, and will lack temporal prosody (Alm, 2011).

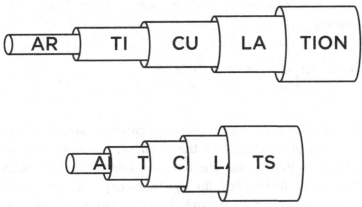

Figure 1.2: Example of Coalescence (see Dinger, Smit and Winkelman, 2008)

> *Coalescence*
>
> For example, when a person says "mation" (two syllables) instead of "limitation" (four syllables), this process of overcoarticulation, in which one syllable is deleted but also parts of syllables run into each other to form a syllable is called coalescence. In order to determine the articulatory rate of the word "limitation," the four syllables are divided by the time that the word was produced in seconds. The rationale is that the speaker intended to say the correct form of the word, but the listener only heard a telescoped or condensed version. The word structure errors resulting from telescoping (omission of syllables) and coalescing can be explained by the speaker's not having the needed time for phonological encoding of the syllables.

> *Coalescence, e.g. Word structure errors*
> *"implations" for "implications."*
> - one syllable is deleted and parts of syllables run into each other to form a syllable.
>
> *Sequencing error, e.g., "untedectable" for "undetectable" or "Magadascar" for "Madagascar."*
> - Syllables are in the wrong order.
>
> *Structure error, e.g., "prossible" for "possible."*
> - Phonemes within the syllables are wrong

In telescoping and coalescing, the articulatory rate is not adjusted to the phonologic demands of the moment. Actually, poor speech intelligibility of PWC is not the only problem to interfere with the understanding of their speech. The high frequency of sentence revisions, incomplete sentences, and word and phrase repetitions can make it very difficult for the listener to understand sentences correctly. The normal disfluencies are a result of the articulatory rate being not well adjusted to the syntactic demands of the moment.

(b) A high frequency of normal disfluencies, not being stuttering (see example)

> "I want to.... I wish ...I had...but actually lets say uhm..uhm..the day of the.. the moment I was healed healed I was not completely not fully recovered."

(c) Errors in pausing
Driven by the fast rate and by lack of inhibition, PWC diminish their pauses to incidences shorter than 0.5 seconds. This results in a lack of preparation for the next utterance, disturbances in the breathing pattern and a lack of processing by the listener.

These three manifestations of cluttering are described by Daly, 1986; Daly and Burnett, 1996; Damsté, 1984; Gutzman, 1893; Mensink-Ypma, 1990; Myers and Bradley, 1992; St. Louis, 1992; St. Louis, Myers, Cassidy, Michael, Penrod, Litton et al., 1996, St. Louis et al., 2007; van Zaalen, Wijnen, and Dejonckere 2009a, b; 2011a, b; Voelker, 1935; Ward, 2006; Weiss, 1964; and Winkelman, 1990.

One of the most interesting features of cluttering is that, generally, its symptoms appear in situations in which the speaker uses a speech rate that is perceived to be fast and/or uses a structure with a high linguistic complexity, especially when PWC are not focused enough on their speech. When PWC focus on their speech output, for a while, no symptoms are audible or visible. An explanation for this will be given in 1.6.3.

1.4.1 Prevalence and incidence

Knowing the prevalence of a specific disorder can help clinicians to be aware of risk factors and to plan clinical services, train professionals, and formulate educational policy (Proctor, Yari, Duff & Zhang, 2008). Prevalence and incidence of cluttering are not well documented in the literature (van Zaalen & Reichel, 2014). Some authors have estimated prevalence rates for PWC (examples appear in Table 1.2). In children diagnosed with speech-language disorders, the prevalence rate ranges from 0.4% to 11.5% for cluttering, and has been found to be 14.8% for cluttering-stuttering. Studies devoted to differential diagnoses in fluency disorders indicate that 5% to 27% of clients exhibit pure cluttering, while 13% to 43% of clients in clinics exhibit signs of cluttering and stuttering.

Ward (2006) postulated that cluttering prevalence numbers vary, depending on age groups and levels of intellectual development. When analyzing the distribution of the disorder, it is important to make a clear distinction between syndromic and non-syndromic presentations of cluttering epidemiology (Drayna, 2011). In clients with organic cerebral insufficiency, prevalence data support rates ranging between 38% and 48%, depending on age. Preus (1973) calculated a 12.7% rate of pure cluttering among those with Down syndrome. Van Borsel and Vandermeulen (2008) found a 78.9% rate of pure cluttering in the same population. These last figures should be considered with caution due to the fact that the authors of the latter study used the Predictive Cluttering Inventory (PCI)(Daly, 2006) as a diagnostic instrument for cluttering. The PCI has been found to be not sensitive and not specific enough to detect cluttering (van Zaalen, Wijnen & Dejonckere, 2009b).

Four major reasons can be advanced for the lack of clarity or agreement on the topic of cluttering prevalence. Firstly, there is no certainty as to which definitions different researchers applied in the diagnosis of cluttering. Secondly, there was a lack of clarity in many studies as to whether cluttering was diagnosed by an assessment, by some prescribed characteristics, or by a questionnaire simply asking people whether they thought of themselves as being PWC. Furthermore, it was unclear whether characteristics such as the articulatory rate and normal disfluencies were considered in the assessments of stuttering or other communication disorders. When the above characteristics were ignored in assessing people with symptoms of both stuttering and cluttering, for example, such people were misdiagnosed as presenting with stuttering only. Finally a lack of agreement regarding the main characteristics and underlying mechanisms of cluttering made a definitive diagnosis difficult (St. Louis et al., 2007; van Zaalen, 2009). A prevalence study based on clinical assessments is feasible now that there is general worldwide agreement as to the main differential diagnosis (St. Louis et al., 2007) and as to the belief that PWC are not capable of adjusting their rate to the linguistic or motor demands of the moment (van Zaalen, 2009) due to an imbalance in coordination in the basal ganglia circuits (Alm, 2008).

According to Dalton and Hardcastle (1993) and St. Louis and Myers (1997), pure cluttering appears to be rare. Becker and Grundmann (1971) found that 1.8% of seven- and eight- year olds in a German school manifested cluttering. In a study of special classes for 208 students between 6 and 12 years of age, with speech and language disorders, Miyamoto and Hayasaka in Japan, and Shapiro in the USA (2006) found that 1% of the students in these classes were diagnosed with cluttering, and 14.9% were diagnosed with cluttering-stuttering. Preus (1981) reported that, in Norway, 32% of adolescents who stuttered also cluttered. Van Borsel & Vandermeulen, both in Belgium (2008), found that 78.9% of children with Down syndrome were diagnosed with cluttering, and 17.1% had cluttering-stuttering. In Russia, Shklovsky (1994) reported that 10% of clients with stuttering who entered his clinic were diagnosed with cluttering. Filatova in Russia (2005) reported that, out of 55 Russian children with fluency disorders, 7% were pure clutterers, and 13% had a mixed form of disorder, with a prevalence of cluttering. Missulovin in Russia (2002) described cases of cluttering in patients who stutter due to organic cerebral insufficiency. In a survey by Missulovin (2002) of people who stutter (PWS) due to organic cerebral insufficiency, cluttering numbers varied depending on age. Specifically, 48% had cluttering between the ages of 12 and 14; 38% of adolescents between 15 and 17 also cluttered, as did 31% of adults between ages 18 and 53. In the USA, Freund (1952) found that, of PWS, 22% also cluttered; and in a later study (1970) of 50 cases of neuro-psychiatric patients with tachylalia, 10% also cluttered. Daly (1993b) found that, in his caseload, about 5% of clients with fluency disorders had pure cluttering and 40% were clients with cluttering and stuttering. Some experts believe that the incidence of cluttering tends to be underestimated because many PWC do not seek speech therapy or consider cluttering to be a minor disorder (Simkins, 1973; St. Louis, Myers, Bakker, & Raphael, 2003; Ward, 2006).

Recent prevalence studies indicate that cluttering is in fact more prevalent than stuttering (van Zaalen, Cook, Elings, & Howell, 2011; Schnell, Abbink, & van Zaalen (2013); van Zaalen, Deckers, Dirven, Kaiser, van Kemenade, & Terhoeve (2012). According to some experts, pure cluttering is present in 5 to 16% of the disfluent population (Bakker, St. Louis, Myers, & Raphael, 2005; St. Louis & McCaffrey, 2005). Prevalence numbers vary within age groups. When analyzing the distribution of the disorder, it is important to make a clear distinction between syndromic and non-syndromic presentations of cluttering epidemiology (Drayna, 2011).

Table 1.2: Overview of estimates of cluttering prevalence in various populations and age groups. Some fields are blank due to an absence of data.

Study	Cluttering	Cluttering-stuttering	Type Population	N
Freund in Germany (1952)		22%		
Freund in Germany (1970)	10%		Neuro-psychiatric patients with tachylalia	50
Perello in Spain (1970)	0.4%		Children with speech and language disorders	7227
Becker and Grundmann in Germany (1970 or 1971)	0.8% to 1.8%		School-aged children (7-8 years)	4984
Preus in Norway (1973)	12.7%	19.2%	Children with Down syndrome	47
Simkins in USA (1973)	11.5%		Children attending special education courses	
Preus in Norway (1981)		32%	Adolescents	
Van Riper in USA (1982)	12%		Children with fluency disorders	256
Daly in USA (1993)	5%	40%	Clients with fluency disorders	
Shklovsky in Russia (1994)		10%	Clients with stuttering who entered his clinic	
Giorgieva & Miliev in Bulgaria (1996)	27%	33%	School age and young adults with fluency disorders	15
Missulovin in Russia (2002)	1	48% (ages 12 -14) 38% (ages 15 – 17) 31% (ages 18- 53)	Patients who stutter due to organic cerebral insufficiency	
Filatova in Russia (2005)	7%	13%		

Miyamoto, Hayasaka, & Shapiro in Japan (2006)	1%	14.9 %	Special classes for children between 6—12 years of age, with speech and language disorders	208
Van Borsel and Vandermeulen in Belgium (2008)	78.9%	17.1%	Children with Down syndrome	
van Zaalen, Wijnen,& Dejonckere in the Netherlands (2009c)	18%	43%	Adult clients with fluency disorders	54
Howell & Davis in England (2011)		17.7%	Pre-adolescents with fluency disorders at 2 different times	96
van Zaalen, Deckers et al. (2012)	1.1%		Children aged 10-12.11	270
Reichel, Cook, et al. (2014)	1.2%		Children aged 10-12.11	85

School-aged children
Froeschels (1946) found that significant numbers of school-aged children with cluttering were enrolled in the speech clinics of public schools. Similarly, Simkins (1973) estimated that, in all probability, 11.5% of the children attending special education classes were clutterers. Becker and Grundmann (1970) discovered 39 (78%) pure clutterers in a group of 4,984 school-aged children. The prevalence number rose with age. The prevalence of pure cluttering in the 7-8 year old group was 0.0-1.8%. According to Winkelman (1990), a high comorbidity of cluttering with learning disabilities was observed in children of high school age; the comorbidity of learning disabilities and cluttering occurred four times more often in boys than in girls.

One of the latest prevalence studies conducted using the working definition of cluttering of St. Louis et al. (2007) and of van Zaalen (2009), found a prevalence of cluttering of 1.8% in a randomized group of 393 10-12 year old Dutch children. This study suggests that the prevalence of cluttering in adolescents is probably higher than the prevalence of stuttering (van Zaalen & Reichel, 2014).

Note: Not all of the studies presented in this chapter were conducted using the same definitions and populations.

1.4.2 Etiology

Although neurological symptoms are not common in PWC, an organic base of cluttering is often considered. Various researchers found abnormal patterns in EEG testing in the early sixties (Langova & Moravek, 1962, 1964). It was assumed that these abnormal patterns were caused by an incomplete maturation of the central nervous system, problems in hemisphere dominance, or abnormal central auditory processing. The hereditary nature of cluttering is pointed out frequently by both researchers and therapists. Weiss (1964) considered heredity as a contributing cause of cluttering. Seeman (1965) described 4 generations in a family in which 16 out of 18 relatives cluttered. St. Louis et al. (2007), in discussing the 85%-90% prevalence of family members in children with cluttering (see 1.2), emphasized that this disorder runs in families, especially those in which a disproportionate number of relatives stutter.

According to Luchsinger and Arnold (1970), cluttering is four times more prevalent in males than in females. Although this finding has not been replicated in other studies, therapists in the Netherlands and Norway who were consulted confirmed this ratio. The male-female ratio is another indication of a genetic cause of cluttering. It should be noted that further research is needed in order to ascertain whether this ratio will also be found in a population using the current definition of cluttering by St. Louis et al. (2007) or of van Zaalen et al. (2009).

Van Zaalen (2009) assumes, based on an fMRI study during repeated production of word and non-word sequences, that cluttering is caused by an inhibition problem in the basal ganglia. The basal ganglia are a collection of nuclei found on both sides of the thalamus. The largest group of these nuclei are called the corpus striatum, made up of the caudate nucleus, the putamen, the globus pallidus, and the nucleus accumbens. Another nucleus of the basal ganglia is the substantia nigra. The first researchers exploring the role of the basal ganglia in cluttering were Seeman (1970) and Lebrun (1996). Miloslav Seeman (1970), a phoniatrician from Prague, contrasted the symptoms of cluttering with the symptoms of other neurological disorders, and concluded that cluttering is caused by a disturbance of the basal ganglia system. Similarly, the neurolinguist Yvan Lebrun, from Brussels, noted, in 1996, that symptons of cluttering after brain damage or disease are usually manifested following damage to the basal ganglia system, as is the case in Parkinson's disease (Alm, 2011). Alm also suggested that the hyperactivation and dysregulation of the medial frontal cortex is an underlying mechanism in cluttering. He considered such processes to be secondary to the disinhibition of the basal ganglia circuits, which can occur, for example, as a result of a hyperactive dopamine system (Alm, 2011). The supplementary motor area (SMA) proper, along with the basal ganglia and the cerebellum, control the timing of articulation, and thereby the speech rate. In fluent speakers, the production of speech is monitored on various levels, mainly by auditory connections to the anterior cingulate cortex (ACC) and the SMA. "Functions associated with the ACC and SMA are (1) Drive, motivation and initiation of action; (2) Inhibition of impulses; (3) Attention; monitoring and correction of behavior; (4) Planning of sequential behavior; (5) Selection of words and word-forms and (6) Execution and timing of sequential behavior" (Alm, 2011, p.21).

Because PWC tend to lack inhibition, they may speak before the language formulation stage and/or before the speech plan is sufficiently ready. Van Zaalen (2009) assumes that impulses for motor activity in cluttering are insufficiently inhibited and/or wiped out after production. Syllables (and sometimes even words) seem "to stick." This will negatively influence the execution of the rest of the phrase (see examples).

Desirée (upon retelling The Wallet story, which is presented in Appendix D):
"It was a rainy day. A young girl called her, crying 'rainy."
Or
Giorgio (in the Screening Phonological Accuracy test):
"Impractable impractations" (instead of "Impractible implications")

1.4.3 Signals of possible cluttering

A clinician generally meets children and adults who clutter only when they experience symptoms of cluttering in their speech. There are signals known to be indicators of possible cluttering in early development. When a child exhibits one or more of the following characteristics, a clinician should be alerted to a possible diagnosis of cluttering:

> Signs of possible cluttering in young children (< 10 years)
> - A fast speech or articulatory rate;
> - Telescoping when using multisyllabic words;
> - Omitting small words (such as articles and prepositions) when reading out loud, when writing or during auditory memory tasks;
> - Semantic or syntactic errors during fast writing or speech, while these disappear in slower writing or speech;
> - Getting stuck while reading; relying on guessing while reading.
> - Many errors occur during reading at a fast rate (but not during a slow rate or when adequately focused)
> - Grapheme substitutions between /b/ and /d/.

1.4.4 Cluttering and normal development

No results of longitudinal studies following speech and fluency development in PWC are known. As discussed earlier, the insufficient adjustment of the articulatory rate to language requirements is a key characteristic of cluttering.

During school years and especially in adolescence, a fast increase of the articulatory rate can be observed. The mean articulatory rate of fluent 3-6 year old children is 3.3 syllables per second (SPS). Children between 6.3 – 11.7 years old have a mean articulatory rate of 4.4 SPS, and between 11.8 and 22 years the mean is 5.6 SPS, which is considered normal. Usually, the mean articulatory rate declines to 4.8 SPS after 22 years of age (see Figure 1.3).

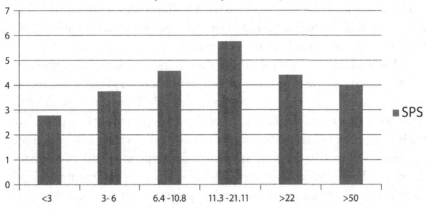

Mean articulatory rate in syllables per seconds

Age in years and months

Figure 1.3: Articulatory rate in syllables per second in children. Modified figure from Boey, 2003; van Zaalen & Winkelman, 2009 based on new unpublished data.

Based on the natural rate increase, many people first discover that they have cluttered speech in adolescence and young adulthood. Mensink-Ypma (1990), Ward (2006) and Daly (2008) observed that cluttering manifests itself only when language development is in an advanced stage and a person has a strong inner urge to speak. Cluttering is therefore difficult to identify in children below 10 years of age. There are two notable reasons for this late onset of cluttering. Firstly, the children's speech rate is still too low to have a significant influence on the fluency and intelligibility of their speech production. Secondly, it is difficult to differentiate whether errors in sentence structures are based on a disorder in language development or only on an insufficient adjustment to rate. The way to differentiate between these two factors is to ask people to write down what they had just said. People with specific language disorders will make sentence structure errors in both writing and speech. When word repetitions and sentence revisions are deleted from the transcribed utterances of PWC, then as a result, syntactically correct sentences remain that do not differ qualitatively from those produced by controls (van Zaalen, van Heeswijk, & Reichel, in preparation; van Zaalen, Wijnen, & Dejonckere, 2011). PWC can produce sentence structure errors and revisions when speaking at a fast rate, but will not when speaking at a slower rate or when writing.

The reduction of the speech rate in adulthood is a natural phenomenon. This reduction in rate is a response to the balance in hormone level after adolescence. If this balance is not present in a person with a predisposition to clutter, cluttering will become chronic.

The increase in the speech rate co-occurs with another important development: a growing level of self-reflection, especially regarding one's appearance and speech. When at first PWC are unaware of their disfluencies or unintelligibility, in adolescence, a vulnerable period in their lives, the gradual realization of speaking differently becomes more apparent. Often, this growing awareness develops as a result of feedback from people in their environment. Adolescents hear comments such as: "Man, it's so hard to understand what you're saying," "You better talk clearer," *and* "What did you say?"

Adolescents understand that they are doing something wrong, but are not aware of exactly what it is that they are doing wrong. Therefore, they cannot change their speech behavior, and tend to become insecure in their speech performance. Winkelman (1990), Ward (2006) and St. Louis et al. (2007) stress that based on this insecurity, PWC can develop stuttering as well.

1.4.5 Prognosis

Longitudinal cohort studies on cluttering are not known. Based on practice-based evidence, clear tendences are noticeable. We will discuss some of them related to age.

> Diedrich (1984) observed that the onset of cluttering occurred about seven years later than the onset of stuttering. This observation is consistent with the finding as to the direction of the age of onset of cluttering in a study conducted by Howell and Davis (2011).

Disfluent young children who regained speech control (after therapy) often return for speech therapy when they are between 10 and 13 years of age. In the early years of adolescence, disturbances in communication often re-occur. Based on natural development, speech rates tend to become much higher while PWC use more complex (multisyllabic) words and sentence structures. Their speech becomes less intelligible and less fluent. If cluttering manifests itself in pre-adolescence, an increase in the severity of symptoms is often noticed in adolescence. After adolescence, the severity of cluttering may decrease, especially when the person involved did not develop negative feelings and emotions during the period of disfluency or diminished intelligibility. It is therefore very important to actively reduce the speech rate of adolescents, by monitoring speech during therapy. The prognosis will be less influenced by the developmental increase of the articulatory rate, and more by the active efforts to modify speech behavior.

Mainly based on practice-based evidence, we further postulate that speech difficulties of PWC increase in the elderly. The reason for this increase in speech problems is still unclear. It is possible that neuro-linguistic processes, which are responsible for speech production, gradually deteriorate as people age. Another explanation can be that the ability to adjust the speech rate in the elderly gradually decreases. To verify the Fluency Profile of elderly people regarding different fluency parameters, de Andrade and de Oliveira Martins (2010) evaluated 128 people, of both genders, above 60 years of age. Participant speech samples were collected and analyzed according to type of speech disruption, and the speech rate and frequency of speech disruptions, based on the analysis of 200 fluent syllables. Participants were compared to each other according to their respective ages. Results indicated significant differences between people of different decades only in the articulatory rate (AR). For the group of individuals above 80 years of age, significant differences were observed indicating an increase in the number of speech disruptions and a decrease in speech rate. Researchers concluded that the effect of aging seems to be more significant after the age of 80.

1.4.6 Subtyping of cluttering

Differences between phonological symptoms and linguistic symptoms in the speech of PWC inspired Damsté (1990) to categorize cluttering into three forms -- dysarthric, dysrhythmic and dysphasic cluttering. Ward (2006) suggested subdivisions of motor cluttering and linguistic cluttering. Van Zaalen (2009) replaced the dysarthric and motor types of cluttering with phonologic cluttering because she found that PWS have problems in phonological encoding rather than in motor execution. Together with data presented by van Zaalen, Ward, Nederveen, Lameris, Wijnen, and Dejonckere (2009) and van Zaalen, Wijnen and Dejonckere

(2011), additional research further alerts clinicians to the existence of cluttering subtypes (Bretherton-Furness & Ward, 2012). The dysphasic, dysrhythmic, and linguistic types of cluttering can be narrowed down to "syntactic cluttering" (van Zaalen, 2009).

Syntactic cluttering
Syntactic cluttering refers to problems in grammatical encoding and word retrieval at a fast speech rate. Such symptoms occur more frequently in linguistically complex situations. The problems are manifested by normal disfluencies, such as word and phrase repetitions, interjections, hesitations and revisions (van Zaalen, 2009). For example: "*I am am very busy wor-working eh on my paper eh thesis,*" instead of "I am very busy working on my thesis."

Phonological cluttering
Phonological cluttering, according to van Zaalen (2009), refers to problems in phonological encoding and is characteristized by word structure errors (e.g., coalescense, telescoping or syllable sequencing errors) at a fast speech rate, especially in multisyllabic words. Similarly to syntactic cluttering, symptoms of phonological cluttering occur more frequently in linguistically complex speaking situations. For example: "Probly we will teetmorrow," instead of "Probably we will meet tomorrow."

In order to determine whether a client's cluttering is predominantly phonological or syntactic, one of the questions on Reichel's Brief Cluttering and Stuttering Questionnaire (BCSQ) (2010) was posed as follows "What interferes more with your communication? Planning and formulating thoughts or fast and unclear speech?" Most of the clients responded that fast and unclear speech interfered with their communication more than planning and formulating sentences. (Exum, Absalon, Smith, & Reichel, 2010). Also see Appendices H and M.

Examples of respondents' experiences with syntactic cluttering

"The cluttered thought processing can be pictured as a crash at a locomotive depot, when a sudden stop causes the thoughts to clash, run over each other."

"I also had to learn how to overcome the wish to never open my mouth again after running sentences in an unknown direction and not looking smart."

"... It became an apparent problem when it became more frequent and when I would intend to say a word, but something completely different would come out. I always attributed this sort of mental dyslexia as normal...

"Why could I not slow down with my speech, and just had to spit it out?"

Examples of respondents' experiences with phonological cluttering

"When cluttering occurs, my speech is fast and unclear or, as I say, a ball of words tumbles out with no beginning and no end."

"I had never heard another person jumble sentences into one verbal mass the way I did."

My thoughts run faster than I can verbalize, resulting in the most mosh-pit words."

"There were instances when my thoughts raced faster than my mouth could catch up. The competition usually resulted in a jumbled mass of words exiting my mouth, leaving both recipient and myself perplexed." (Exum et al., 2010)

1.5 Cluttering in the ICF and the ICD-10

In the International Classification of Functioning (ICF), human functioning can be observed from three perspectives. These are:

1 The perspective of the human organ (functions of the organism and anatomical characteristics);
2 The perspective of human behavior (activities and participation);
3 The perspective of a person as a participant in social life (environmental factors).

By combining aspects of a disease/disorder with data about human functioning, broader and more meaningful images of PWC can be created. These data form the basis for the decision-making processes in the diagnosis and treatment of cluttering.

According to the ICF (WHO, 2007), cluttering can be coded as:

ICF: cluttering a problem in rate control

Body function

b 3300: fluency of speech; b 3301: rhythm of speech; b 3302: speed of speech; and b 3303: melody of speech;

Activities and Participation

d 330: speaking, d166: reading, d170: writing; and d 3601: using writing machines;

Environmental factors related to individual attitudes

e 310: immediate family; e 315: extended family; e 320: friends; e 325: acquaintances, peers, colleagues, neighbors and community members; e 355: health professionals; and e 555: associations and organizational services, systems and policies;

personal factors:

- hasty – uninhibited – impulsive – low level of speech monitoring.

To better understand the relationship between these codes, we introduce Figure 1.4:

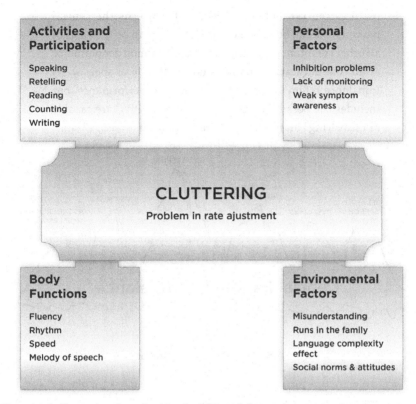

Figure 1.4: Cluttering described in the ICF model

Based on the 10th revision of the International Classification of Diseases (ICD-10, WHO, 2007), cluttering can be coded and defined as:

cluttering = F98.6

A rapid rate of speech with a breakdown in fluency, but no repetitions or hesitations, of a severity to give rise to diminished speech intelligibility. Speech is erratic and dysrhythmic, with rapid jerky spurts that usually involve faulty phrasing patterns (WHO, 2007).

1.6 Explanatory models of cluttering

1.6.1 Central language imbalance (Weiss, 1964)

In 1964 Deso Weiss described cluttering as a Central language imbalance (CLI). He gave the following explanation of CLI:

(C) It is central, not only because it concerns the central nervous system, but also because it appears to be the basis of all other symptoms. (L) Language is the common denominator of all communication channels (and not only of speech). (I) Imbalance refers to the lack of balance in performance, but includes the possibility of recovery as well. PWC are capable of recovering balance with focused attention (Weiss, 1968).

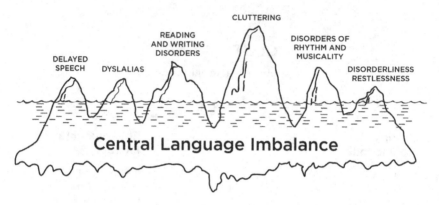

Figure 1.5: Central Language Imbalance

1.6.2 Linguistic Disfluency Model

Based on Weiss' concept, Daly and Burnett (1999) described cluttering as a syndrome in their Linguistic Disfluency Model. In a syndrome, different symptoms are displayed at the same time. Daly and Burnett described symptoms according to specific categories: cognition, language, pragmatics, speech and motor. They concluded that cluttering can be diagnosed if one or more of theses categories is affected. But, as is shown in the picture below, many clients can be assigned to more than one category, and therefore diagnosed with cluttering. The model explains all the different possible symptoms, but is not specific and sensitive enough.

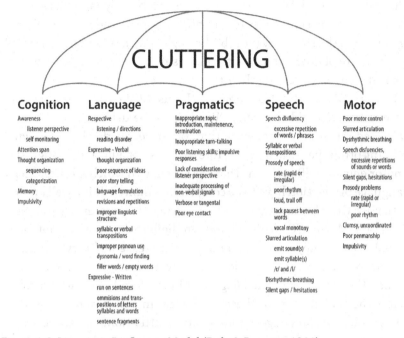

Cognition	Language	Pragmatics	Speech	Motor
Awareness	Respective	Inappropriate topic introduction, maintenence, termination	Speech disfluency	Poor motor control
listener perspective	listening / directions		excessive repetition of words / phrases	Slurred articulation
self monitoring	reading disorder	Inappropriate turn-talking		Dysrhythmic breathing
Attention span	Expressive - Verbal	Poor listening skills; impulsive responses	Syllabic or verbal transpositions	Speech disfuencies,
Thought organization	thought organzation		Prosody of speech	excessive repetitions of sounds or words
sequencing	poor sequence of ideas	Lack of consideration of listener perspective	rate (rapid or irregular)	Silent gaps, hesitations
categorization	poor story telling	Inadequate processing of non-verbal signals	poor rhythm	Prosody problems
Memory	language formulation	Verbose or tangental	loud, trail off	rate (rapid or irregular)
Impulsivity	revisions and repetitions	Poor eye contact	lack pauses between words	poor rhythm
	improper linguistic structure		vocal monotony	Clumsy, uncoordinated
	syllabic or verbal transpositions		Slurred articulation	Poor penmanship
	improper pronoun use		emit sound(s)	Impulsivity
	dysnomia / word finding		emit syllable(s)	
	filler words / empty words		/r/ and /l/	
	Expressive - Written		Disrhythmic breathing	
	run on sentences		Silent gaps / hesitations	
	ommisions and trans-positions of letters syllables and words			
	sentence fragments			

Figure 1.6: Linguistic Disfluency Model (Daly & Burnett, 1999)

1.6.3 Language automatization deficit model (van Zaalen, 2009).

To explain the nature of the disfluencies and speech intelligibility problems in cluttering, it is important to understand the processes of language formulation before the moment of language production. Van Zaalen utilized Levelt's model of language production to explain the underlying processes of cluttering, and referred to her version as a language automatization deficit model (2009). According to Levelt (1993), the expression of ideas is a three-step process (see Figure 1.7). The first step after the communicative intention deals with planning the idea or message and monitoring whether this is an accurate moment to express this message. Everyone will recognize that when people are careless, they may say things that they will later regret. In those cases, this monitoring process does not function adequately. The second step is formulation of the message in correct grammatical sentence structures. The sentences in such messages are built with words that are gathered from the lexicons of the respective speakers. Every word within such sentences has to be built up itself as well. Words are built with syllables. Syllables have to be pronounced in the right order (so "bi-bli-o-gra-phy" and not "bli-bi-gra-phy-o") and in the right way (not "bli-bli-o-gra-phy'). When the sentences and words are planned and a motor plan is ready, people can proceed to the third step by expressing their thoughts.

Bakker, Myers, Raphael and St. Louis (2011) suggest that, as with excessively rapid speakers, PWC tend to be driven to speak with accelerated rates more frequently than other people do. A person with cluttering often speaks at a speech rate which is not adjusted to linguistic or motor demands. This means that the speed with which all three steps of language production have to be completed is limited. It is a well known fact that PWC can be fluent and intelligible when they concentrate on their speech rate. Most PWC are fluent and intelligible when reading out loud, especially when they wear headphones to increase auditory feedback. Furthermore, cluttering behavior seems to increase in circumstances in which the person is relaxed (e.g., within the family, or with friends). What is the explanation for these differences in performance? We refer to three concepts: language automatization, attention, and speech rate. In the next section of this chapter we will highlight the most important facts as to all three concepts.

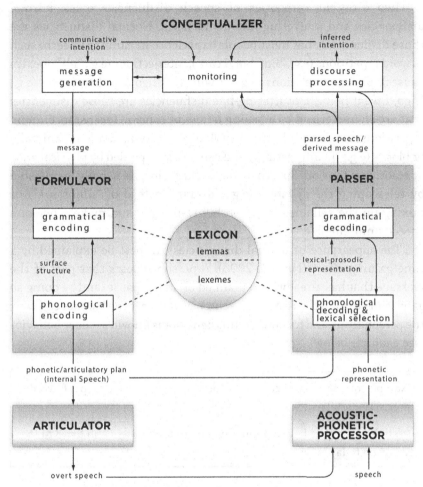

Figure 1.7: Levelt's model of language production

Language automatization/dissynchrony
Firstly, correct sentences can be produced at a fast speech rate if the process of language formulation is synchronous. Sentences are constructed, using appropriate words that are planned and produced as intended. When people have cluttering, their language formulation processes are not in synchrony with language production. The sentence or the word structure has not been planned or completed within the available time. When language formulation is insufficiently synchronous, errors in language production can be expected. Errors in language production can be manifested by an excessive number of disfluencies or speech errors.

33

Two different categories of speech disfluencies exist: normal disfluencies and stuttering-like disfluencies. Normal disfluencies are those disfluencies that most people experience in running speech, such as word repetitions (e.g., "But, but, I can"), interjections (e.g., "uh" or extra pauses), phrase repetitions (e.g., "I will, I will go") and revisions (e.g., "I go, I went home"). Stuttering-like disfluencies are those disfluencies that are characterized by a feeling of loss of control, for instance sound repetitions (e.g., "b-b-b-butter"), prolongations (e.g., "a-a-a-a-a-animal") or blocks (e.g., "I....nteresting") and can be accompanied by physical and/or emotional tension. Speech errors in cluttering are usually manifested by telescoping the syllables (e.g., "disaur" instead of "dinosaurs") or mixing up the syllables (e.g., "bli-bi-gra-phy-o") and make a person's speech unintelligible.

The appearance of normal disfluencies can best be explained by a time gaining effect (Howell, 2008). A person repeats that part of the message that has already been planned or adds a pause, and by doing so gains time to plan the rest of the sentence. It is as if the listener can hear the person think and formulate. This behavior is known as maze behavior (see example below).

> Example of maze behavior (revisions, repetition of group of words, interjections/fillers):
>
> "Well, lets say, that I want, uhm, I will go to the to the, I will drive to the aquarium today."

Speech errors occur because they are not detected by PWC when their speech rate is fast. Normally, a person detects and then repairs speech errors. Although PWC are able to recognize speech errors in their recorded speech, they are unaware of such errors in running speech. In running speech, PWC are unable to pay enough attention to such errors. St. Louis et al. posit that sustained monitoring and modulation of speech production requires careful vigilance by PWC. These skills do not come naturally or automatically to them, especially when they speak spontaneously on topics that they find to be exciting or complex (St. Louis et al., 2007).

To summarize, in cluttering a dissynchrony of language formulation and production occurs due to speech rate regulation problems. The language production dissynchrony in PWC results in either a higher than normal frequency of normal disfluencies or unintelligible speech.

Attention

In order to detect and repair an error, an appropriate monitoring system is necessary. For PWC, much attention is needed for planning a sentence or word; consequently, fewer resources remain for other processes, particularly monitoring and articulation. Therefore, errors and other production difficulties are not detected and repaired.

A lack of responses to speech errors or disfluencies can be a sign of weak monitoring (control and repair) skills. PWC are able to monitor their speech when attentional resources are not taken away for language formulation (sentence and word structure), as, for instance, in producing nonsense syllables, retelling a memorized story or describing daily activities.

PWC are usually more disfluent and less intelligible when talking in a home environment, compared to, for instance, when talking in a classroom situation. The same child can be mostly fluent in a classroom and mostly disfluent at home or with friends. In addition to the speech and communication rate, attention plays an important role. When PWC are tired or at home, their attention to speech production tends to decrease compared to when speaking at school or at work.

When attention is fully focused on language formulation, as is the case in complex speech formulation tasks, fewer resources are left for recognizing and repairing speech errors. Thus, it is hypothesized that a "double deficit" exists in cluttering: a deficit in language formulation due to inadequate synchronicity, and as a result of that, weak monitoring, because the processing capacity is used up for the formulation processes.

In summary, formulating sentences and articulating words in running speech are difficult enough, so that monitoring speech production sometimes becomes very challenging for PWC.

Speech rate

Language formulation problems audible as repetitions or repairs in PWC, also known as maze behavior, disappear during slow speech, and are detected by PWC when listening to their own recorded speech. To rule out the possibility of a language formulation disorder, PWC should be asked to write down a story. If no errors occur during the writing task, a language disorder can be ruled out. People without cluttering adjust their speech rate to the difficulty of the message. They speak slowly when the story, sentence or word structure is complex, and fast when language production is relatively simple. PWC are not able to quickly adjust their speech rate to the language complexity. It is common that the focus of PWC on speech production is adequate during the first 40 seconds and is lost after 2 minutes of conversation.

As noted earlier, members of families of PWC often clutter themselves. The speech rate in such families can be fast and can negatively influence communication of the adolescent or adult. It is very difficult for one member of a group to change his/her behavior when the others in the group continue the behavior.

PWC do not seem to monitor what they say sufficiently during running speech. To articulate all syllables clearly, much attention is needed. In running speech, PWC are not able to remain at the slower rate for a long time, because all of their attention capacity is used up for language formulation.

Monitoring in language production by Levelt
Levelt's model (1983) explains the steps of monitoring and their common relationship to language production in phases.

The Conceptualizer
During the Conceptualizer phase, a preverbal message is generated. This preverbal message is the result of several processes involving the conception of an expressive intention, selection of relevant information, sequencing this information, and keeping track of the conversation (Olsthoorn, 2007). Checking for the appropriateness and accuracy of the idea which has been formulated by the speaker is called internal monitoring (level 1). During this Conceptualizer phase, the speaker checks whether the message is intended, whether it is useful, and whether the speaker wishes to share this information with others.

The Formulator
First, the proper words corresponding to the meaning of the concepts to be expressed are retrieved from the Mental Lexicon in the form of lemmas and put into a syntactic frame resulting in a surface structure. This is called grammatical encoding. During the second step of formulation, which is called phonological encoding, the sounds (lexemes) and stress patterns are selected that accompany the string of lemmas produced in the

previous stage. The end result of the Formulator phase is an articulatory or phonetic plan, used in the final stage of language production.

In the lexical selection process, the one and only correct word must be selected from among thousands of alternative choices. The programming of phonologic and prosodic patterns is planned based on the phonologic code related to the selected item.

Articulator

In the Articulator phase, the resulting speech plans are translated into movements of the speech organs, resulting in overt speech.

Acoustic phonetic processing

After execution of planned speech, auditory feedback (audition) makes the speaker aware of the spoken message. Based on what the speaker hears, the message is again monitored for accuracy, by comparing it with the intended speech and language pattern. This monitoring can lead to overt repairs at the syllable, word and sentence level, but also to repairs of the content of the intended message. In running speech of PWC, this monitoring is diminished due to the lack of remaining attention capacity.

Summary

Cluttering is a language-based fluency disorder. When language production is relatively easy, PWC are capable of producing fluent and intelligible speech. When language production is more difficult, the speech rate should be adjusted to the language complexity. Because PWC need to focus their attention on formulating sentences and words, inadequate attention capacity remains for them to control their speech rate. When the level of language automatization is inadequate, the result is either a higher than normal number of speech disfluencies or unintelligible speech.

1.6.4 Cluttering and Stourneras' four component model

The four component model of Stourneras, discussed in relation to stuttering in Bezemer, Bouwen and Winkelman (2006), helps to explain the interaction of different communication factors in cluttering as well. The model makes it possible to display the different communicative characteristics of cluttering and suggests new approaches for treatment planning.

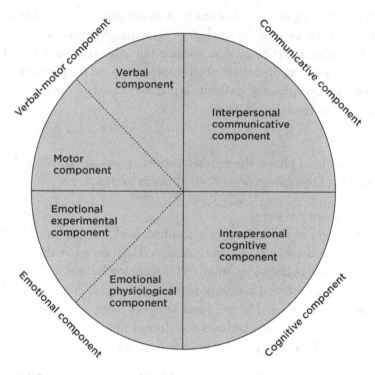

Figure 1.8: Four component model of cluttering (originally developed by Stourneras, 2006, for stuttering)

The four components of cluttering influence each other. The verbal-motor component consists of a motor subcomponent and a verbal subcomponent. These subcomponents relate to all characteristics of speech behavior, such as a fast and/or variable speech rate, errors in word or sentence structure (telescoping and abnormal syllable sequence) and a high frequency of normal disfluencies (e.g., word- and phrase repetitions, interjections, revisions).

Regarding phonological cluttering, the motor subcomponent is the one that is affected the most (e.g., syllable sequencing and planning). As to syntactic cluttering, the verbal subcomponent is the one that is affected the most (e.g., sentence structure, story structure).

The interpersonal and social component reflects the effects that abnormal speech has on the listener. Poor speech intelligibility and a fast rate of communicative exchange between the speaker and the listener interfere with the listener's ability to adjust to the speaker. The message of PWC is therefore often misunderstood.

The emotional component relating to the effect of speech on PWC consists of two subcomponents. The experiential subcomponent concerns the experiences the person with cluttering has accumulated over the years. If a person with cluttering is often misunderstood, fear of communication can develop. A person is often unaware of this process, which makes it a hidden problem. The fear starts when a person is frequently not taken seriously, because the speaker's message is not understood and no relationship is formed between the response of the listener and the speaker's own speech. Fear of sounds, words, or speech overall is not likely to develop in pure cluttering.

Inhibition of behavior can be seen as the physiological subcomponent of cluttering. When speech is initiated, it is hard for PWC to stop it. The lack of inhibitory control does not disturb or stop the person who clutters; this is contrary to what happens to PWS, for whom the loss of control during speech can have a debilitating effect. The lack of inhibition in PWC is noticeable in their body restlessness during speech, but not during listening. This restlessness can distract the listener from the message as well.

The cognitive component of cluttering is somewhat diffuse and therefore difficult to recognize. The self-image of most people with normal speech is generally moderately positive. Based on a low symptom awareness, PWC generally judge their speech positively and are under the impression that listeners who have problems understanding them might not be paying enough attention to their speech. The original positive self-image changes for the worse as soon as the connection is made between listeners' negative feedback and the speakers' speech. During therapy, a client's symptom awareness (focused speech) and resistance to talking differently (habituation) are distinguished. The cognitive components are addressed implicitly and explicitly in the therapeutic process (see Chapters 4, 5 and 6).

1.7 Awareness of and attitudes toward cluttering

1.7.1 Negative stigma toward cluttering in early literature

Dalton and Hardcastle (1993) observed that a few pioneers in the field attributed negative personality traits to PWC. This was done, occasionally, based on impressionistic perceptions. At the intersection of speech and personality, Froeschels (1946) described the personality of PWC as impulsive, careless, forgetful, and messy. Freund (1966) portrayed PWC as aggressive, expansive, explosive, extroverted, impulsive, uncontrolled, and hasty. In addition, Freund stated that the speech of PWC had negative effects on listeners, who frequently felt tension, frustration, and confusion, and had to concentrate intensively in order to be able to follow what the person with cluttering said. Weiss (1964) described the personality of PWC as poor listeners, impatient to express their thoughts, superficial, inconsiderate of the interests of other people and of the consequences of their behavior. Weiss pointed out that PWC take the initiative in conversations, and ignore thoughts and feelings of listeners. According to Weiss, PWC annoy people by their lack of sensitivity and childlike egocentricity. Weiss also noted that many adolescents who clutter express anger, possibly because of their generally poor performance in school. PWC, according to Weiss, are worried, frustrated, short-tempered, explosive, and difficult to manage at home.

Ward (2006) cautioned, in opposition to these stereotypes, that the personalities of PWC have not been empirically or systematically researched. Ward postulates that poor attention and self-monitoring skills can result in inadequate listening, which in turn can lead to misunderstandings and inappropriate responses. Van Zaalen (2009) explains that at the time of language formulation difficulties of PWC, limited attention capacity is left for them to monitor their own speech output and react to listener responses. Dalton and Hardcastle believe that the negative stereotypes of PWC have never been rationally explained.

Early pioneers in the field of cluttering arrived at their impressions about the personalities of PWC based exclusively on clinical observation. Their perceptions were influenced by their reactions to the difficulties of communicating with PWC. Mullet (1971) commented that pioneers in speech pathology, "[by seeking] to loosen the tongue, ... sought also to untie the mind" (p. 149). Mullet believed that they "...reflected the compelling and manifold urges of their time" (p. 149). But times have changed. More people have now concluded that negative stereotyping, prejudice, and stigma result in pain, hurtfulness, and hatred. Such destructive attitudes are still virtually universal, even though they vary considerably across historical periods, countries, and cultures (Reichel & St. Louis, 2007).

1.7.2 Public awareness of cluttering

The public's awareness of a communication disorder may significantly influence attitudes toward the people who suffer from such disorders (Pireira, Rossi, & Van Borsel, 2007). In order to measure the awareness of cluttering and stuttering, an Experimental Edition of the Public Opinion Survey of Human Attributes (POSHA-E) was conducted with a sampling of the general public in the United States, Russia, Bulgaria, and Turkey (St. Louis, Filatova, Coskun, Topbas, Ozdemir, Georgieva et al., 2010). Lay-oriented definitions of cluttering and stuttering appeared in the questionnaire.

The respondents estimated that 40% of people with fluency disorders had combined cases of cluttering-stuttering, and 60% only had stuttering. Respondents from the four countries surveyed considered cluttering and stuttering to be different fluency disorders, and were under the impression that both of these disorders may coexist. The most common coexisting syndrome in people with cluttering and stuttering, regardless of age, was believed to be attention deficit hyperactivity disorder. Other reported coexisting communication disorders were language impairments, articulation disorders, and unspecified conditions.

1.7.3 Public attitudes about cluttering

Many people continue to have some measure of a negative image of PWC to this day (Green, 1999). When speaking with PWC, listeners can be annoyed and stop listening, due to the speakers' compulsive talking pattern, unclear articulation, monotonous tone, and/or seemingly never-ending flow of "verbal drive" (Simkins, 1973). Some of the negative beliefs and stereotypes are common in most countries and cultures, while others, particularly in non-Western countries, are culture-specific, especially those where the belief is harbored that certain illnesses and disorders are caused by an "act of God" or "ghosts, demons, or spirits" (Al-Khaledi, Lincoln, McCabe, Packman, & Alshatti, 2009; Reichel & Draguns, 2011; St. Louis et al., 2007).

A survey of attitudes of people in the general public toward cluttering and stuttering (St. Louis, Filatova, Coskun, Topbas, Ozdemir, & Georgieva, 2011) in the same four countries as in the companion survey of public awareness referred to above (1.7.2) was administered simultaneously. The POSHA-E was also utilized to compare the disorders of cluttering and stuttering with eight other human conditions deemed to be positive, neutral, or negative. The respondents perceived cluttering and stuttering as negatively as they perceived being overweight, using a wheelchair, or having a mental illness; more negatively than being old or left handed; and significantly more negatively than being intelligent, multilingual, or a good talker. The respondents believed that cluttering is caused by psychological and related factors, such as emotional trauma and tension at home; however, all of these causes were believed to be less influential than they are for PWS. In addition, the respondents did not necessarily reject the idea that cluttering is caused by a virus, a disease, or an "act of God," ghosts, demons, or spirits. A negative stigma toward cluttering and stuttering existed in all four countries. Respondents also believed that PWC may be nervous, excitable, fearful, or shy, and cannot work up to par in jobs requiring a significant amount of talking and/or responsibility. Such responses confirm a negative stereotype resembling the well-known negative stereotype toward people who stutter (St. Louis et al., 2011; 2013).

1.7.4 Speech therapists' awareness of cluttering

Awareness of the existence of cluttering and the methods for intervention has always been and continues to be limited among speech therapists. Surveys of speech therapists' awareness suggest that their knowledge about cluttering is generally limited in the United States (St. Louis & Hinzman, 1986) and in Great Britain (St. Louis & Rustin, 1992). Responses to these surveys indicate that speech therapists lacked confidence in their ability to plan and conduct therapy for PWC.

Another questionnaire was presented to speech therapists in Bulgaria, Greece, Great Britain, and the United States (Georgieva, 2004). The survey included questions comparing cluttering and stuttering. The respondents indicated that they were familiar with the symptoms and the causes of cluttering, but did not have a clear understanding of the differences and similarities between cluttering and stuttering, nor did they have significant experience with therapeutic techniques in clinical settings. They felt uncomfortable with their abilities to work with PWC, due to inadequate academic preparation and limited access to relevant publications.

More recently, an International Cluttering Survey (ICS) of 25 international representatives of the ICA was conducted (Reichel & Bakker, 2009). Many of the participants were speech therapists with a special interest in cluttering. Of the 25 representatives surveyed, 10 (from Australia, Belgium, Bulgaria, Canada, Denmark, England, Faroe Islands, Israel, Sweden, and the USA) believed that in their countries, most speech therapists are aware of cluttering, but do not consider themselves knowledgeable enough to identify its symptoms, arrive at a diagnosis, or provide therapeutic procedures. The speech therapists reportedly lacked awareness of cluttering in eight countries (Argentina, Indonesia, Japan, Lithuania, Netherlands, Russia, Sudan, and Thailand).

1.8 Conclusions

This completes a historic overview of different definitions and explanations of models of cluttering. For a very long time, cluttering was an overlooked or misunderstood disorder. In order to describe the main characteristics of cluttering in correlation to other disorders, van Zaalen (2009) created a four-component language automatization deficit model of cluttering, utilizing the models of Levelt (1989) and Stourneras (in Bezemer et al., 2006). Now, the disorder of cluttering is better understood and placed in a theoretical framework.

2

Chapter 2

Cluttering symptoms

2.1 Introduction

This chapter places the variety of symptoms discussed in Chapter One into a theoretical framework. This framework will guide clinicians in their assessment, diagnosis and treatment of cluttering.

> "Diagnostic markers are measurable characteristics used to classify persons as affected by the disorder" (Shriberg, 2003, p. *510*).

Based on Shriberg's definition, measurable and strong characteristics are necessary in order to differentiate cluttering from other disorders. The term "cluttering" encompasses a combination of symptoms and characteristics manifested in varying degrees by different individuals. A diagnosis of cluttering cannot be made based on a single symptom or characteristic (Alm, 2011). People who are diagnosed with cluttering exhibit at least the following key characteristics: a perceived fast and/or irregular speech rate combined with at least one or more of:

o high frequency nonstuttering-like disfluencies, also called normal disfluencies;
o excessively frequent pauses and prosodic patterns (syllable stress or speech rhythm) that are inconsistent with syntactic and semantic rules;
o an inadequate (and mostly excessive) use of coarticulation, especially in multisyllabic words (telescoping) (see also 1.3).

St. Louis and Schulte (2011, p. 241) added the concept of native language to the definition of cluttering when they defined cluttering as "a fluency disorder wherein segments of conversation in the speaker's native language typically are perceived as too fast overall, too irregular, or both." Assuming cluttering to be a problem in rate adjustment, the concept of native language is not decisive, but of course speaking in a second or even a third language will slow down the rate of the speaker as long as the speaker is not fluent in the new language. But because cluttering is a rate adjustment problem, cluttering will emerge in non-native languages as soon as the speaker is able to speak in any of these languages fluently.

In addition to the symptoms referred to above, other symptoms are often observed in PWC that are not necessarily unique to this group of clients. Examples of these symptoms include excessive use of word fillers, monotony, verbosity, mumbling, change of vowel color, and indistinct pronunciation.

Cluttering is diagnosed in only those cases where the frequent presence of the above mentioned key characteristics disturb verbal communication, especially when intelligibility and message sharing is concerned (Winkelman, 1990). Not every speaker with reduced speech intelligibility or with an extremely fast speech rate should be diagnosed with cluttering. Reduced speech intelligibility, especially in professional speakers such as teachers and journalists, can be attributed in most cases to only one of the characteristics of cluttering and not to a combination of symptoms. In many cases, reduced speech intelligibility occurs in stressful circumstances. This was also mentioned by Myers and St. Louis (1992) when they wrote that some parameters, such as an abnormal speech rate, disfluency, language disorders and coarticulation, may be present independently of each other.

2.2 Characteristics and symptoms

In the following paragraphs, views based on the general international consensus on the different characteristics of cluttering and the symptoms of coexisting disorders are discussed. See the web site of the International Cluttering Association, http://associations.missouristate.edu/ica/.www. associations.missouristate.edu/ica/

2.2.1 Fast and/or irregular speech rate

When assessing the speech rate of a speaker, it is important to know the difference between the speech rate and the articulatory rate (AR). Some scientists see the articulatory rate as an indicator of speech-motor behavior (Kent, 1984; Van Riper, 1982). The articulatory rate measured in syllables per second is a better measure of speech execution time than the speech rate measured in words per minute (Hall, Amir, & Yairi, 1999). The articulatory rate is defined as the number of syllables or phonemes per second in a speech sample, after removal of pauses and disfluent episodes. In determining the speech rate in words per minute, pauses are included in the time measured.

In our view, the speech of PWC is characterized by a high frequency of irregular and short pauses in linguistically unexpected places. Pauses influence time duration in cluttering to a great extent. We therefore consider the articulatory rate as the best measure for the assessment of PWC.

Example of pauses that are different from sociolinguistic norms
I go with .... my friends for dinner because .... when I ... do... not do that I will certainly be... hungry.

In the working definition of cluttering formulated by St. Louis et al. (2007), the perceived fast and/or irregular articulatory rate is considered to be an obligatory characteristic of cluttering. St. Louis et al. observe that the articulatory rate can be perceived to be too fast, but when measured, the articulatory rate can actually be within normal limits. Rate disturbances are manifested by:

○ a high frequency of normal disfluencies;
○ frequent use of pauses or incorrect prosodic patterns;
○ a high frequency of coarticulation, especially in multisyllable words.

2.2.2 Word structure

Words are composed of syllables. The order in which syllables are sequenced can determine the meaning of the word. In order to compose words by combining syllables, a certain amount of planning time is needed. Due to the fast rate of PWC, they have insufficient time left for phonological planning, before the completion of phonetic planning and motor execution (articulator). See Levelt's model (1.6.3).

When speakers have insufficient time for planning, they are prone to make errors, including errors in syllable sequencing. For example, PWC can say "magfinicent" instead of "magnificent." Also, an error within a syllable structure can occur. For example, PWC can say "dangle" when they mean to say "tangle." This phenomenon is manifested in the fast speech rate of PWC. Errors in word structure can occur due to insufficient planning time or because earlier produced syllables are still present in the speaker's mind.

CASE EXAMPLE:
When Bertram spoke slowly, he hardly experienced syllable sequencing errors. When excitedly telling a story about his vacation in Bellport, he said "There were prossabilities" when he intended to say "possible probabilities." When telling the rest of the story, this type of error increased. Bertram produced similar sequencing errors in other words on the SPA test. He had a high syllable error score on the Screening Phonological Accuracy Test (SPA) (van Zaalen, 2011).

PWC generally experience faster reaction times in phoneme monitoring compared to controls (Garnett, Adams, Montgomery, St. Louis, & den Ouden, 2012), while PWS had significantly slower reaction times (Sasisekaran, de Nil, Smyth, & Johnson, 2006). But PWC and PWS both made errors more frequently than controls when performing a phoneme monitoring task. These findings indicate that both groups have a self-monitoring deficit that adds to speech output errors. For an accurate diagnosis of cluttering, it is necessary to make sure that phonetic errors produced by the client are related to planning errors and not to phonetic deficits. In light of this, regular phonetic exercises are not recommended for therapy planning, while increased self-monitoring is (see Chapter 5).

Phonological errors similar to those that are typically made by people with verbal apraxia are often observed in the speech of PWC. Some experts consider these errors to reflect the most important characteristic of cluttering (Ward, 2006). Typical among PWC are the so-called speech anticipation errors, such as "grees gras" or "ficefellow." Phonetic substitutions, such as "brink deer" or "freel fee" can also be apparent in cluttering. PWC tend to have significant problems with so-called "tongue twisters," even if the speech rate is decreased.

Tongue twisters
Peter Piper picked a peck of pickled peppers.
Betty Botter bought a bit of butter. "But," she said, "this butter's bitter!"
A canner can can anything that he can, But a canner can't can a can, can he?
She sells sea shells by the sea shore.

During the production of these classic "tongue twisters," errors can be heard that are similar to those present in clients with developmental apraxia of speech. So it is possible that within tongue twisters:

Excessive coarticulation (telescoping) is audible. For example:

- o "politsian" (politician)
- o "pleas" (police);
- o "Many thinkle peep so" (Many people think so);

Syllables or sounds are substituted:

- o "Magadascer" (Madagascar)
- o "presisent" (president)
- o "tevelision" (television)

Sounds or syllables are added, such as

- ○ "spossible" (possible).

2.2.3 Speech pauses

Pauses between sentences and between speakers usually range from 0.5 to 1.0 seconds (van Zaalen & Winkelman, 2009). It is well known that PWC have reduced intelligibility. This is due, in part, to the fact that the pauses of PWC between phrases are significantly shorter than the pauses of other people in normal speech. These pauses are important in order for the listener to comprehend spoken language. The pauses are of equal importance to the speaker. They provide time for the speaker to formulate and plan the next sentence. They also provide time for the speaker to let go of the breathing tension which had been built up during the previous phrase and to regain enough oxygen to be able to produce the next phrase. The speaker who skips a pause has a limited amount of time to prepare and plan the next phrase. As a result of this time limit, speakers must adjust their utterance formulation during speech. Such an adjustment can be manifested by normal disfluencies, e.g., revisions, interjections, or word- and phrase repetitions. The next example clarifies this.

> Desirée, a 30-year old comedienne, shows up in a clinic with major concerns about her speech performance. She is a very fast speaker and a language juggler. She spends many hours writing her sketches. After the show, she talks with her fans. She notices that her fans love her but do not seem to understand a lot of what she says in her act. People who are not among her fans hate her style. They say: "This girl is so full of herself talking, but that is what it is; it is only talking talking." Desirée feels misunderstood. She often loses much of her audience due to her lack of pauses. Often, people who try to understand her give up, because she simply does not give them time to understand what she is saying. The high frequency of disfluencies are interpreted by her fans as being funny. As a result, a language juggler is judged to be a clown.

Another characteristic of cluttering is abnormal pause placements within sentences. Because PWC speak with a fast speech rate, their pauses tend to be very short, which in many cases causes them to be out of breath.

In the course of normal language development, most people have no need to be taught where to pause in their sentences. The rapid speech rate of PWC prevents them from developing this inner concept of phrasing and pauses. But PWC have a need to be taught where to pause because they even have problems identifying appropriate pause placements and sentence beginnings in a text without punctuation marks.

2.2.4 Disfluencies

The common occurrence of interjections and revisions has implications for the nature of fluency breakdowns in cluttering. According to Starkweather (1987), in St. Louis et al. (2007), interjections present a more mature version of normal disfluency contrasted with word and phrase repetitions. Logan and La Salle posited (1999) that revisions may be caused by conceptual or formulative breakdowns occurring during language programming (St. Louis et al., 2007). Although the previously prevailing opinion that speech disfluencies are caused by a disruption in time dependent processes of phonological or phonetic encoding could not be determined in a population of fluent speakers (Eldrigde, 2007), we speculate that a number of disfluencies of PWC are motivated by linguistic rather than motoric difficulties. These disruptions are often called "linguistic maze" behaviors (Howell & Au -Yeung, 2002), resulting in linguistic disfluencies or normal disfluencies (van Zaalen, Myers, Ward, & Bennet, 2008). As proposed by Howell and Au-Yeung (2002), normal disfluencies are produced in order to gain time to plan the next structure. The speaker repeats what was already planned and executed. As soon as the next plan is ready, the disfluency will end, and the intended structure will be executed. Therefore, the repetitions that are considered normal disfluencies are less tense, and produced in normal rhythmic patterns. But, contrary to stuttering-like disfluencies, normal disfluencies do not break up the syllable structure. The syllable remains intact. Repetitions that are considered to be normal disfluencies are syllable-, word-, and phrase repetitions produced without tension, at a regular rate and without additional stress.

Most disfluencies of PWC are normal disfluencies (Myers & Bradley, 1992; St. Louis, 1996a; Ward, 2006; van Zaalen, Wijnen, & Dejonckere, 2009a, b). Recent studies of Myers and St. Louis (2007) and van Zaalen, Wijnen and Dejonckere (2009c) show that as a group, PWC produce normal disfluencies to the extent that normal speakers do. But these findings are based on observing only those people who attend speech clinics. Sometimes the frequency of normal disfluencies is much higher in PWC. In addition, there seems to be a difference in the frequency of disfluencies between the two subtypes of cluttering. In people with phonological cluttering, the frequency of normal disfluencies is comparable to that of fluent speakers. By contrast, in people with syntactic cluttering, the frequency of normal disfluencies is significantly higher compared to other groups.

Normal disfluencies, such as interjections, revisions, and word- and phrase repetitions are produced with mild tension and a normal speech rhythm. Due to formulation difficulties and a fast speech rate, a high frequency of word and phrase repetitions is observed. Part- word repetitions (e.g., "pa-pattern") in which the number of repetitions is fewer than two, occur frequently in PWC as well. Stuttering-like disfluencies, such as tensed word repetitions, prolongations and tense pauses rarely occur (< 3% SS) (Sasisekaran et al., 2006). The frequency of normal disfluencies in fluent speakers is reported to range between 3.1% in a group of young children and adolescents (De Nil, Sasisekaran, van Lieshout, & Sandor, 2005), and about 9.7% (Eggers, 2010; Blokker, Vos, & van Wingerden, 2010). In some PWC, normal disfluencies can be as frequent as 35% (van Zaalen, Wijnen, & Dejonckere, 2009b). In contrast, PWS tend to produce fewer than 5% normal disfluencies (van Zaalen, Wijnen, & Dejonckere, 2009b). Damsté (1990) explained this phenomenon by suggesting that PWS repair even utterances which normally do not need to be repaired.

Note: The combination of fast speech rate, short pauses, disfluencies and excessive coarticulation makes the perception of disfluencies even higher than the actual number of disfluencies when measured (van Zaalen & van Heeswijk, 2012). For an explanation of this phenomenon, see 2.3.

2.2.5 Disorders of communication

Communication rules are important in order to conduct a normal conversation between two or more people. For PWC, normal communication rules (pragmatics) are not taken for granted. For example, turn taking or turn giving can be extremely challenging. PWC start talking impulsively or keep on talking without noticing the responses of listeners, in part because their attention is focused intensely on language production.

Because of inadequate speech intelligibility and/or the high frequency of disfluencies, stories told by PWC can be misunderstood or not understood at all. PWC are often not fully aware of the reason why they are not understood. When asked for clarification, PWC will often repeat what they have just said in the same way. This can frustrate the listener, but this can also frustrate the PWC upon realizing that they are not understood again. Some PWC who are aware of their symptoms will pronounce the words more clearly the second time they say them. This can happen as a result of the response of the listener, for example, when the listener frowns.

Introducing and maintaining a conversational topic is often difficult for PWC. A speaker needs to take the knowledge of the listener into account in order to introduce and discuss a topic adequately. Weiss (1964) interpreted this lack of adequate response to the listener as an indication of disinterest in real communication. At the present time, we realize that the fast communication rate of PWC makes adequate judgment of the knowledge or informational need of the listener almost impossible. When the listener's perspective is not adequately taken into account by PWC, the communication becomes, in effect, a monologue instead of a dialogue. In the literature, however, no empirical evidence is found that PWC are less able, under the pressure of communication, to judge the knowledge or informational needs of the listener differently than fluent speakers.

2.2.6 Melodic patterns

Natural speech consists of the following aspects:

o   speech intelligibility;
o   adequate phrasing;
o   use of sufficiently long pauses between linguistic units;
o   use of melodic patterns and stress.

Therefore, the impaired communication typical in cluttering can also be a result of abnormal melodic and prosodic patterns. These are paralinguistic parameters associated with the communication described above. A number of examples are provided for clarification. Abnormal phrasing, fast speech rate and atypical sentence formulation can lead to superficial changes of pitch and monotony. The monotony makes the message difficult to understand, and the listener's concentration diminishes as a consequence.

A frequent variation of monotony in cluttering is melodic monotony. In monotony, the differences in pitch are minimal (below 100 Hz within a 2-3 second phrase). In melodic monotony (see Figure 2.1), the speaker uses the same intonation pattern in every sentence, regardless of the meaning of the sentences. If the listeners are aware of this speaking style, it may distract them from the message. The listener will not always be able to identify the nature of the abnormal speech pattern, but is likely to lose attention anyway because the speaking style sounds boring.

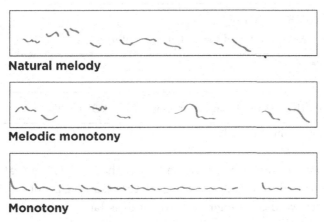

Natural melody

Melodic monotony

Monotony

Figure 2.1 Different speaking melodies, produced with Praat software (see 3.3.7)

In addition to prosodic difficulties at the sentence level, problems can also occur at the word level. These are related to syllabic stress. For instance, "irrespon'sible" is pronounced as "ir'responsible."

Furthermore, unstressed syllables are often omitted, such as "irresponsel." If this phenomenon occurs frequently or regularly it can distract the listener's attention from the content of the message.

In an attempt not to be boring, numerous speakers – not only PWC -- stress short words at the beginning of their thoughts that happen to be of less semantic interest. Often stress is put on prepositions instead of on meaningful words in the sentence. The following example clarifies this:

> "ALSO this phenomenon that occurs IN the army, is IN this case A bad example that happens ON a daily basis."

Abnormal stress patterns

Due to the wrong stress pattern, the message "that happens on a daily basis" can elude the listener. Stress in the above mentioned example was made with variations in loudness and pitch. The trailing off of the volume at the end of a sentence (night candle effect) is a most frequent phenomenon in cluttering (see first box, below). This can also occur as an isolated phenomenon, even in professional speakers. This phenomen has a negative influence on the speaker's intelligibility and the listener's ability to understand.

> Example of the night candle effect:
> "SADLY I HAVE not heard the end of the sentence."

Night candle effect

> Example: "IN riots in Moscow four people ARE WOUNDED."

Stress not on meaningful words

In the above example, the written words that are not capitalized are spoken with reduced loudness. Stress in this example is not on the most meaningful words. Listeners ask themselves later: "Where were these riots?" and "How many people were wounded?"

Another example:

> "Yesterday IN China hundreds OF children GOT sick after using poisoned milk powder."
> Two listeners talk about it:
> "In ... Iowa?"
> "No, China."
> "Oh good heavens, I was shocked."

Stress is not on meaningful words

2.2.7 Rhythm and musicality

A lack of or disrupted speech rhythm, possibly combined with tachylalia (speech that is too fast) or bradylalia (speech that is too slow), is considered by many to be a good indicator of cluttering (Daly, 1996; St. Louis, 1992; St. Louis et al., 2003; Ward, 2006; van Zaalen et al., 2008). Speech intelligibility can be affected by spurts of fast speech. Speech impairment becomes more apparent when the spurts of fast speech are combined with short pauses between sentences and the abrupt way that sentences are begun. These abrupt starts sometimes lead to a staccato-like style of speech.

The problems become even more severe for PWC when they need to memorize or retell children's poems because these poems are mainly based on repeated, rhythmic patterns. The reduced coherence between the rhythmic pattern and the pauses (phrasing) leads to severe phrasing problems, interfering even more with speech intelligibility. If such problems are caused by a lack of musical (sensory) characteristics, treatment can be very difficult. This only becomes clear when the treatment has very minimal effects. These musical characteristics should not be misinterpreted as musicality.

Nonmusical phenomena can appear in musicians as well. For example, there are drum players whose speech appears dysrhythmic. Production of music probably has a different brain activation than the brain activation for communication (and motor memory). A different level of focused attention is needed in music performance compared to speech. A similar concept applies to people with severe stuttering, most of whom can sing fluently (Alm, 2004, 2007, 2008). There are famous piano players who have an absolutely musical ear, but who are not able to control their pitch when singing. A difference in perception and production of tones during singing seems to be present in these cases. Muscle control of the vocal cords is organized differently than muscle control applied to the use of drum sticks or piano keys. The ability to produce different musical tones is determined by prosody. A lack of musical skills can also lead to monotony, often heard in PWC.

2.2.8 Handwriting and writing problems

Sufficient language skills (reading, speaking, writing and listening) are important for efficient, easy and effective communication with others.

It is widely known that PWC can experience problems in any one of the four language skills. Problems in writing are mentioned by multiple researchers and authors (Daly & Cantrell, 2006; Bezemer, Bouwen, & Winkelman, 2006; Dinger, Smit, & Winkelman, 2008; Ward, 2006; van Zaalen & Winkelman, 2009). A strong relationship exists between different movement rates, such as in walking, speaking and writing, or, as some mothers may say: "You walk fast, you talk fast, and you think fast."

Writing is learning how culturally determined signs are represented, based on certain distinguished shapes, relationships, and sizes. Writing is correlated to speech production; it is simply another way of expressing the same speech and language code. Verbal language production is a development of consecutive movement patterns of breathing, vocal cords, labial, and lingual muscles. Handwriting is a trace-tracking form of movements that visualize internal speech through sound symbols. Where a phonetic plan leads to a speech-motor plan of spoken language, a phonetic plan leads to a grapheme motor plan in written language. The legibility depends on the shape, the movement trail and the space on the paper. The rate of writing is correlated to the speed of a person's acting and thinking. A child, at age three, is already able to execute fine, grapheme motor movements. Long before children of this age group go to kindergarten, they are capable of executing finger movements with eight millimeter precision. These finger movements, which are used in writing and drawing, are usually well developed before the age at which children go to kindergarden. This does not mean that fine motor development is completed at that age. Writing is still an important skill for adequate functioning in school.

> Lloyd, age 10, claims: "If I pay attention to my writing, I do not remember how the word has to be written. And if I pay attention to how the word has to be written, I cannot write neatly anymore."

In recent years more attention is paid to teaching how to write, but the prevalence of writing problems is nevertheless increasing. Currently, 30% of boys and 10% of girls have major or minor writing problems.

PWC often produce errors in writing that are correlated to errors in speech. No scientific studies have been published on handwriting and fluency disorders, to our knowledge. The clinical experience of the authors indicates that writing problems in PWC are evident. Practice-based evidence demonstrates that a person with syntactic cluttering produces a high frequency of word repetitions and revisions in both written and spoken speech; a person with phonological cluttering presents with a higher than normal number of illegibility problems due to telescoping of graphemes. PWC inhibit their high speed during writing, leading to increased pressure on the paper on which they are writing and complaints of fatigue during writing.

2.2.9 Self-evaluation, speech control and monitoring

In the seventies of the former century, many authors viewed the sensory component as a cause and maintaining factor of cluttering (St. Louis et al., 2007; Ward, 2006). According to these authors, self-monitoring by PWC was impaired. This explanation is very plausible considering that PWC tend to be unaware of their problems in fluency and in speech intelligibility, which is consistent with the belief that the sensory component is a maintaining factor of cluttering. The poor intelligibility is therefore caused by a specific deficit in language formulation, fast articulatory and speech rates, abnormal timing, and irregular rhythm. But it is very important to stress that when the language formulation component is not a problem, PWC are fully able to self-monitor their speech. Therefore, the sensory component is ruled out as the major cause of cluttering.

In addition to the inability of PWC to influence and control musical aspects, they have an insufficient ability to self-monitor in running speech. One of the first steps in treatment planning is to have clients identify their symptoms. This can be done by having clients listen to recordings of their speech. See Chapter 5.

2.2.10 Attention and concentration

Kussmaul observed, in 1877, that more focused attention improves speech production in PWC. Instances of less focused attention clearly expose more cluttering symptoms. Many parents or other family members of PWC have confirmed these observations, over the years.

> The wife of a person with cluttering observed: "Lately, when Peter speaks to me, he is completly unintelligible. When he speaks to my friend, suddenly he is intelligible. Sometimes it feels as if he is not willing to do his best for me any more."

Speech production of PWC usually deteriorates during relaxation. When an additional person, especially one who is unfamiliar, joins a conversation, focused attention to speech production will increase. The reason for this speech improvement is that the person with cluttering becomes more alert because of this additional person's presence. This aspect of cluttering can mislead the referring medical doctor or clinician during the diagnostic evaluation. Often, people do not feel at ease during their first sessions with the therapist. They experience problems with speech, but are often focused on showing what they are capable of. As a consequence, they focus their attention on their speech and exhibit fewer cluttering symptoms than they normally would. In later sessions, when speakers experience less tension, they will be less alert, and their cluttering will increase. To be able to detect cluttered speech within the first sessions, the Predictive Cluttering Inventory-revised (PCI-r) (Appendix A) and the Screening Phonological Accuracy (SPA) (Appendix E) may be used. In addition, speech should be assessed in less structured conditions, where clients are unaware of their speech being recorded. See 3.1.4 regarding procedures to obtain consent forms.

2.2.11 Auditory skills

The correlation between cluttering and possibly reduced auditory processing skills has recently drawn increased interest among researchers. One of the explanations is the temporary positive effect of auditory feedback through headphones, by using heightened auditory feedback (HAF) or delayed auditory feedback (DAF). When the reading skills of children with cluttering are examined, HAF can reduce the instances of word omissions, guessing when reading and phonologic paraphrasias. But it is not known whether PWC have abnormal auditory memory, problems in auditory analysis, synthesis, discrimination, or processing. PWC make errors in verbally repeating sentences, giving them a low score on auditory memory tasks. But when the PWC are asked to write down the sentences, they make no errors or omissions. Considering that PWC do not generally have problems focusing their attention, any difficulties they may experience in auditory skills have to be considered an additional problem or a correlated problem.

2.2.12 Planning difficulties

Many speech language pathologists are familiar with the phenomenon that a stuttering client is usually on time while a cluttering client is often late for therapy as is explained in the example below.

> Wednesday morning, at 7:45 A.M., Eli has an appointment with the dentist. It is a ten minute bike ride from his house to the dentist. At 7:35, Eli decides that he would like to take a shower. A shower only takes five minutes. Later, he is completely surprised that he is late again for his appointment with the dentist.

We assume that PWC experience planning problems not only in their speech but also in their writing and daily general and financial activities. Although interesting, no research data is available on this issue. A definite conclusion on the occurrence of planning problems in PWC cannot be reached at this time.

2.3 Influences on speech rate

2.3.1 Linguistic factors

A variety of linguistic factors influence the speech rate. It is common knowledge that syllables within the first words of utterances are produced faster than the same syllables at the end of utterances. The complexity of the phrase influences the speech rate as well; the more complex the sentence structure, the more interjections and pauses take place, slowing down the speech rate. Furthermore, various researchers have determined that longer sentences are produced somewhat faster than shorter sentences (e.g., Kelly & Conture, 1992). The speech rate is influenced by the conversational interaction rate, also called the speed of turn taking. During a conversation where the normal pause duration of 0.5 – 1.0 sec. is reduced, the speech rate of the next utterance will be faster than it is in a dialogue where sufficiently long pauses are used.

2.3.2 Phonetic and phonological aspects

Syllable duration depends on the number of sounds per syllable, the stress pattern, and the word length. The duration of a syllable, composed of different consonants and a vowel, such as "spread" (mean 0.58 sec), is considerably longer than that of a syllable composed of two consonants and a vowel, such as "job" (mean 0.26 sec). A syllable will also last longer when produced in front of the mouth, such as "pip" (mean 0.22) compared to when it is produced in the back of the mouth, such as "kick" (mean 0.19 sec). In addition to the adjustment of the pitch, the stress on a syllable is also made by the adjustment of a syllable's duration. Syllables within a long multisyllabic word are generally spoken at a faster rate than syllables that are within a short word.

2.3.3 Relevance of the subject to the speaker

The speech rate is highly dependent on the relevance of the subject to the speaker. When speakers are asked to give their opinion, the rate in which this will be performed will be strongly dependent on the relevance to the theme. A student member of the school board will express her opinion on the amount of contact hours much faster than a student who is not a member of the board.

The number of times that an opinion is formulated influences the speech rate. The more that people tell the same story, the more their speech rate will increase. During a diagnostic evaluation, this difference can also be apparent when the speech rate varies depending on the speech task.

2.3.4 Influence of the speech rate on perceptions about the speaker

The speech rate can vary depending on the social context. A person with a slower speech rate tends to be perceived as "professional" or "self-confident," but a person with excessively fast speech tends to be considered "passionate" or "nervous." On the other hand, a person who speaks rapidly without disfluencies can be viewed as very self-confident or even dominant.

Within families, often unsaid remarks are implied. An expression such as, "He talks like a real McClain" is an example of this. Self-image develops mostly from the time of adolescence. It is therefore expected that people's self-image can influence their speech rate primarily after adolescence.

▓ 2.3.5 Rate in people with intellectual disabilities and neurological impairments

Contrary to generally prevailing expectations, individuals with intellectual disabilities (ID) appear to have an articulatory and speech rate comparable to controls (Coppens-Hofman, Terband, Maassen, van Schrojenstein Lantman – de Valk, van Zaalen-op't Hof, & Snik, 2013). These authors found that since the mean articulatory rate of the adults in the study is similar to the articulatory rate of adults without intellectual disabilities, there is no evidence that their speech rate is affected by their disability. The authors did not observe a significant correlation between the speech rate and the number or type of disfluencies. So the idea that people with intellectual disabilities necessarily speak slowly is not substantiated and is probably based solely on listeners' perceptions. The speech of people with intellectual disabilities can be perceived as slow based on the high frequency of normal disfluencies and the message content related to their intellectual levels.

Changes in the speech rate may be observed in people with some neurologic conditions, especially those where the basal ganglia or language formulation are involved. The speech rate can either decrease or increase as a result of such conditions. Examples of disorders associated with a fast speech rate are Parkinson's disease, Wernicke aphasia, Fragile X syndrome, ADHD, and patients within a phase of manic depression.

▓ 2.3.6 Emotional state and motivation

The intrinsic motivation of a speaker to share a message has an influence on the speech rate. When speakers are not fully interested in a topic, their speech rate will be much slower than when the same speakers are addressing topics about which they are passionate.

2.3.7 Effects of age

There is a correlation between speakers' speech rate and their age. Very young children and very old adults speak considerably slower than adolescents and young adults (Zonneveld, Quené & Heeren, 2011; van Zaalen & Winkelman, 2009). Variations of speech rates may be related to other differences, as well, such as gender, the speakers' education level, regional background, average length of utterance, average lexical diversity Zonneveld, Quené & Heeren, 2011, ethnicity, and life experiences.

Quené, as cited in Zonneveld, Quené & Heeren (2011) found that older listeners' perceptions may be influenced by their own speaking rate, due to age-related reductions in their articulatory and cognitive capacities. Quené presumed that the stimulus speech rate that listeners consider to be most comfortable is identical to their own speech rate. More on the influence of speech rate on fluency, speech intelligibility, and reading is described in 1.3.

Figure 2.2: External influences on speech rate

2.4 Conclusion

In this chapter, a wide variety of symptoms related to cluttering were presented. The type, frequency, and degree of different symptoms determine the severity of the disorder. Knowledge and insights about the symptoms assist in assessment and in making clients aware of why their communication is negatively influenced by symptoms of cluttering.

DIAGNOSTICS

Chapter 3

Assessment

▨ 3.1 Introduction

The determination of the presence of cluttering depends on whether a client manifests cluttering in a relatively pure form or in conjunction with other disorders, and particularly stuttering. In the latter case, it is important to recognize that cluttering sometimes does not emerge as a salient condition until stuttering has remitted, either spontaneously or as a result of treatment, or at least until treatment for stuttering is underway. Also, it is important to document the possible presence of other coexisting problems with communication or learning, or attention deficit hyperactivity disorders (ADHD) (van Zaalen, Myers, Ward, & Bennett, 2007).

Norm-referenced instruments to diagnose cluttering are not available yet and based on the multifaceted nature of cluttering will probably never be devised. The main reason is that cluttering is a syndrome with a wide variety of symptoms that only in combination can lead to a cluttering diagnosis. Some norm-referenced tests that differentiate certain aspects of cluttering from stuttering or other speech disorders do exist. The Fluency Assessment Battery (van Zaalen & Winkelman, 2009) has been developed to interpret the speech behavior of people with fluency problems in all aspects of communication and speech production. The different components of the Fluency Assessment Battery will be elaborated on in 3.2. An instrument to assess the severity of cluttering developed by Myers and Bakker (2011) is described in 3.3.9. All the available instruments will be presented in this chapter and further explained in the Appendices. To give the reader a visual re-enactment of the assessment procedure, some video and audio files are available on the website, www.NYCSA-Center.org.

We want to emphasize that, according to ICF, an assessment should not only focus on the limitations of the client but also on the client's potential for change and development. The assessment should focus on functioning and participation, as well as recognizing the importance of personal and environmental characteristics. A major objective in the diagnostic phase is to study the different processes of language production in relation to each other, in order to differentiate between stuttering, cluttering, and other fluency disorders. A second major objective is to consider or rule out any other disorders, such as learning disabilities, dyslexia, ADHD, verbal dyspraxia of speech or intellectual disabilities.

Because cluttering may encompass all of the above mentioned problems, the Fluency Assessment Battery has been developed in such a way that data gathered in this assessment instrument can easily be applied to other diagnostic tools, such as the Stuttering Assessment Protocol.

3.1.1 Predictive Cluttering Inventory-revised

In 2006, Daly and Cantrell presented their newest checklist of cluttering symptoms, which they referred to as the Predictive Cluttering Inventory (PCI). This checklist was based on the opinions of international experts regarding symptoms related to cluttering. The checklist contains 33 items that are clinically observed in various PWC. The 2006 version of the PCI was not normed and did not appear to be specific and sensitive enough to detect possible cluttering (van Zaalen et al., 2009c). Based on its items analysis, ten items appeared to demonstrate significant differences between cluttering and other disorders. These items are used in the PCI-revised, a normed checklist for cluttering signs (see 3.2 and Appendix A). This checklist can help the clinician to identify possible cluttering symptoms, and to determine whether further evaluation is indicated, using the Fluency Assessment Battery (see Appendices A--F). The PCI-revised also gives the clinician a clear insight into the linguistic and communicative characteristics of the client. Both the instruction and the interpretation are described in the PCI-revised form (Appendix A).

3.1.2 Case history

The differential diagnosis between cluttering and co-existing disorders, such as specific language imbalance (SLI), learning difficulties or ADHD is difficult to make in children until they reach 10 years of age. Because language development is "never" finished, the diagnosis of cluttering is not clear-cut. For further information on the differential diagnosis between different fluency disorders, see 3.3.

As in most speech-language evaluations, the case history should include information regarding the following five aspects:

(a) clients' complaints and expectations,
(b) birth and developmental history,
(c) medical history,
(d) timeline of efficacy of previous treatment, and
(e) family history of speech or language disorders, including fluency disorders and tachylalia.

Clients' complaints and expectations
In taking a case history, the clinician at the outset should ascertain the primary reason why clients have presented themselves for assessment (and potentially for treatment) at this moment in their lives. The reason clients seek assessment and treatment strongly influences intervention goals and the clients' internal motivation to change. Clients' complaints can be a result of either a tension they felt within communication settings or external feedback to their speech. The question of whether clients understand the impact of their speech production compared to their experienced difficulty or external complaints of listeners should be addressed. This can give an idea to the clinician about clients' insights to deficits underlying their communication problems. Before the clinician

begins any intervention, it is important to ask clients in which situations they want to change their speech. Cluttering is not easy to treat, and full recovery is not likely. The therapy will benefit tremendously if treatment goals will reflect the expectations and needs of the client.

Birth and developmental history
Although no birth risk factors have been identified for cluttering and other fluency disorders, gathering information on birth is helpful to better understand the disorder of cluttering, and can provide other important information about the causes of the condition. Information on developmental history is significant because signals of cluttering are described and influence clients' perceptions of their own behavior. Developmental history can also provide ideas for potential treatment goals, in addition to speech production, that need to be addressed. For instance, trouble with handwriting is not related to speech outcome in many adult clients who start therapy, and feels like a separate disorder, when in fact it is part of the same compromised speech and language delivery system. In our experience, adult clients are relieved to find out that some of their symptoms are part of the same underlying deficit and not independent different disorders.

It is also helpful to study the history of any potentially relevant symptoms, whether or not they have led to any formal diagnoses, such as behavioral problems or attention disorders, such as ADHD or ADD in school or work settings, learning disabilities, and an auditory processing disorder. These additional problems can have a serious impact on the client's assessment and treatment planning (see Chapter 5). More on the differential diagnostics will be discussed later in this chapter.

Medical history
Information concerning medical history is significant for two reasons. This information can influence the treatment planning and/or treatment outcome, and gathering information about PWC as a group can help researchers in the future. An important aspect of medical history is whether or not a client uses medications that can influence either the client's attention or speech rate.

Medications, such as Levodopa, Ritalin, and antidepressants are known for their influence on speech and fluency. Little to nothing is known on the effects of other medications on speech rates and speech control. If clients use medications that can influence attention or speech, clinicians should consult their clients' doctors to ascertain whether adjustments of their clients' medications or dosages would be beneficial.

(d) Timeline of and efficacy of previous treatment.
The date of the initial treatment can give clinicians a clear idea of the time in their clients' speech development when the first critical symptoms were clear enough to lead them to seek an assessment. Clients who start therapy to improve rate-related symptoms will have a better chance of improving if they start therapy during adolescence than if they start therapy in early childhood (see Figure 3.1).

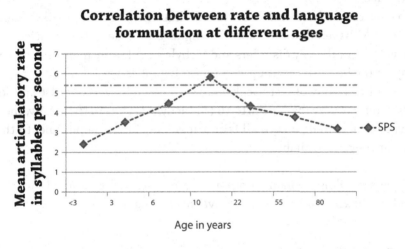

Figure 3.1: Example of the effect of correlation between rate and language formulation at different ages: The unbroken line indicates the maximum rate at which client A is able to speak fluently or intelligibly. In the case of client A, cluttering symptoms will be apparent from age seven to eight, and will not really change during this client's childhood and early adulthood. Client B (broken line with dashes and dots) is disfluent or unintelligible at a rate of 5.3 syllables per second (SPS). Client B will experience cluttering symptoms in early adolescence (when the speech rate reaches 5.4 SPS) and is likely to recover in early adulthood when the rate will naturally decline. A person with normal rate is represented by the broken line consisting of dashes and squares.

Those clients who seek cluttering treatment often had some experience with previous therapy. One of the explanations for this "hop on hop off" approach to therapy is clients' inconsistent desire to control their speech rate. Another explanation can be found in the treatment of only some of the symptoms related to cluttering, such as language production training, or working on the production of specific sounds.

Effective methods, such as audio-visual feedback training (see 6.5.1.) in previous treatment have a good chance of being effective again later in life. Although there is no assurance that the method will work again, there is no need to use different treatment methods in the beginning of therapy. This is especially true when clinicians follow clients' ideas about effective treatment. If clients are convinced that a method will be effective, their internal motivation will be heightened.

Family history of speech or language disorders including fluency disorders and tachylalia

Various researchers have concluded that there is a high likelihood that PWC have additional speech-language disorders. Information on prevalence of fluency disorders and tachylalia in family members is very important because of group dynamics. E.g., it is very difficult for one person in a family of fast speakers to slow down if everyone else speaks and interacts very fast. If cluttering or tachylalia runs in the family, then it is advisable to deal with all family members at the same time, to the extent they are available.

Note: All assessment procedures are described thoroughly in 3.2. Additional assessment forms are available in Appendices A-F.

3.1.3 Bilingual considerations

Dalton and Hardcastle (1993) pointed out that their bilingual clients with cluttering in India and Pakistan showed some rhythmic noncluttering patterns of their first language. Moreover, Dalton and Hardcastle's Asian clients were found to present cluttering patterns of speech more frequently than stuttering. It is well worth reiterating that these theories are based upon clinical observation rather than empirical evidence. Dalton and Hardcastle suggest re-examining clutterers' first languages in order to adjust treatment strategies to their clients' particular problems. They also recommend assessing the relationship between the types of disfluencies presented by speakers of different languages and the characteristics of those languages, such as rhythm and articulatory patterns. According to Hernandez (2009), switching between languages results in a more effortful cognitive retrieval process. These increased demands may cause changes in symptoms of bilingual speakers with cluttering.

3.1.4 Recordings

Assessment procedures should include samples of spontaneous and conversational speech (with a duration of between 3 to 10 minutes), perhaps in unconventional settings (e.g., when speakers do not know they are being recorded, subject to the procedure described below), and perhaps at different levels of language complexity, to analyze instances of cluttering. We recommend digital video- and audio recording of people with possible cluttering in a variety of speaking tasks for subsequent analyses of fluency, rate and rate adaptation, sentence and word structure and voice. Clinicians should be aware that the client may try to "normalize" speech behaviors when being recorded, so clinicians should prevent this from happening by comparing clients' communication behaviors when being recorded with their communication behaviors when speaking extemporaneously and not being recorded.

Note: It is considered unethical to record clients without their knowledge that recordings will be made. At the first face-to-face meeting of the clinician with the client and the client's parent(s), if applicable, the client, and the client's parent(s), if applicable, should be asked for permission, in advance, for the clinician to make and/or authorize audio and/or video recordings. Once a consent form has been signed, family members can record the speech of the client at times when the client is unaware of being recorded, typically at home either with a laptop, a mobile phone, or an I-pod. As long as permission was granted by the client, in advance, these recordings can be shared with the clinician.

The differential diagnosis conducted during the administration of the Fluency Assessment Battery should be included as part of the cluttering assessment. The Fluency Assessment Battery consists of a variety of tasks, including oral reading, spontaneous speech, retelling a memorized story, writing, screening phonological accuracy, a test of oral-motor coordination, and questionnaires. Additional receptive and expressive language tests can serve as further diagnostic tools to rule out a language disorder.

Cluttering severity may vary depending on the nature of the speaking task, and can be determined by the Cluttering Severity Instrument

(Bakker & Myers, 2011). See 3.3.9. Cluttering behaviors are more likely to surface when the speaking task is more extemporaneous and informal, less structured, more emotional, and linguistically more complex, or in situations when the client is unaware of being recorded.

3.1.5 Speech rate adjustment

Cluttering is a fluency problem in which people are not able to adjust their speech rate to the linguistic (syntactic or phonological) demands of the moment. In a linguistically challenging context, people normally speak more slowly; they adjust their speech rate to gain time to retrieve and formulate what they want to say. As a general rule, fluent people tend to speak faster when they talk about simple things or tell the same stories for the third or fourth time. The reason for a slower rate in more difficult speech conditions is obvious: expressions that are used on a regular basis have a shorter retrieval time than expressions that are used for the first time or with a long time interval in between usage. Fluent people speak more slowly particularly when communicating in a second or third language. PWC present with a deficit in adjusting their rate to the demands of the moment. When performing a complex language task, their output system remains at the same rate, even if retrieval or formulation takes much longer. Their articulatory rate is equal at different levels of language complexity. Based on our clinical experience, we know that people who are fluent speak at different rates when reading, retelling a story and speaking spontaneously, with speech rate differences ranging between 1.0 and 3.3 syllables per second (SPS), measured as a product of the highest and lowest mean articulatory rate produced. In PWC, the adjustment of the mean articulatory rate in the three just mentioned speech conditions is below 1.0 SPS. Another way to assess the potential for rate adjustment is to ask a client to speak or read faster. Fluent speakers and PWS will indeed increase their articulatory rate, while PWC will exhibit hasty or relaxed behavior without actually talking faster or slower.

> Assessment of cluttering should be conducted with tasks at various rates and at different levels of language complexity.

3.1.6 Fluency

Common instances of interjections and revisions have implications for the nature of fluency breakdowns in cluttering (Starkweather, 1987; Logan & LaSalle, 1999; see 2.2.4). It has been postulated that a number of the disfluencies exhibited by PWC are caused by linguistic rather than motoric difficulties. These disfluencies are often called "linguistic maze" behaviors (Howell & Au-Yeung, 2002), resulting in linguistic or normal disfluencies (van Zaalen, Myers, Ward, & Bennett, 2008). As proposed by Howell and Au-Yeung (2002), normal disfluencies are produced to gain time to plan the next linguistic structure. PWC normally say what was already planned. As soon as the next plan is ready, the disfluency will stop and the intended structure will be executed. Therefore, repetitions that are considered to be normal disfluencies lack tension and are produced in normal rhythmic patterns. But, contrary to stuttering-like disfluencies, normal disfluencies do not break up the syllable structure. The syllable remains intact. Normal disfluencies consist of one or two repetitions of words and/or phrases produced at a regular rate, without tension and additional stress.

When considering fluency disorders, it is important to study the effect of language complexity on the type and frequency of the disfluencies. The language formulation is more or less affected by the fast rate of PWC, depending on the level of language complexity. A way of testing the correlation of speech rate and language formulation is by asking clients to express themselves under different speech conditions, such as spontaneous speech, retelling a story and reading and comparing the effect of the linguistic task with the frequency and type of the disfluencies, both normal and stuttering-like. Normally, a more complex task is associated with more normal disfluencies. But even within one condition, e.g., spontaneous speech, different levels of language complexity are at risk, depending on the context of the topic, duration of the talk or the number of people talking. (For a full description of language complexity, see 6.5.9.) The complexity level of the task should be high enough to elicit the normal disfluencies and easy enough to enable the client to be successful without causing resistance.

3.1.7 Intelligibility

Reduced speech intelligibility is a core characteristic of a subtype of cluttering referred to as phonological cluttering (see also 1.4.6). Assessment of intelligibility should include tasks that range from short and structured, to longer and less structured. Examples of the former include rote tasks, such as counting or retelling a story. Clinicians should be alert to errors in syllable- and word structure and should measure the articulatory rate. Some PWC tend to present with phoneme-specific errors. Most PWC exhibit reduced non phoneme-specific speech intelligibility as their speech becomes more informal and extended. Speech intelligibility can be compromised by elisions of sounds and syllables, neutralization of vowels, and cluster reductions. Reduced speech intelligibility is frequently associated with a limited jaw movement while talking. This limited jaw movement improves automatically when the client speaks slower, as when reading out loud.

Simple tests to assess intelligibility:

- ○ Ask the client to count from 20 to 29.
- ○ Ask the client to count backwards.
- ○ Ask the client to count backwards, skipping two numbers each time, e.g., 100-97-94-91....

Clients up to 10.8 years of age should read some words that are difficult to pronounce (e.g., "statistical," "chrysanthemum," "possibilities," "tyrannosaurus") and produce these words three times in succession, first at a comfortable speech rate and then at a faster rate. An advanced test to assess intelligibility and phonological encoding, entitled Screening Phonological Accuracy, appears as Appendix E. Older PWC should read some words with changing stress pattern sequences, such as "apply, application, applicable" (a_ply' / a_pli_ca'_tion / a_pli'_ca_ble).

3.1.8 Awareness and Lack of Awareness

When PWC focus on speech production, their speech intelligibility improves for a short period of time, usually for 30 to 40 seconds. In contrast, PWS find that extra focus can lead to more tense and disfluent speech productions. PWC sometimes complain that when they initially sought professional help, clinicians could not detect any speech disturbances and sent them home without offering treatment. Parents and other family members sometimes tell the clinician that it seems that the client is not willing to pay enough attention to their speech. They come to this conclusion because, when at home, unfocused speech production is less fluent and less intelligible than it is when other people are around. Assessment recordings should include moments of focused speech at times when the client was aware of being recorded, as well as moments of unfocused speech at times when the client was unaware of being recorded. Differences between these two sets of conditions provide important information to the clinician regarding the clients' potential to change. For a discussion about consent for recording, see 3.1.4.

3.1.9 Linguistic skills

PWC commonly experience language problems in addition to their articulatory problems. Language difficulties in individuals who clutter include word-finding problems, poor syntactic structure, lack of coherence and cohesion in discourse and narratives, and compromised pragmatics (e.g., poor pre-suppositional skills, such as not taking into account the listener's viewpoint or knowledge, or frequent interruptions of a conversational partner's turn). But in cluttering, most language difficulties disappear in linguistic contexts that are not complex. Many language problems that appear in spoken language do not necessarily appear in written language. So language problems in cluttering are related to the rate of speech production and not to language deficits. Therefore, it is imperative to assess the language skills of the client. Language tests should be administered to rule out additional language problems as reasons for abnormal fluency. If a client has receptive or expressive language problems in addition to cluttering symptoms, the client's communication disorder should be considered and treated as a double deficit.

3.1.10 Oral-motor coordination

The diadochokinetic tasks of the Oral-Motor Assessment scale (OMAS, Riley & Riley, 1985) provide clear guidelines for observation of oral-motor coordination skills. During the oral-motor assessment, no lexical retrieval and only limited phonological encoding is necessary. The oral-motor assessment provides information on the clients' ability to coordinate muscle movements in repeated strings of syllables, productions of which require no linguistic meaning. The OMAS was normed at a time when digital recordings were unavailable. The OMAS was not normed for adolescents or adults. In the revised version of OMAS by van Zaalen and Winkelman (2009), the norms are available for all age groups and based on digital speech analysis performed by using Praat speech analysis software (Boersma & Weenink, 2012). Motor execution problems are not a characteristic of cluttering. The OMAS is administered, therefore, to exclude motor execution problems as bases of poor intelligibility. A client who has trouble on the OMAS as well as cluttering symptoms should be treated as a client with two independent deficits.

3.2 The Fluency Assessment Battery

3.2.1 Introduction

The Fluency Assessment Battery (van Zaalen & Winkelman, 2009) includes analysis of rate (3.2.3), fluency (3.2.4), intelligibility (3.3) and structure in different speech tasks: spontaneous speech (3.3.1), oral reading (3.3.2), retelling "The Wallet story" (3.3.3), the "Screening Phonological Accuracy" (3.3.5), writing (3.3.4) and the Oral- Motor Assessment Scale (3.3.6). Because many of the assessment instruments used in fluency disorders are language related, the assessment forms of the Fluency Assessment Battery are available in many different languages, such as Dutch, English, Finnish, French, Norwegian and Polish. Translation into other languages is in progress and additional translations will be posted at www.NYCSA-Center.org upon their availability.

3.2.2 Analysis of recordings and questionnaires

The clinician should analyze the recordings and questionnaires and decide on rate (adjustment), fluency, articulation, language and cognitive/ emotional components of the disorder. Comparing the client's perspective with the clinician's perspective can inform the clinician regarding the client's awareness of the disorder and motivation to overcome it. Clinicians should use the assessment forms as provided in Appendices A-F to keep records of their findings.

Table 3.1: Assessment of cluttering and stuttering (van Zaalen, Myers, Ward, & Bennet, 2010).

Cluttering Assessment	Findings and Interpretations
○ Rate	Mean articulatory rate (AR) in SPS (in 10-20 consecutive fluent syllables) Rating of the degree or irregularity in speech output (i.e., whether the pauses coincide with phrase or clause boundaries)
○ Fluency	% normal disfluencies % stuttering-like disfluencies Stuttering Severity Instrument-4 (Riley, 2008)
○ Articulation	Accuracy of syllable and word structure; appropriate stress patterns, speech naturalness (using appropriate prosody), overall speech intelligibility.
○ Language	Word, sentence and story structure; cohesion and coherence of narratives, pragmatics
○ Cognitive and emotional aspects	Feelings and attitudes towards communication; self-awareness of clients' speech and language behaviors.
○ Perspective	Comparison of results of speech tasks and clinician's perceptions on various checklists with clients' perceptions of their communication behaviors. Use the Fluency Assessment Battery. Clinicians should use Appendix F to record their findings and perspectives.

3.2.3. Mean Articulatory Rate (MAR)

After making the recording, the clinician should complete the Form for Analysis of Spontaneous Speech, Reading and Retelling (see Appendix B). This recorded sample can be used to analyze the articulatory rate, fluency, word and sentence structures and the usage and duration of pauses.

Many researchers (Hall, Amir, & Yairi, 1999; Pindzola, Jenkins, & Lokken, 1989) agree that the measurements of the articulatory rate are meant to illustrate how quickly sounds are produced in consecutive segments of speech, without pauses. In fluency assessment, the articulatory rate is calculated primarily in syllables or phonemes per second in perceptually fluent segments. Perceptually fluent productions do not include disfluencies, hesitations or pauses longer than 250 milliseconds (Yaruss, Logan, & Conture, 1994). Measuring the duration and counting the number of syllables is most easily done using the Praat speech analysis software (Boersma & Weenink, 2012). During the assessment, it takes a clinician two minutes for the recording and four minutes for the analysis. For a detailed description of how to measure and interpret the articulatory rate, see Appendix C.

In counting syllables, the clinician has to choose between the linguistically correct word form planned before speaking and actual speech-motor output. In other words, should the clinician count what the client intended to say or what the client actually said? Based on the assumption that the client has a correct word form planned before speaking, the linguistic word form is used in the determination of the articulatory rate. If the client says "libry," in counting the syllables, the number of syllables necessary to produce "library" will be used. The rationale for this assumption is that it is important to know how much time a person has planned for producing the word, in order to determine whether a problem in speech planning exists (Verhoeven, Pauw, & Kloots, 2004).

In the interpretation of articulatory rate scores, the following norms for fluent speakers can be used as an indication of the mean articulatory rate for various ages:

Table 3.2: Norms for mean articulatory rate, measured at random in a speech sample of 3 minutes, in different age groups within strings of 10-20 consecutive fluent syllables (van Zaalen et al., 2009b; van Zaalen & Winkelman, 2009)

Age	Syllables per second (SPS)
6 - 11 years	2.5 – 5.0
12 - 22 years	2.5 – 5.5
23 - 64 years	2.5 – 5.3
> 65 years	2.5 – 4.8

Example: A clinician measures the articulatory rate of an 8-year-old boy. The mean of five random recordings is 7.2 SPS. As is shown in the table, this means that the boy's rate is higher than the rate of his peers. But in itself the fast rate does not make the boy a person with cluttering.

If the client does not show at least one of the three characteristics – poor intelligibility, normal disfluencies or errors in pausing -- then the diagnosis cannot be cluttering and should be tachylalia.

It should be stressed that the mean articulatory rate is only used as an indicator of speed and is needed for the interpretation of the effect of language complexity on rate (see Appendix B). In cluttering, an imbalance between rate and language formulation is present, meaning that in some people although their articulatory rate is within the norm, it can be too fast for their speech production system to handle. This is especially true among people with intellectual disabilities.

When mean scores of the articulatory rate are below the norm, the condition is called bradylalia. When mean scores of the articulatory rate are above the norm, the condition is called tachylalia. The procedure to determine the mean articulatory rate is thoroughly discussed in the Fluency Assessment Battery (van Zaalen & Winkelman, 2009) in Appendix C.

3.2.4 Analysis of disfluencies

Frequency
In order to determine the frequency of disfluencies, a speech sample of at least 100 words is necessary. Cluttering and stuttering often coexist. It is necessary to count the normal disfluencies in a manner that is similar to the form in which the clinician counts stuttering disfluencies. We advise clinicians to use the modified Stuttering Frequency form used in the Stuttering Severity Instrument-4 (SSI-4, Riley, 2008) as part of the Fluency Assessment Battery (see Appendix B). A limitation of the SSI-4 is that normal disfluencies are completely ignored. Damsté (1987), Janssen (1985), Howell and Au-Yeung (2002) and St. Louis et al. (2007), among others, advise clinicians to take normal disfluencies into account in the interpretation of fluency disorders. The number of normal disfluencies is an indication of the extent to which the speech rate relates to language planning skills. Based on studies by Eggers (2010), and Blokker et al. (2010), a mean percentage of 8.97 (SD 5.5) normal disfluencies in a sample of 100 words is seen in spontaneous speech. This is not significantly different from the amount of normal disfluencies in retelling a story (M= 9.17; SD 5.38) but both are different from reading

a text (M=3.32; SD 2.33). According to Yairi and Ambrose (2005), 3% of stuttering-like disfluencies indicate stuttering. Juste, Sassi, and de Andrade (2006) examine differences in early adolescence (3.65% normal disfluent syllables) and late adolescence (1.35% stuttering-like disfluent syllables).

Type of disfluencies
Stuttering-like disfluencies (SLDs) are those disfluencies that interrupt the speech flow, e.g., tense word-, syllable-, or sound repetitions, prolongations and blocks. Normal or nonstuttering-like disfluencies (NDFs) are those disfluencies that happen within the flow of speech and occur with no additional uncontrolled muscular tension, e.g., relaxed and slow word, syllable- or phrase repetitions, revisions and interjections. People are usually aware of SLDs and unaware of NDFs.

Ratio disfluencies (RDF).
   Scientific research has shown that the ratio of disfluencies differentiates cluttering from stuttering more than the percentages of stuttering-like and normal disfluencies (van Zaalen, 2009). The ratio is determined by dividing the percentage of normal disfluencies by the percentage of stuttering-like disfluencies. For the interpretation of the ratio of disfluencies, see Table 3.3.

Table 3.3: Mean scores on the Stuttering Severity Instrument (Riley, 2008) and ratio disfluencies in the cluttering, stuttering and cluttering-stuttering groups (van Zaalen, Wijnen, & Dejonckere, 2009b).

	Cluttering	Cluttering stuttering	Stuttering
Stuttering Severity Instrument-4	No stuttering – mild stuttering	Mild - moderate stuttering	Mild – severe stuttering
Ratio disfluencies	RD ≥ 2.7	0 < RD > 2.7	≤ 0

3.3 Analysis of various speech conditions

The following sections will describe procedures for the analysis of rate, fluency and intelligibility in various speech conditions.

3.3.1 Spontaneous speech

The clinician should engage the clients in a relaxed exchange on a subject that is of great interest to them. This can include explaining a videogame, discussing their favorite sport or leisure activity, or telling a story about a recent exciting event that the clients experienced. The clinician should record at least 10 minutes of this language sample. The language sample should consist of a narrative rather than a listing of events. We have found that cluttering behaviors become more evident the more informal, spontaneous and extensive the conversation may be. When the client is not aware of the recording, the clinician will have the best chance of recording "uncontrolled" cluttering speech. Such speech may also be observed when recording the interaction between, for instance, a parent and a child, or an adult and a partner when the clinician is not in the room (van Zaalen et al., 2007). During the clinician's first telephone contact with the client, the speech performance of the client can be examined by the clinician's asking questions about the client's symptoms. The clinician should keep in mind that the client's heightened concentration in this first contact can influence the speech production. Immediately after getting a consent form duly signed (see 3.1.4), the clinician should take a more detailed background history, including the client's complaints, while recording it (see video of Baruti at www.NYCSA.org). Recordings make it possible to have an open conversation with the client and afterwards to process all the initial information.

After making the recording, the clinician should ask the clients (not tell them) what their impressions of their speech performance was in this recording. A comparison of the clients' perception and the clinician's perception provides insight as to the level of speech awareness of the clients. It is commonly known that the speech of PWC in their first session is much more focused than it generally is and only a little bit disfluent or unintelligible (see 2.2.10). It can be assumed that clients also may have "practiced" their speech before the first visit. A way to diminish this learning effect is to ask clients in the first session to describe something that they did not expect to talk about. It is advisable for the clinician to ask something at a high level of language complexity, as is described in 6.5.9. Processing of the spontaneous speech sample takes about fifteen minutes.

3.3.2 Oral reading

The nature of the oral reading task will limit the possibilities for language formulation difficulties in PWC. It is advisable for the clinician to use a reading text in which communication between people is included (see Appendix J for a sample of a reading text). However, different errors are likely to occur in prosody or during word production. Omission or substitution of syllables and words (particularly pronouns and articles) may be noted. Take note of errors in syllable and word structure, such as telescoping of syllables or guessing at words. Three samples of at least two minutes of continuous reading of the same text should be evaluated. Rate, fluency and intelligibility are measured using the Fluency Assessment Battery Forms (Appendix B and C). Oral reading and spontaneous speech are processed the same way (Appendix I), making a comparison of the task's effect on rate, fluency and intelligibility easy.

Because the level of the reading material may influence the severity of cluttering, clinicians should present their clients with appropriate reading material that varies in complexity. The more difficult passages, containing more multisyllabic words and linguistically more complex sentences, may produce more cluttering behaviors compared to the less difficult passages. It is also suggested that the client should be asked to read one passage with preparation and one without, to compare the results of both readings.

Unlike people who do not clutter, PWC who read the same material four times in a row show a decreased level of focused attention during their repeated readings. The result of less attention is audible and is manifested by an increase in guessed reading, telescoping of multisyllabic words and disfluencies compared to prior readings, especially when a reading text is significantly below the reading level of the client. In PWS, speech output upon repeated rereading of the same text is unaffected at times, though at other times the blocks or prolongations related to fear of specific sounds become longer and more severe.

Because the level of auditory monitoring in PWC is below normal during speech, clinicians should ask their clients to evaluate their intelligibility, rate, and fluency immediately after reading any appropriate text. Secondly, reading out loud using headphones (heightened auditory feedback) is known to compensate the weak monitoring during speech and thereby reduces moments of unintelligibility, disfluencies and errors in reading.

Reading offers important information regarding the emotional component of the speech disorder. Do clients feel comfortable when reading? Are the clients under the impression that they can control their speech better when reading, compared to spontaneous speech? Comparing the perceptions of clients with the perceptions of the clinician provides not only diagnostic data, but also the first insight into clients' monitoring skills. This can be confrontational but also a therapeutically valuable experience for the client.

3.3.3 Retelling a memorized story

Many clinicians have observed that PWC experience problems in telling stories. PWC are often tempted to provide more detailed information than necessary. They are also reported to have problems in maintaining the line of the discourse. But these impressions have not been substantiated by empirical research. To the contrary, in a retelling task called "The Wallet story" (Appendix D), PWC narrated side issues similarly to the fluent controls. A study conducted by van Zaalen, Dejonckere and Wijnen (2009a) showed that PWC distinguish themselves from PWS by adding side issues and making extra comments, not supportive to the story.

"The Wallet Story" (Appendix D) is specifically designed to gather information on speech output when less focus is placed on language formulation compared to spontaneous speech. Such a goal is achieved by the storyteller who provides both the story structure and the sentence structure when presenting a story to the client. If the auditory memory is normal, such an approach will help in memorizing the story constructs as well as parts of the sentence structures. The story was developed by van Zaalen and Bochane (2007) based on the basic principles of the Bus story (Renfrew Language Scales) and on the story construct of the Arizona Battery for Communication Disorders of Dementia test (ABCD). The Bus story can still be used for children younger than 12 years of age.

During the retelling of the story, the clinician should analyze the story's components, articulatory rate, ratio of disfluencies and the structures of the sentences. Judging a story's components and speech outcome in a structured setting makes it possible to compare the results of the analysis of the client with the analysis of other people, but also of the client herself in different situations. Comparison of the scores of rate, fluency and intelligibility provides the clinician with more information about the influence of the client's language formulation on the quality of her speech. Sometimes a client is able to imitate or use complex language structures while retelling a story, but may not be able to produce the same structures in spontaneous speech. The errors in language formulation in those cases are not related to a lack of language production skills, but are related to a lack of formulation skills while retelling a story with a fast articulatory rate. In such a case, working on sentence structure would be less effective in changing the speech outcome than working on speech rate and language planning.

3.3.4 Writing and handwriting

Writing and reading are the highest levels of speech and language development (van Zaalen & Bochane, 2007). It seems to us that the articulatory rate is highly correlated to the writing rate. Similarly to linguistic weaknesses, poor handwriting is one of the earlier behaviors associated with cluttering. Some older PWC use the compensatory strategy of printing the written code. It is suggested that clients should be asked to write, both in script as well as in print, for comparison purposes. Writing errors may mirror difficulties in the speech domain, so the client should be asked to write a short paragraph, after which the clinician should look for untidy or illegible writing, weak spelling, poorly constructed grammar, and transposition and omissions of letters as evidence of cluttering related behaviors.

The handwriting speed can be determined using the Handwriting Speed Test (Wallen, Bonney, & Lennox, 1996). In this test, the client is asked to write a standardized sentence ten times in quick succession during a pre-set time period. The handwriting should then be analyzed, consulting the handwriting observation lists of van Hartingsveldt, Cup, and Corstens-Mignot (2006/2010). According to Van Hartingsveldt et al., the clinician should analyze characteristics such as fluency in movement, amplitude of the movement, the pressure on the paper, the spatial positioning, the readability and the writing rate. If the client appears to have severe grapho-motor problems, such as, for instance, an illegible handwriting, this should be considered when planning therapeutic intervention. A consult of a physical or occupational therapist is recommended in those cases.

3.3.5 Screening Phonological Accuracy

Every disfluent speaker can be examined regarding possible problems in the area of speech-motor control and phonological encoding. Speech-motor control problems in stuttering can be identified by using the Oral-Motor Assessment Scale (Riley & Riley 1985; van Zaalen & Winkelman, 2009) (see 3.3.6). If a client is unintelligible or stumbles in multisyllabic words, then it is advisable to assess phonological planning at the word or phrase level, and to assess speech motor skills.

PWC often demonstrate abnormal phonological encoding skills at the word level, because their inhibition problem prevents them from being able to adjust their rate to the higher level of planning skills in low frequency multisyllabic words. Low frequency words take longer lexicon retrieval time than high frequency words. Words that are frequently used can be retrieved much faster based on the linguistic motor memory. Words that are infrequently used need to be planned before execution is initiated. Although this planning takes time, PWC are "forced" to speak fast, because they don't have adequate planning time. PWC finalize the syllable planning at the same time as they are already producing the word. In repeated attempts, the client cannot benefit from an earlier well performed production, contrary to what happens while the client plans the new sequence, at which time equal problems in lack of balance between planning and production occur. While fluent people are able to produce the SPA words (see next paragraph and Appendix E) three times fast, equally, and intelligibly, PWC plan for each of the three sequences by making three separate attempts.

To assess clients' phonological planning and execution skills, the Screening Phonological Accuracy (van Zaalen, Cook, Elings, & Howell, 2011) was developed as a modified translation of the SPA (Dutch: Screening Pittige Articulatie) developed by van Zaalen et al. (2009b). Meanwhile, in addition to being available in Dutch and English, the SPA is available in different languages, such as German, French, Norwegian, Polish and Finnish, and translations of the SPA into more languages are in progress, see www.NYCSA-Center.org. A full description of the SPA test instruction, normative data, and interpretations are presented in Appendix E.

3.3.6 Diadochokinetic rate

The Oral-Motor Assessment Scale (OMAS), at the sound level, was originally developed by Riley and Riley (1985), and was later modified to digital recording and analysis by van Zaalen (2009). The OMAS is the most effective instrument to rule out oral-motor difficulties as an explanation for intelligibility problems. The norms and interpretations of OMAS are described in Appendix G.

It is important to learn as much as possible about the oral-motor skills of clients. This information gives the clinician insight as to how far the clients are able to adjust their articulatory rate to the oral-motor demands of the moment. In other words, it helps to measure how fast the oral-motor system is able to produce sound sequences without a linguistic content. The ability of PWC to adjust their syllable sequencing (temporal ordering) and syntactic formulation skills (grammatical order) to the speech rate is inadequate. The articulatory rate that PWC can maintain in order to control their syntactic planning and motor movements can be selected as a goal for facilitating an appropriate speech rate in therapy. It is obvious that a mean articulatory rate may depend on various speech situations or level of language complexity. The mean rate produced in the OMAS task should therefore be considered to be the absolute maximum mean rate. If a person is able to speak clearly when linguistic demands are low, the speech rate should be slower for situations with higher language complexity.

Speech-motor control includes the following aspects (Riley & Riley, 1985; van Zaalen et al., 2009):

Table 3.4: Speech-motor control

Aspect	Variable	Correct production	Errors
Accuracy	Distortion	a good articulation position and correct force	In voiced sounds the voice onset is not well adjusted to the articulatory movements: voice-onset time (common in stuttering)
	Voicing	Normal voicing	Voiced sounds are produced without voicing and vice versa

Smooth flow	Coarticulation	A gradual flow from one speech movement to the other	Extra pauses between syllables or tense vocal onset
	Flow	Equal rhythm and normal stress	Dysrhythmic production
	Telescoping	A correct number of syllables	Deletion of syllables within a sequence (e.g., pa-ta-ka produced as paka-paka).
	Sequencing	A correct sequence of sounds/sequence of syllables	Order of syllables is changed (e.g., "pataka" as "pakata"; "pata'as "pa-at").
Rate	Syllables per second	Mean rate over three attempts of ten syllable combinations	Extreme slowing down (below 3 SPS), possibly with extra pauses

The characteristics of speech-motor control are related to verbal-motor elements (syllables) and not to nonverbal elements, such as tongue movements, lip rounding and jaw movements.

When Edwin (age 22.3 years) talks about his vacation, a mean rate of 6.0 SPS is an adequate rate for the motor control of his speech output. When Edwin wants to express his opinion about the access policy of the swimming pool, the rate of 6.0 SPS leads to a high frequency of telescoping and normal disfluencies. Edwin was able to produce "pataka" at a rate of 6.5 SPS. After a suggestion made by the clinician, Edwin lowers his speech rate (when measured it appeared to be 5.1 SPS) and he is able to control his speech once again.

3.3.7 Speech analysis using Praat software

Praat is a program for speech analysis and synthesis written by Paul Boersma and David Weenink at the Department of Phonetics of the University of Amsterdam. The Praat website is www.fon.hum.uva.nl/

praat. The program is constantly being improved and updated. Praat provides assistance in speech analysis (spectral, pitch, formant and intensity analysis, jitter and shimmer), speech synthesis (from pitch formant and intensity and articulatory synthesis), listening experiments (identification and discrimination tests) and speech manipulation (change of pitch and duration contours). Praat provides free downloadable software. The Praat user manual for beginners is downloadable via www. NYSCA.org. The digital speech analysis helps to make the measurements objective and to provide insight into the speech of clients. See Chapters 5 and 6. The speech analysis procedure can serve as a therapeutic feedback instrument. Installation of the software takes only two minutes. Most clients who are at least eight years old are able to use Praat after one or two ten-minute sessions of instruction.

3.3.8 Cluttering self-assessment checklists

Self-evaluation of speech is possible using different instruments or assignments (see Appendix J). Self-evaluation gives insight into clients' cognitive and emotional factors of cluttering. Instruments especially developed for PWS can be adjusted and used for PWC. An example of this is the Speech Situation Checklist of Brutten and Shoemaker (1974) as adapted to cluttering (see Appendix O).

The Stuttering Prediction Instrument (SPI) (Riley, 1981) assesses a child's history, reactions, part-word repetitions, prolongations, and frequency of stuttered words to assist in measuring severity and predicting chronicity. The impact of stuttering in a person's life can be assessed with the help of The Wright and Ayre Stuttering Self-Rating Profile (WASSP, Wright & Ayre, 2000) and the Overall Assessment of the Speaker's Experience of Stuttering (OASES, Yaruss & Quesal, 2010). Some questions on the WASSP and SPI relate to the physical aspects of disfluencies. When these questions are related to cluttering behaviors, comparisons can be made between the observations of the clinician and those of the client. For instruments assessing feelings and attitudes (such as Erickson's Speech Situation Checklist, subsections of the WASSP and the "expectancy" and "avoidance" statements on the SPI), the clinician can go through the responses together with the client once the client has completed the questionnaires and can use the client's responses as a springboard for subsequent therapy.

The clinician can ask clients to assess their own speech during various recorded tasks, which should then be compared to the clinician's feedback. A 5-point rating scale (ranging from 1 being fluent, with no complaints, to 5 being severely disfluent) is often useful to judge the recorded samples on each of the major areas of the clients' speech and language.

3.3.9 Computer-based Cluttering Severity Instrument

Because of the multidimensional nature of cluttering, it is necessary to supplement assessment of the individual dimensions, such as rate and fluency, with a means to rate the overall severity of cluttering based on the perception of the experienced clinician. A freeware assessment tool was developed for this purpose by Klaas Bakker and Florence Myers (2011), the *Cluttering Severity Instrument (CSI)*. It is available at the Resources and Links section of the International Cluttering Association website, http://associations.missouristate.edu/ica/.

This diagnostic tool allows the clinician to determine the percentage of speaking time cluttered. While listening to a speech sample, speaking time is measured by pressing the left mouse button of the computer as long as the speech is perceived to be either fluent or cluttered. The perception of cluttering is marked by holding down the right mouse button for the duration of perceived cluttering. More information about the program is available at the download site.

The CSI is built on the assumption that cluttering needs to be measured by (1) using perceptual assessment procedures, (2) addressing the multifaceted aspects of the problem, and (3) being sensitive to individually different severity patterns. The quantified nature of results from the CSI allows clinicians to determine the baseline severity as well as the degree of gains made for the eight separate clinical dimensions that are assessed, as therapy progresses. It should be noted that improvements in one dimension can have a beneficial effect on another dimension since cluttering is a systemic disorder (Bakker & Myers, 2011).

The CSI, on one hand, produces a severity value that represents overall cluttering severity, which is its primary objective. Nevertheless, it also provides the option to analyze the severity of individual dimensions of cluttering and to consider how they interact in producing an overall severity result (Bakker & Myers, 2011).

The CSI software, code and manual are available to anyone as freeware without any restrictions. A Code is available upon request, from Klaas Bakker. For more information, see http://associations.missouristate.edu/ICA/.

3.4 Differential diagnosis

Differential diagnosis relates to the diagnosis in which a choice is made between strongly related alternatives. In this chapter we will discuss differential diagnostics between cluttering on the one hand and stuttering, learning difficulties, tachylalia, developmental apraxia of speech, specific language impairment, neurologic cluttering, and dysarthria. Furthermore we will discuss the prevalence of cluttering in a number of disorders and syndromes, like Down syndrome, Autism Spectrum Disorders, Fragile-X syndrome, Gilles de la Tourette syndrome, Neurofibromatosis-1 and Attention Deficit Hyperactivity Disorder (ADHD).

3.4.1 Introduction

Cluttering usually co-exists with other disorders such as stuttering, articulation disorders, attention-deficit hyperactivity disorders and learning disabilities. The available literature as a whole suggests that an essential difference between cluttering and stuttering is based on the speaker's level of preparedness for saying intended utterances. PWS know what they intend to say but have a breakdown at the motoric level in their attempts to produce various words, whereas PWC do not necessarily know all of what they want to say (or how to say it) but continue talking anyway. Part-word repetitions, prolongations and blocks are typically produced by PWS, whereas excessive but normal disfluencies often characterize the speech of PWC. The latter include interjections, incomplete phrases/words, and revisions.

PWC exceed the normal qualitative and quantitative limits of changes in phonemes and tend to delete or neutralize syllables that standard speakers do not neutralize, especially in fast speech. Although symptoms of ADD or ADHD are often considered indicative of cluttering, individuals diagnosed with ADHD do not necessarily clutter. Specific Learning Difficulties (SLD) have been reported to co-exist with cluttering, especially difficulties in oral expression, reading, writing, handwriting and music; however, corroborating data for these observations are anecdotal.

3.4.2 Differential diagnostic criteria

Eisenson (1986) described cluttering as a "cousin" of stuttering, with both disorders stemming from the same family tree. Van Riper (1970) stated that confusion between cluttering and stuttering has characterized the field of speech pathology since the "proverbial pre-dawn darkness" (p. 347). Historically, cluttering was considered to be the same disorder as stuttering (Georgieva, 2010; Van Riper, 1970). Several experts from Germany (de Hirsch, 1970; Freund, 1966; Froeschels, 1946) and Austria (Weiss, 1964) expressed the belief that stuttering is caused by cluttering. De Hirsch (1970) pointed out that children with cluttering-like behavior whose linguistic systems are immature and disorganized are likely to become stutterers due to emotional conflict and stress.

Clinicians perform diagnostic assessments within their clinics to evaluate clients' speech output. In order to plan effective treatment, it is important to differentiate between types and subtypes of disorders and at the same time to rule out potentially co-existing disorders. A differential diagnosis in fluency disorders is also important in identifying cluttering or stuttering components, and at the same time in understanding the effect of rate on the client's speech output. But as described above, there are many syndromes in which disfluencies or problems with intelligibility occur. To distinguish between the syndromes, a thorough assessment is necessary under various speaking conditions. Making a diagnosis based on only one or two symptoms is not sufficient for all types of fluency disorders. It is the profile of speech behaviors in different conditions that will give clinicians answers about their clients' underlying problems and consequently will lead to the correct diagnosis.

Note: Symptoms can change during a therapy program. It is possible that a cluttering component is overlooked in a person with severe blocks, because the blocks prevent the person from speaking without inhibitions. It is also possible that PWC suffer from severe negative reactions toward speaking based on their communication experiences, but do not express these thoughts at the outset of therapy because they are unaware of the relationship between their speech problems and negative thoughts. We will now take a closer look at the similarities and differences between cluttering and other communication disorders.

Objective acoustic speech analysis is not commonly performed within the speech pathology community. Assessment of speech is generally performed based on perceptual findings. It is possible that a client's speech can be perceived as fast in the opinion of one clinician while the same speech segment can be perceived as normal in the opinion of another clinician. Clients do not benefit from this difference in perception, which may interfere with a correct diagnosis. Clinical decisions can be made based on objective measurements, using, for example, speech analysis software such as Praat (Boersma & Weenink, 2012).

In Chapters 5 and 6, the use of Praat in exercises is explained. Scoring forms and test instruments are all described in this chapter. The interpretation and form for the use of Praat appear at the www.NYCSA. org website.

Diagnostic markers.

As described in Chapter 1, cluttering is characterized by an articulatory rate that is too fast or too variable, resulting in a high frequency of normal disfluencies, and errors in pausing or word structure. But not every fast speaker is considered to be a person with cluttering. In addition, some non-cluttering people also produce errors in pausing or word structure or have a high frequency of "normal" disfluencies. In other words, no single characteristic independently justifies a diagnosis of cluttering, contrary to the different responses to changes in language complexity that characterize cluttering. Recent research (van Zaalen, Heeswijk, & Reichel, in preparation) has shown that PWC produce significantly more normal disfluencies and word structure errors than fluent individuals. But this is also true for people with intellectual disabilities, dysarthria, Parkinson's disease, or people with some types of aphasia. The extent to which the underlying mechanism for the disfluencies in the above mentioned syndromes is comparable to the underlying mechanism for cluttering, if at all, will be discussed in the next sections.

When PWC do not adjust their speech rate to the linguistic complexity of multisyllabic words, then word structure errors can easily occur. The most obvious errors are sequencing errors and overcoarticulation (telescoping). In producing complex multisyllable segments three consecutive times, the planning normally takes place before production. When planning takes place before production, each production will be executed separately according to the same plan. When planning is done during production, each production is different. The Screening Phonological Accuracy test (van Zaalen et al., 2011) is sensitive to these processes, and can be used as a diagnostic instrument indicating phonological cluttering.

3.4.3 Stuttering

Cluttering is a fluency disorder that is similar to stuttering, but is also very different in many aspects. Cluttering and stuttering, when occurring simultaneously, also called *balbuties e paraphrasia praecipe* (Freund, in Weiss, 1964), were known and described as comorbid disorders in the early years of the former century by Scripture (1912). Although the first detailed description of these two coexisting disorders was already made a century ago, many clinicians still know very little about cluttering. They confuse cluttering with stuttering or with other disorders (Ward, 2006).

St. Louis, Hinzman, and Hull (1985) studied the differences between stuttering and cluttering symptoms. They ascertained that people with combined cluttering and stuttering disorders produce a high frequency of disfluencies. PWC produce significantly fewer repetitions of sounds and syllables, prolongations and struggle behaviors than PWS. Among PWC, the speech disruptions seem to be attempts to gain time for linguistic planning. Among PWS, the speech disruptions reflect the tension and struggle to produce what was already planned.

The differences between cluttering and stuttering

PWC are differentiated from PWS by:

1. A fast or variable articulatory rate;
2. Weak speech motor control in multisyllabic words;
3. A high ratio of disfluencies;
4. No rate adjustment to linguistic complexity;
5. Focused attention makes speech better;
6. Relaxation makes speech worse.

All six characteristics that distinguish cluttering from stuttering will be discussed more thoroughly below.

1 A fast or variable articulatory rate
In our clinical experience, we have found that PWC are not able to control their speech rate for longer than about 40 seconds. This is especially true in speech conditions of high language complexity or when the person is very tired.

2   Weak speech-motor control in multisyllabic words

PWC, especially those with phonological cluttering, have great difficulty in maintaining correct syllable structures when they produce complex multisyllabic words at a fast rate. This is especially true for low frequency words (see also Screening Phonological Accuracy, 3.3.5). PWS also experience difficulties performing this task. They can have trouble starting production, but keep the word structure intact.

3   A high ratio of disfluencies

The ratio of disfluencies is defined as the relationship between the frequencies of normal disfluencies to stuttering-like disfluencies (see 3.2). PWC usually produce seven times more normal disfluencies than stuttering-like disfluencies. Among PWS, the ratio of disfluencies is always below 3 and often even below 1.

4   No rate adjustment to linguistic complexity

It appears that people with syntactic cluttering are not able to adequately adjust their speech rate to the linguistic demands of the moment. In comparing the mean articulatory rate in different speaking situations, the mean rate varies by less than 1.0 SPS. PWS, in contrast, are capable of adjusting their articulatory rate in various linguistic contexts. The difference in articulatory rate between speaking situations in those who are able to adjust their rate usually ranges between 1.0 – 3.3 SPS (van Zaalen & Winkelman, 2009).

5   Focused attention makes speech better

While PWC present better output when focused on their speech, among PWS extra attention usually tends to increase tension, making speech output more difficult and disfluent.

6   Relaxation makes speech worse

Among PWS, relaxation has a positive effect on speech output. By contrast, among PWC, relaxation makes speech output worse. For example, when communicating with close relatives and friends, PWS have fewer problems, while PWC experience more problems.

Cluttering and stuttering also have many *similarities*. These are:

1 Speech fear;
2 Word fear;

3 Less achievement in society;
4 Problems in social encounters;
5 Coping with negative stigma.

We will elaborate on these five differentiating characteristics as well.

1   Speech fear
Contrary to what many clinicians think, communicative or speech fear is present in both PWC and PWS. Both types of disfluent speakers are afraid of the listener's responses. Among PWS, this fear is related to the anxiety of getting stuck while speaking (fear of stuttering). PWC can develop anxiety of not being understood. The extent to which this fear can develop is the same for both types of disfluent speakers. Some PWC develop stuttering as a result of this fear. We will discuss this more thoroughly later.

2   Word fear or fear of difficult words
PWS with word fear experience difficulties in producing words that start with a particular sound, often plosives or vowels. They can also develop fear of words on which they stuttered before. PWC can develop fear of the production of multisyllabic words or reading out loud.

3 and 4 Underachievement in society and problems in social encounters
Speakers with stuttering and cluttering can underachieve in many areas of life because of their speech problems. Avoidance of job hunting, for instance, can contribute to vocational underachievement. A job that requires a lot of telephone conversations or client interactions can be difficult for a person with fluency disorders. PWC can find it extremely difficult to express their thoughts during a team meeting in an intelligible and comprehensible manner. As one of our clients, a 34-year-old man by the name of Wilco, confided, "It is so difficult for me to produce the name of the deceased correctly that I have decided to give up my job as a funeral director and became an ambulance driver."

5   Coping with negative stigma
It is widely known that PWC and PWS are negatively stigmatized by the general public. Dalton and Hardcastle (1993) observed that "[L]isteners are usually spared the anxiety transmitted by many stutterers, but they often produce their own in their effort to grasp the clutterer's meaning"

(p. 127). A recent study found that respondents from four countries believe that PWC and PWS may be nervous, excitable, fearful, or shy, and cannot work satisfactorily in jobs requiring a significant amount of talking (St. Louis et al., 2011).

When asked whether cluttering or stuttering is more negatively stigmatized, respondents to the previously referenced Brief Cluttering and Stuttering Questionnaire (BCSQ) answered: "People stigmatize cluttering and stuttering in different ways." "With stuttering it's a pity/amused look, but with cluttering it's a confused look or the long silent pause on the other end of the phone. And both disorders draw an emotional reaction, whether it's laughter or tears, it's a reaction that you never forget." "If stuttering is mostly associated with speech, cluttering, due to its unusual nature, is often associated with non-coherent thinking, a low IQ, absence of cognitive skills, low emotional intelligence, etc." And finally: "Inability to express the thoughts effortlessly and explicitly causes puzzled listeners' facial expressions and comments" (Exum et al., 2010).

In Table 3.5, an overview is given of the characteristics differentiating between various fluency disorders.

Table 3.5: Speech characteristics of different disorders in various conditions

Differential diagnosis for various disorders				
Linguistic and psychological factors	**Cluttering**	**Stuttering**	**Learning problems**	**ADHD**
Mean articulatory rate	Rapid and/or irregular	Slow-to-moderate	Normal	Normal to fast
Ratio disfluencies (NDFs to SLDs) in monologue or retelling	High in favor of NDFs	High in favor of SLDs	High in favor of NDFs	High in favor of NDFs
Pauses	Too few, too short, or in linguistically inappropriate places	Appropriate, too many and too long	Many	Too short, in normal places
Adjustment of rate to language complexity	No	Yes	Yes	No
Errors in word structure	Possible	No	Possible	Possible
Possible causes of errors in sentence structures	Sentence formulation under stress in time	Avoidance behavior	Sentence formulation underdeveloped	Absent
Attention makes speech:	Better	Worse	Better	Better
Relaxation makes speech:	Worse	Better	Better	Better
Speaking a foreign language makes speech:	Better	Varies	Worse	Better
Reading out loud from a known text is:	Worse	Mostly better, but worse in cases of speech fear	Better	Worse
Reading out loud from an unknown text is:	Better	Worse	Mostly worse	Mostly worse
Fear of communication:	Possible	Present	Absent	Absent
Awareness of symptoms	Mostly not	Mostly yes	Mostly not	Present
Awareness of speech disorder	Often	Mostly yes	Absent	Absent
Word fear mainly in case of:	Multisyllable words	Mostly emotionally loaded	Absent	Absent
Sound fear	Absent	Frequent and varies with individuals	Absent	Absent

3.4.4 Specific learning disorder

Tiger, Irvine, and Reis (1980) examined similarities between cluttering and learning disabilities. Daly (1992) also noted such similarities, and pointed out that many symptoms experienced by PWC are also present in people with learning disabilities. Daly referred to symptoms such as impulsiveness, lack of order and awareness, inattentiveness, underachieving in school, specific reading problems and language disorders. Additional common factors, according to Daly (1992) and Mensink-Ypma (1990) are problems with writing and dysrhythmic speech. Although the symptoms are comparable, the underlying processes leading to the symptoms of both disorders are different, and the rates of improvement may vary as well.

Because difficulties in language formulation are present in both PWC and people with intellectual disabilities, Preus (1996) concluded that cluttering has more in common with the speech of people with intellectual disabilities than with the speech of PWS. This idea was previously expressed by Mensink-Ypma in 1990. All the above mentioned characteristics are based on clinical observations by clinicians and are described in relatively vague terms, such as "difficulties in language formulation" or "unaware of speech symptoms." Recent research shows that differences in type, severity and underlying processes in the linguistic performance do exist. How the different speech and language characteristics of PWC and people with intellectual disabilities differ will be described below.

In a Dutch study (N= 150; age range 10.6 – 12.11 years), van Zaalen et al. (2009d) found that adolescents with cluttering scored similarly to people with intellectual disabilities in terms of their articulatory rate.

Children with cluttering differ from children with learning disabilities by:

1. higher frequency of normal disfluencies;
2. a greater number of instances of semantic paraphasia;
3. making grammatical errors in speech but not in writing;
4. higher percentage of main issues, side issues and noise while narrating a story;
5. fewer errors in story sequence.

We will now discuss the differences in speech output between PWC and people with learning disabilities.

1. The types of normal disfluencies
The normal disfluencies of PWC are mainly word- and phrase repetitions. They are possibly used for gaining time to convert their thoughts into speech sounds. The repetitions are used to gain time for speech planning and execution. People with intellectual disabilities use 'uhm'-interjections mainly in order to gain time for lexical retrieval. In addition, building "the idea" or "the message" appears to be troublesome for this group. In addition to their normal disfluencies, people with intellectual disabilities produce disfluencies that are not typical and cannot be categorized as stuttering-like or normal disfluencies, e.g., repetitions of the final syllable (Coppens-Hofman et al., 2013).

2. The number of semantic paraphrasias
PWC use both semantically related words as well as phonological paraphasias. In the latter, a speaker constructs a word with a high level of phonological similarities, e.g., "I book a fight" when "I book a flight" was meant. After production, these errors are not corrected, but they are detected by the speaker when a recording is played back. Children with intellectual disabilities use semantic paraphasias quite often. When making this type of error, PWC have the right concept in their thoughts and want to express it, but eventually a sentence with a different meaning is unintentionally produced. For example, Tatyana, a person with cluttering, recalled, "I also had to learn how to overcome the wish to never open my mouth again after running sentences in an unknown direction..." (Exum et al., 2010). Clients fail to retrieve the correct word from the lexicon and are unaware of the error unless it is pointed out to them. They discriminate the error when a recording is played back repeatedly. For example, Charlene described such an experience, as follows: "The competition usually resulted in a jumbled mass of words exiting my mouth, leaving both the recipient and myself perplexed" (Exum et al., 2010).

3. Making grammatical errors in speech but not in writing
Sentence structure errors in cluttering are only apparent in spoken language. In written language the errors are not present. PWC do not produce grammatical errors when they are able to focus adequate

attention when speaking. This is contrary to what happens with people with intellectual disabilities who produce grammatical errors in written and spoken language.

4. A high percentage of main issues, side issues and noise
Research by van Zaalen, Wijnen and Dejonckere (2009a) showed that children with intellectual disabilities produced fewer main and side issues and much more noise, such as interjections "I do not remember it anymore" or "What did you tell me?" or additional sentences that were not originally in the story. PWC tend to use main and side issues as much as fluent speakers do, but generally produce some noise as well.

5. Few errors in story sequence.
Children with intellectual disabilities have big problems retelling stories in sequence. In retelling stories, they make errors in the sequence of story elements, errors of which they are unaware. (E.g., "My father drives to Amsterdam and sat down in the car.") PWC do not notice such story structure errors in their own speech, although the story of PWC can be perceived as chaotic due to the high frequency of disfluencies and telescoping combined with a fast speech rate and frequent instances of noise.

3.4.5 Tachylalia

Tachylalia is speech with a fast speech rate without a neurological or psychological etiology. Tachylalia and cluttering can easily be differentiated. In the fast speech rate of a person with tachylalia, the fluency of speech remains intact (Weiss, 1964). People with tachylalia will always speak at a fast rate, while PWC often speak at a variable rate. Another obvious difference between people with tachylalia and PWC is that PWC have high incidences of telescoping, while in tachylalia the word structure is not affected. A fast rate in cluttering often co-occurs with short pauses in linguistically wrong places, while pauses by people with tachylalia are shorter but occur in appropriate places. Some PWC in the DVD entitled Cluttering presented with tachylalia as well (Myers & St. Louis, 2007).

3.4.6 Developmental apraxia of speech

Developmental apraxia of speech (DAS) refers to a disorder in which the coordination of sequenced speech movements is disturbed. DAS means the inconsistent ability to perform certain goal-oriented motor movements. It involves problems in the planning and coordination of muscle movements. The distinctive feature of apraxia is that people with this condition can fail to make certain movements intentionally but can only make them involuntarily, while being unaware of them. For example, DAS children can blow in their tea cup when the tea is too hot, but can have difficulties in producing the [f] phoneme in isolation.

Apraxia-like errors are sometimes made by PWC, such as sound distortions, which are common among people with apraxia and cluttering, and may indicate abnormal synchronization of articulatory sequencing and serial ordering in the speech of PWC (Ward, 2011). Although DAS and cluttering have distinct etiologies, these disorders also have noticeable similarities. We will discuss the similarities before we will discuss the differences.

Common characteristics of cluttering and developmental apraxia of speech

1. Speech rate adjustment to different speech conditions
The speech rate of children with DAS and of PWC does not adjust to different speech conditions. In DAS, the speech rate is often slow, while in cluttering the speech rate is often fast (Dannenbauer, 1999).

2. Search behavior in oral motor movement
The groping movements of the lips while a person searches for the correct articulatory position, so well known in DAS, happens in cluttering only when the speech rate is too fast.

3. Variability of repeated production in multisyllabic words
People with DAS as well as PWC demonstrate a high variability of repeated productions of the same word. For people with DAS, this happens in both low and high frequency words, while for PWC only the low frequency words are affected.

Table 3.6: Characteristics of cluttering and verbal dyspraxia of speech

Characteristics	Cluttering	Developmental Apraxia of Speech
Variability in reproduction	Fast	Fast
Speech rate	Fast	Slow
Searching mouth movements	Yes, only during fast rate	Yes
Initial sound substitutions	None	Possible
Final sound omissions	Possible	Possible
Sound additions	Yes, in fast rate	Yes
Age with the most symptoms	Early adolescence	Toddler years

4. *Frequent occurrence of final consonant deletion*
Deletion *of* the *final consonants* can occur in both DAS and PWC.

5. *Additions of sounds*
Additions of sounds can hinder the speech intelligibility of children with DAS. In cluttering this tends to happen only when the speech rate is too fast or when complex multisyllabic words are used.

▨ 3.4.7 Specific Language Impairment

"Cluttering is a verbal manifestation of central language imbalance, which affects all channels of communication (e.g., reading, writing, rhythm, and musicality), and behavior in general" (Weiss, 1964, p.1). Myers and St. Louis (2007) concluded that PWC demonstrate normal scores on language tests. Ward (2004, 2006), however, observed linguistic disturbances in spontaneous speech. The influence of linguistic complexity on cluttering symptoms was also described by Mensink-Ypma (1990), Winkelman (1990), and van Zaalen and Winkelman (2009). The more complex the speaker's message is, the more likely it is that language formulation difficulties will occur. Based primarily on clinical observation, we claim that PWC's language difficulties do not necessarily indicate a language

CLUTTERING

disorder. Such language difficulties disappear when PWC speak at a slower rate or when they write (van Zaalen, 2009e).

Language formulation problems are related to the complexity of the linguistic output in almost every speaker. PWC are no different in this respect. People with language production problems, such as semantic permutations, word finding problems or syntax problems, can be differentiated from PWC. The most important distinction is that production problems of people with specific language impairment (SLI) do not disappear when they speak at a slower rate or when they write. They simply do not possess necessary grammatical construction or lexical selection skills (word finding strategies). Although the skills of PWC will improve when speaking at a slower rate, their language formulation skills will not be the same as those of fluent speakers.

3.4.8 Neurogenic cluttering and dysarthria

Cluttering that develops in adulthood as a result of a neurological disorder is called neurogenic cluttering. In the literature, some cases of neurogenic cluttering are described regarding people who experienced cluttering symptoms in addition to multiple sclerosis (MS) or Parkinson's disease (PD) (see also 3.4.13). PD originates in the death of cells in the substantia nigra and the loss of dopamine and melanin produced by those cells. It progresses to other parts of the basal ganglia (see 1.4) and to the nerves that control the muscles, involving other neurotransmitters. The main characteristic of people with neurogenic cluttering is their fast rate of speech (De Nil, Jokel, & Rochon, 2007; van Borsel & Tetnowski, 2008). Baumgartner (1999) introduced some speech tasks to differentiate between cluttering and neurogenic fluency disorders. Although the disfluencies of PWC are more variable compared to the disfluencies of people with neurogenic fluency disorders, an aggravation of the symptoms in simple speech tasks is a sign of a neurogenic disorder.

PD may be more closely related to PWC than most people realize, according to van Zaalen and van Wanseele (2012). These researchers attempted to compare the jaw stability of clients with PD with the jaw stability of clients with phonological cluttering and fluent speakers, using kinematic measurements. Mandibular control has been described as fundamental to good articulation (Hayden, 1994). Stable mandibular movement has been described as a stable movement pattern, amplitude and duration (Hartinger & Mooshammer, 2008). It has been noted that stable jaw movement has a positive influence on speech intelligibility (Smith, Goffman, Zelaznik, Ying, & McGillem, 1995). Van Zaalen & van Wanseele (2012) concluded that moderate temporal variability with high spatial variability -- in other words, flexibility -- in jaw movement is essential for intelligibility. PWC, as PD, showed limited amplitude results (i.e., less jaw opening than fluent speakers). In other words, the accurate but limited jaw opening during speech production of PWC and PD has a negative effect on their intelligibility, although the reason for this limited jaw movement is probably different.

3.4.9 Down syndrome

Back in 1866, John Langdon Down referred to the speech of individuals with the syndrome which was later to be named after him in terms that seem to be consistent with a diagnosis of cluttering (van Borsel, 2011). "Disfluency in speech of adults with intellectual disabilities mostly is considered to be 'stuttering' in official reports and patient records and treatment is focusing on 'stuttering.' Remarkably, only little research has been published to differentiate aspects of disfluencies in this specific group of persons" (Coppens-Hofman et al 2013, p. 485). One theme recurs throughout the literature in this area, namely, the issue of whether the disfluent speech in people with Down syndrome [DS] is characterized by stuttering or cluttering (van Borsel, 2011). It is likely that underlying causes of the speech disfluencies in DS are different from disfluencies of people without intellectual disabilities and may be related to other problems, such as cognitive functioning, knowledge of language and words, concentration, memory difficulties, medications, auditory input problems, and co-morbidity. In addition to normal and stuttering-like disfluencies, people with DS also demonstrate atypical disfluencies, such as final syllable repetitions. These atypical disfluencies are normally not observed in PWC or PWS.

Devenny and Silverman (1990) stated that 42% to 59% of their participants with DS were disfluent. In addition to cluttering, stuttering, or cluttering-stuttering, other types of disfluencies are observed in people with DS. People with DS lack secondary behaviors or other behaviors typical for stuttering. Several studies revealed a high number of disfluencies in people with DS, but data on different types of disfluencies are rarely provided in them (Bray, 2003; Devenny & Silverman, 1990; Van Borsel & Vandermeulen, 2008).

Researchers such as Otto and Yairi (1975) and Coppens-Hofman et al. (2013) focused on differentiating disfluencies. They assumed that people with DS present with cluttering and cluttering-stuttering more frequently than with stuttering. Where Stansfield (1990) concluded that 14-77% of the total DS population were disfluent, with a ratio of 13 PWS to 2 PWC, Van Borsel and Vandermeulen (2008) reported 78.9% of children with DS were diagnosed with cluttering, and 17.1% were classified as combined cases of cluttering and stuttering. Bray (2003) made a similar assumption, and collected observational data on disfluencies of 27 speech-language therapists treating clients with DS. Most of the observed disfluencies were normal, such as word repetitions or multiple phoneme repetitions, interjections, or telescoping, but blocks were also present at times.

3.4.10 Autism spectrum disorders

Little is known about cluttering and autism spectrum disorders (ASDs). Research in the speech of people with ASDs, though admittedly limited, indicates that cluttered speech is not a symptom in all people with ASDs, although a higher incidence of cluttering symptoms is expected in this group than in a comparison population of controls (Scaler Scott, 2011). Clinicians who work with children with ASDs often comment "I see many children with a diagnosis of ASDs that have other comorbid disorders." A diagnosis of ASDs can be confused with a diagnosis of cluttering. The similarities can be misleading, especially when the lack of symptom awareness is considered to be only a cluttering symptom. Children diagnosed with ASDs are unable to take the perspective of the listener, which can be associated with the bad pragmatic skills of PWC, who are known to blame the listeners for the breakdown in communication. Also, switching from one topic to another, often considered a symptom of cluttering, seems to characterize children with ASDs. Children with PDD-NOS, for example, are bothered by chaotic thinking and a lack of insight while processing information.

Studies focusing on individuals with autistic features (Shields, 2010; Thacker & Austen, 1996) and on Asperger's disorder (Scaler Scott, 2008; Scott, Grossman, Abendroth, Tetnowski, & Damico, 2006) suggest that cluttering is a syndrome that clinicians will need to consider as a potential coexisting condition when evaluating the communication pattern of individuals with ASDs (Scaler Scott, 2011).

3.4.11 Fragile X syndrome

Children with Fragile X syndrome (FXS) often present with short bursts of speech and disruptions in the flow, including repetitions of sounds, words, and phrases. The speech of these children has been described as compulsive and often perseverative. Speech of children with FXS has also been described as "cluttered." Gillberg (1992) stated that cluttered speech characterized the FXS and was not observed in any of the other ASDs groups. Poor topic maintenance with frequent tangential comments may occur. Syntax is usually appropriate for the mental age of the people with this syndrome; they usually demonstrate a high receptive vocabulary score; however, their auditory sensory and processing skills are weak (Scharfenaker & Stackhouse, 2012). Boys with FXS, regardless of their autism status, exhibited phonological characteristics (consonant production accuracy, presence of simplifying phonological processes) similar to those of younger normally developing children but nevertheless were less intelligible in connected speech (Barnes, Long, Martin, Berni, Mandulak, & Sideris, 2009). The occurrence of cluttering in clients with FXS is disputed by van Borsel, Dor and Rondal (2008). In their study investigating the disfluencies in the speech of French-speaking individuals with FXS, van Borsel et al. (2008) found a mean speech rate below the norm, meaning that a fast rate is not a constant characteristic in this population. In response to the above referenced finding by van Borsel et al., we would like to observe that the process of adjusting the rate to the language complexity is much more complicated than simply measuring the rate without looking at the variability and the effect that the rate has on sentence and word structures. We believe that the latter is more important. As St. Louis et al. (2007) stated, in cluttering, the speech rate may be perceived to be fast, even when the rate is within normal limits when actually measured.

In a comparison study by Zajac, Harris, Roberts and Martin (2009), boys with FXS and ASD were judged to speak faster than similarly chronologically aged controls. Multiple linear regression indicated that the articulation rate with the final word of the sentence excluded and sentence-final F0 drop accounted for 91% of the variance for the perceived rate. Zajac et al. (2009) concluded that atypical sentence-final prosody may be related to the perceived rate in boys with FXS and ASD. For more information on the perceived rate, see Chapter 1.

3.4.12 Gilles de la Tourette syndrome

No research has been published about cluttering in relation to the Gilles de la Tourette syndrome (TS). The putamen, part of the basal ganglia, appears to be involved in coordinating automatic behaviors such as riding a bike or driving a car. Problems with the putamen may account for the symptoms of TS. The most obvious reason for the lack of discussions on cluttering and TS is that TS, similarly to developmental stuttering, may be related to the extrapyramidal motor system that causes involuntary reflexes and movements. The extrapyramidal motor system is not known to be impaired in PWC. Developmental stuttering, however, shares many clinical similarities with TS. Abwender, Como, Kurlan, Parry, Fett, Cui et al. (1996) discussed the extrapyramidal involvement in developmental stuttering and raised the possibility that DS and TS are pathogenetically related (1998). Although De Nil, Sasisekaran, Van Lieshout, and Sandor (2005) revealed an overall higher frequency of more typical (normal) disfluencies in a detailed analysis of fluency of 69 children with TS during reading and spontaneous speech compared to controls, the disfluencies of people with TS differ from stuttering-like and normal disfluencies, and occur primarily in the medial and final word positions. These findings are supported by a study conducted by van Borsel and Vanrijckeghem (2000), who observed that interjections were the predominant type of disfluency, accounting for 48.2% of all disfluencies demonstrated in a case study of an 18-year-old male with TS. Cluttering in clients with TS may be characterized predominantly by a significant number of non-stuttering disfluencies, such as phrase- and whole-word repetitions, interjections, frequent revisions and incomplete phrases, resulting in disorganized wording (van Borsel, 2011). No prolongations and blocks were observed in clients with TS (van Borsel & Vanrijckeghem, 2000).

3.4.13 Neurofibromatosis Type 1

The first study that digitally measured the articulatory rate in adults with neurofibromatosis type 1 (NF-1) concluded that differences in speech fluency between NF-1 patients and controls are most notable in the articulatory rate (Cosyns, van Zaalen, Mortier, Janssens, Amez, Van Damme, & van Borsel, 2013). Although the frequency of disfluencies was similar between groups, NF-1 patients exhibited a faster MAR and their pauses were longer and more frequent than those of people in a control group. As a result, patients with NF-1 had a slower speech rate and a more varied articulatory rate. Cosyns et al. (2013) determined that the disfluency pattern displayed by NF-1 patients corresponds more closely to patterns of cluttering than to patterns of stuttering.

3.4.14 Attention deficit hyperactivity disorder (ADHD)

Although symptoms of ADD/ADHD are often considered indicative of cluttering, individuals diagnosed with ADHD do not necessarily suffer from cluttering (van Borsel et al., 2008). People with ADD or ADHD have a normal-to-fast mean articulatory rate. Their ratio of disfluencies is high in favor of normal disfluencies, while appropriately placed pauses are often too short. Similarly to the experiences of PWC, people with ADD/ADHD find that attention makes their speech better, while relaxation makes their speech worse. Fifteen participants with cluttering in a study by St. Louis and Schulte (2011) demonstrated irregularities on an attention subsection of the ADHD questionnaire. Alm (2011) observed that PWC exhibit opposite responses to dopaminergic medications compared with individuals with ADHD, possibly indicating the presence of a different type of dysregulation of attention deficits, though found in the same attention system.

No general differences in communication characteristics between ADHD and cluttering were evidenced. Some patients with a diagnosis of ADHD described experiencing "multiple tracks" of thought. These tracks of thought were experienced simultaneously and sometimes in rapid succession, switching between two or more different topics. These patterns of thought may be described by an external observer as internal distractibility or difficulty maintaining focus on a topic in conversation (Jerome, 2003). This phenomenon of multiple tracks of thought is not described for cluttering.

The ability of people with ADHD or ADD to adjust their speech rate to the language complexity will determine whether they also exhibit cluttering or not. Assessment in different speech conditions and with and without medication is necessary to confirm or reject this diagnosis. Another important aspect to consider is the effect of ADD/ADHD medications on speech production. Considering the fact that medications such as Ritalin inhibit hyperactive behaviors in general, such medications can also be administered to reduce the rate of speech and thereby reduce the symptoms of cluttering.

3.4.15 Reliability data of cluttering in other syndromes

Characteristics of the different syndromes often determine the quantity of the disfluencies, whether for normal or stuttering-like disfluencies. Disfluencies are mentioned mostly as a single variable, without information on rate, intelligibility, etc. In addition, disfluency analysis has been criticized in part because several different schema of disfluencies have been described. "Agreement among highly experienced judges, and congruence between their binary judgments of stuttering and categorizations based on disfluency types, were relatively high using some definitions and very low using others" (Bothe, 2008, p. 867). These results suggest the use of measurement methods other than those based on disfluency types for quantifying or describing children's disfluency (Bothe, 2008). Other differential diagnostic characteristics, such as rate and rate variation or sentence and word structures are seldom considered. Further research using the current definitions of cluttering in the above mentioned disorder groups, considering fluency, rate, phonology and intelligibility, within different speech tasks, especially in connected speech samples, is necessary to adequately advance our knowledge of disfluency subgroups, especially when different subtypes of disfluencies are considered and will contribute to a better understanding of the verbal potential of these individuals (St. Louis et al., 2007; van Zaalen, 2009).

3.5 Conclusion

An accurate comprehensive diagnosis is suggested to differentiate between a variety of disorders that have cluttering characteristics as secondary symptoms. The characteristics, analysis and interpretations described above make a valid differential diagnosis possible.

TREATMENT

4

Chapter 4

Therapeutic considerations

▨ 4.1 Introduction

This chapter provides an overview of some general considerations of cluttering therapy, such as changes in social communication, problems in monitoring, the four-component model of Stourneras (1972) and cluttering therapy, priorities in the treatment of people with cluttering and stuttering, exercise hierarchy and intensity of the treatment. The impact that cluttering therapy can have on PWC is examined in relation to the short-term and long-term results. The short-term results can be seen as to the immediate impact on speech behavior, cognitions and emotions. It is difficult to achieve long-term results in the treatment of cluttering; therefore, results can only be achieved by brief periods of intensive training within communicative contexts. In addition, the four component model of Stourneras (1972) consisting of cognitive, emotional, verbal-motor and communicative components will be explained in terms of how to assist PWC to improve their performance in all four of these components.

The chapter presents therapeutic considerations relating to issues such as planning a client-centered intervention, daily practice with exercises focusing on improving identification, speech, attention skills, and memory. Special attention is given to facilitating expressive and receptive language abilities, and increasing organizational, pragmatic, word-retrieving and conversational skills. The chapter closes with a discussion on exercise hierarchy and intensity of treatment.

4.2 Impact of therapy

Cluttering therapy, similarly to stuttering therapy, involves more than changing a client's speech. It creates transformations in many areas of communication that transcend routine speech exercises. Examples of such work include training focused speech, formulating the message, and developing a different listening attitude or focus on a partner. PWC who have poor speech intelligibility may not be able to accurately interpret listeners' feedback. They respond differently compared to the way PWS are likely to react to the listener's reaction to their speech. The following example illustrates how a person with cluttering was unable to correctly read clues from a listener's reaction to her speech.

> Anouschka, a 23-year old student of geography, says:
> "I was in a bar two weeks ago with a friend I hadn't seen in a long time.
> I drank two beers and we had a very lively conversation. I had a wonderful night. A couple of days ago I saw her again. She told me: 'Wow, you were so drunk! I could not understand a word you said, wasn't that fun?' I was stunned. My world broke down. I really thought she understood me while we were talking, and I was not drunk at all."

4.2.1 Short-term and long-term impact

The short-term results of the treatment of cluttering are influenced by two main components: a positive impact on speech behavior and a positive impact on cognitions and emotions. The impact on speech behavior can be significant, especially when a client becomes capable of transfer and stabilization of new behaviors. It is difficult to achieve long-term results in the treatment of cluttering because speech is an automatized behavior. In order to achieve SMART goals, i.e., that are specific, measurable, attainable, realistic, and timely, as discussed at 5.3, below, and therefore long-term results, brief periods of intensive training are highly recommended.

4.2.2 Changes in social communication

Being unaware of the reasons for their communication difficulties, PWC often try to modify their communication pattern and social behavior. In rare instances, these intuitive modifications may be enough to resolve the cluttering. In such instances, there is no need to do anything differently. Similarly to PWS, PWC also often avoid difficult speaking situations. This avoidance often takes place while PWC are not conscious of the fact that their disfluency or poor intelligibility is the main reason for the avoidance behavior (see example below).

> Example:
> Ariella, a 35-year-old curriculum developer at a university, is working on the development of a new curriculum for the first year students together with seven of her colleagues. During meetings, Ariella suggests a number of creative solutions and ideas. Her colleagues in the group smile at her but do not really respond to the content of her suggestions. When another colleague in the same group introduces almost identical ideas, this colleague is applauded for her inventive mind and her ideas are adopted in the curriculum plan. After this happens several times, Ariella decides to become the secretary of the group and no longer shares her ideas with the group. Although this is a short-term solution, after some time Ariella starts to have misgivings about the meetings, knowing that she is not able to adequately perform. Two months later she decides to go for speech and language evaluation and therapy. One of the first goals in therapy is to train Ariella to speak and respond in a focused manner during work group meetings. As a result of the implementation of the lessons she learned in her therapy, her colleagues are surprised by her knowledge and creativity. Ariella gives up her role as secretary and becomes part of the brainstorm group again.

Example of avoidance behavior in a person with cluttering.

4.3 Problems in monitoring

As pointed out above, one of the most important characteristics of cluttering is an uncontrollable fast and/or irregular speech rate (see 2.2.1), leading to problems in planning and execution of the verbal-motor and the linguistic structures, and secondly, to an inability to monitor the linguistic output accurately. When errors are detected, PWC may have difficulties making corrections due to problems related to their abnormal speech rate.

Fluent speakers recognize problems by the so-called internal "feedback loop," which is unnoticeable to the listener (covert monitoring). They are aware of the quality of their own speech, and, if necessary, will improve it. Many slips of the tongue in fluent speakers are recognized before the utterance is fully produced. An example of overt monitoring is: "I w –cycled home." Sometimes these types of problems are corrected after producing the utterance (e.g., "I walked; no, cycled home").

Although discussed in the literature, no evidence has been noted that PWC have monitoring problems. But clinical experience has made it absolutely clear that PWC have a limited ability to monitor their speech in complex language tasks. At the same time, there is no doubt that PWC adequately monitor their speech in basic speaking situations (e.g., reading out loud, and counting from one to ten). In other words, the inability of PWC to adjust their speech rate to the complexity of the linguistic task also detracts from their ability to adequately monitor their speech and language output. This is called a double deficit (van Zaalen, 2009).

Monitoring weakness at different levels of language complexity and a person's capacity to be trained determine the prognosis for the effectiveness of cluttering intervention. Development of monitoring skills at different levels of language complexity is the first priority in cluttering therapy. Such therapy starts at monitoring, after language execution. At this level, the speaker hears a part of the message and compares it with linguistic rules and content of the intended message. At this level of monitoring, PWC can benefit from auditory, visual and sensory identification of symptoms. Arranging for PWC to listen to their own recorded speech is an excellent way to make them aware of their speech pattern. This can be supported by visual information, as is possible with *PRAAT* software, which is described under Audio Visual Feedback training *(6.5.1)*. See www.nycsa-center.org.

4.4 The four-component model and cluttering therapy

In the Introduction and in Chapter 1, the four component model of Stourneras (1972) is described. The model includes cognitive, emotional, verbal-motor and communicative components. PWC should aim to improve in all four components of communication. In therapy, attention should not only be paid to the verbal-motor and communicative components, but also to the cognitive and emotional components. In this section, the importance of the four components within therapy is highlighted.

4.4.1 The cognitive component

Based on our experience, we believe that PWC fall within a wide continuum of self-awareness and feelings (from denials to incessant concerns; from frustration stemming from one's own deficits in speaking to frustration at the deficits of others in keeping up with what they are saying). PWC often have low self-esteem, and feel misunderstood and incompetent. For example, two school teachers were concerned about the inability of their students to understand them. An SLP graduate student was anxious about her future employment. A car mechanic was saddened due to his losing customers because of his unsuccessful communication. A high school student was annoyed by frequent requests to repeat what he said. This young man blamed stuttering for all his problems of communication even though his speech was highly unintelligible and fast due to his cluttering. Another high school student was frustrated about his poor grades and constant conflicts with peers due to his poor social control. A 13-year-old boy was timid and confused due to his mother's insistence that he do his speech exercises instead of playing video games. In sum, the negative thoughts and feelings of PWC were not as profound as such thoughts and feelings in cases of PWS, but they were present nonetheless and contributed to concerns about the future, lack of hope for successful treatment, poor self-esteem and low motivation.

The cognitive component of the Stourneras model has two sub-components: "attention" and "habituation."

Attention

A spontaneous, short feedback loop can lead to self-correction. When working on improving the awareness of speech, clients will, in response to the therapist's feedback to their cluttered speech, repeat the utterance as advised by the therapist. Later, the clients will be able to recognize, detect, and correct the cluttered speech by themselves in order to sound intelligible or fluent. In therapy, the speech therapist strives to make the feedback loop more automatic for the client. The aim of therapy for PWC is to enable clients to adequately plan and program their speech prior to speech execution. If a speaker has sufficient time for sentence formulation, the second level of monitoring can also take place in time to limit or eliminate deficiencies at the formulator phase. As a result, audible (overt) repairs will occur less frequently, and the number of word- and phrase repetitions as well as revisions will decrease. A precondition of covert self-correction is that the speaker has enough time to make the correction. Slowing down the speech rate enables the client to better plan and self-correct.

> *Short feedback loop*
> "Selfcrecie ... excuse me self-correction" is an example of a short feedback loop, overt monitoring.
>
> *Covert repair*
> Before execution of a multisyllabic word, the speaker takes precautions by slowing down the rate to ensure speech intelligibility. E.g., "I walk in the ... *li-brai-ry* searching for a book."

Using a digital audio or video recording increases the effectiveness of the first therapy phase. Later, spontaneous monitoring takes place without external feedback.

Habituation

The cognitive component "habituation" needs constant attention during the treatment process. While practicing rate reduction, PWC will not feel at ease, especially at the beginning of therapy. They will feel that speech is no longer "natural." Such a negative response by the speaker will overshadow the positive effect of improved fluency and speech intelligibility (see example below).

> In a group therapy session, one of the participants with cluttering used his focused speech and was fully intelligible. Another participant observed, "if you would speak like this all the time, your communication will benefit so much!" The first participant responded "That may be true, but for me it sounds sooooo slow. I feel like a turtle."

The new manner of speech can elicit negative thoughts (e.g., "it sounds weird!"; "they think I am boring"; "they will think I am too slow") and negative feelings, such as embarrassment or impatience due to unnatural speech. A clinician should always be aware of clients' cognitions and negative self-evaluation. The clinician should play back segments of the client's speech, using audio and video recordings, and thereby show the client that the new speech pattern is much easier to listen to. Habituation to the "new" speech pattern is considered an important objective of treatment. It is very important for a clinician to positively encourage feelings of accomplishment and satisfaction. A sentence like "You have to get used to it" may be used frequently in the beginning of therapy. Later, the clinician can use sentences like "Are you getting used to it?" or more provocatively, "Did your listeners fall asleep when you spoke more slowly?" With such casual encouragement, the client's resistance can be diminished at an early stage and the process of habituation can continue. When the speech rate is noticeably very fast, a provocative paradoxical comment may help, as, for example, "slower speech goes faster." This may jolt the client into a quick improvement in communication. When a client speaks at a slower rate, fewer misarticulations and word- or phrase repetitions take place, which results in a more intelligible and comprehensible message. PWC often have a low self-image. They may say, for example, "Nobody wants to hear what I have to say." In therapy, such comments should be replaced by positive encouragement, for example, "You already speak more intelligibly and more fluently in many situations."

4.4.2 The emotional component

Affective and cognitive aspects of cluttering have not yet been extensively considered in the international literature. Several authors (Bennett, 2006; Dalton & Hardcastle, 1993; Daly, 1986, 1993; Daly & Burnett, 1999; Winkelman, 1990, 1993) emphasized that PWC may respond to their failure to speak clearly and to be understood by experiencing anxiety, frustration (Dalton & Hardcastle, 1993), negative thoughts (Daly, 1993, 1986), nervousness, sadness, and low self-esteem (Reichel, 2010). Green (1999) suggested that clinicians provide positive psycho-social conditions in order to improve the fluency and self-monitoring skills of PWC. Langevin and Boberg (1996) incorporated cognitive-behavioral skills training in their therapy in order to change attitudes, perceptions, and self-confidence of clients with cluttering and stuttering.

An affective component of cluttering in many PWC is manifested by negative emotions such as fear, anger, or sadness, as well as physiological responses to the cluttered speech. These emotional responses are not learned the same way as the responses of PWS. According to Sheehan (1975), stuttering is what people do in order not to stutter. PWC do not exhibit secondary behaviors or tension or a feeling of loss of control which is typical for PWS. The lack of awareness of the symptoms helps PWC to experience fewer difficulties during speech. PWC, by contrast, do not have situational fear, fear of specific sounds, or fear of getting stuck.

On the other hand, the confidence of being able to make appropriate changes by oneself (locus of control) is less prevalent in PWC than in PWS. Therefore, PWC do not experience such severe fear of symptoms. Even to the extent that they experience fear, it generally does not develop quickly, either. Normal disfluencies and a fast articulatory rate do not interrupt communication. Cluttering does not "sound" or "feel" as disturbing as stuttering. Generally, the speaker and the listener will not consider cluttering as a "speech disorder" or as a sign of loss of control. Because PWC do not directly associate their speech with unwanted social responses, they will not develop severe speech fear, if any. But sometimes negative response from a listener can give PWC communicative fear (fear experienced before or during communication). The fear develops because PWC are not understood without any reason that is obvious to them or they are ignored in communicative situations. PWC may be perceived to be "noisy" or selfish. Such negative attitudes result in communication fears that can lead to avoidance and other adjusted behaviors.

Daly (1993, 1986) proposed a combination of cognitive training, counselling, attitude change, relaxation, affirmation training, and positive self-talk in working with PWC. Reichel (2010) adapted Bar-On's (2000) ten emotional intelligence (EI) competencies for the use of clinicians who work with PWC. Individuals with a preponderance of cluttering-like symptoms are introduced to the following five skills: (1) Emotional self-awareness, (2) Impulse control, (3) Reality testing, (4) Empathy, and (5) Interpersonal relationships. The development of such skills is designed to improve awareness of emotions and communication behaviors, to facilitate the ability to manage emotions to help achieve self-control, to cognitively process emotions, to assess situations realistically, to consider the feelings of listeners, and to maximize the ability of clients to receive and to give emotional closeness in relationships which may result, in turn, in increased responsibility for meeting expectations.

In mild cases, PWC may not even develop communicative fear. They can only present with the verbal-motor component. The more intelligible the client's speech gets, the more desensitized the client becomes to communication fear. For clients with moderate and severe cases of cluttering, working on the verbal-motor component is especially important. Addressing the cognitive component is also essential with these clients. Improvements in the speech of such clients results in their awareness about their improved communication abilities and increases their motivation to work on their speech.

4.4.3 Verbal-motor component

Due to the fact that emotional and cognitive components of cluttering differ from the same components in stuttering, the focus on the verbal-motor component is much stronger in cluttering and in cluttering-stuttering therapy. In most cases it is possible to address the fast articulatory rate by slowing down the speech rate with syllable tapping. Such work on speech rate reduction needs to be performed in a carefully structured manner, with both auditory and visual feedback. Besides moderating or tempering the speech rate, the clinician should also consider the degree of motoric and linguistic loading involved in the speaking task, in order to facilitate better cohesiveness or synergy of speech and language output (Myers, 2011).

Frequently occurring errors in articulation which can appear in many disorders including cluttering are reduced movements of the lips, tongue, and jaw. Use of traditional approaches may be adequate for other disorders, but may not be sufficient in the treatment of cluttering.

> PWC *are able to make all verbal-motor movements*
> *adequately, but not when the speech rate is too fast.*
> (van Zaalen & Winkelman, 2009)

PWC manifest a problem in the planning and not just in the execution of oral-motor movements, as, for example, jaw movements. It is important to address the verbal-motor skills at the word level. Priority is given to working on accurate sequencing of syllables, especially in multisyllabic words at a fast speech rate. The next step is to practice such skills at the sentence level.

Priorities in the treatment of people with cluttering and stuttering
When cluttering is accompanied by stuttering in adults, the specific symptoms of cluttering need to be addressed first unless people have anxiety or fear of speech as a result of stuttering. St. Louis et al. (2003) and van Zaalen and Winkelman (2009) claim that fluency enhancing techniques, such as rhythmic speech with breathing exercises, can be used for this purpose (see exercise counting backwards, 5.4.4). Once PWC will realize that their speech is improving, their overall confidence will improve. The fear of stuttering is a maintaining factor in cluttering-stuttering cases. By increasing the confidence in their clients' speech, clinicians will help their clients' fear of stuttering to decline as well. A second reason to start treating the cluttering component first is that if it is not addressed, the cluttering symptoms will continue and eventually result in a relapse of stuttering. This vision of the treatment of cluttering-stuttering cases was already widely introduced by Weiss (1964). A third reason to start with the cluttering component before the stuttering component is the lack of cluttering symptom awareness. Accurate awareness of a person's speech symptoms is necessary in order to lead to a permanent behavior change. And finally, when a person slows down the speech rate, it is much easier to apply the stuttering modification techniques.

In children with a combination of cluttering and stuttering, it is better to start therapy by devoting a few sessions to stuttering (stuttering modification) in order to prevent the development of a fear of speech. Working on stuttering is consistent with what children expect to address in therapy and thereby helps to establish the needed client-clinician rapport. After a couple of sessions, the clinician can make children aware that, at that point, cluttering symptoms should be addressed. Another reason for addressing stuttering in children first is because cluttering is difficult to differentiate from developmental language disorders.

4.4.4 Communicative component

Weiss (1964) described a number of stigmatizing characteristics of PWC, such as not being interested in communication, a negative life attitude, and laziness. These characteristics can be explained by a communicative focused system theory. This distinguishes the level of content from the level of relationship (Watzlawic, Bavin, & Jackson, 1970).

> *The level of content includes the meaning of the words, or semantics. The level of relation applies to the relationship between two conversational partners.*

A question like "Can you say that in a more friendly way?" seeks content feedback (level of content) in the relationship between two people. The sentence "I am happy that you finally agree with me" puts both speakers closer together. But one speaker also informs the other one that she always knew better. This addresses the speakers' level of relationship (Korrelboom & ten Broeke, 2004). Watzlawic et al. (1970) point out that the level of relationship has a higher emotional impact on communication than the level of content. The negative characteristics described by Weiss (1964) are related to dysfunctional communication at the level of relationship, such as poor listening, abnormal turn-taking and verbosity. Above all, the level of relationship is especially determined by metalinguistic and nonverbal behaviors ("analogue" communication), such as mimics, loudness, pausing, stress and gestures. PWC can send out unintended and unwanted messages. This leads to the misinterpretations of characteristics of PWC as described by Weiss (1964).

Therefore, there are various reasons to explicitly address and train the above aspects of communication focusing on the level of relationship in cluttering therapy. From the point of view of system theory it is also known that the communicative context is of the essence to the communication of all individual speakers and their conversation partners. Especially in cluttering, a period of frequent and direct feedback from the environment (partner, colleague) can contribute to an increase in speech awareness. Partner-focused communication (adjusting the message to the listener) is a skill which needs to be developed in PWC.

4.4.5 Therapeutic considerations

Planning a client-centered intervention depends on the results of the comprehensive evaluation and assessment of the diagnostic exercises. Treatment of PWC requires a clear structure. It is important for the client to practice daily, beginning on the first day of therapy, according to the SMART criteria. It is also crucial that the amount of exercise each day should be tailored to the symptoms, skill level, and needs of each individual client.

Treatment plans for phonological and syntactic cluttering (for sub-typing, see 1.4.6) should both start with identification exercises. It is certainly not necessary to do all identification exercises with every client. In many cases, the repertoire of identification exercises has a therapeutic effect on speech production. After the identification exercises, the clinician should discuss exercises that improve speech, memory and attention skills of the client. We also provide suggestions as to how to work on language formulation and, briefly, on the social use of language skills.

It is crucial to praise and reinforce each client every time a goal is achieved. The sense of success and of mutual journey will bring them hope, pride, and courage to attempt to overcome any remaining symptoms of cluttering, such as improving speech intelligibility (articulation and prosody), expressive and receptive language abilities, and increasing organizational and word-retrieving skills. Special attention will be given to increasing awareness of speech and improving pragmatic skills such as turn-taking, topic maintenance, and story-narrating abilities.

4.4.6 Exercise hierarchy

To determine the order of the exercises, a client should fill in the Speech Situation checklist by Brutten (1979), which was adjusted for PWC (Appendix I). When this is done, the client as well as the clinician should have a better understanding of the client's ability to communicate in various conversational situations. Without a doubt, the exercises will be implemented first in the situations that are known to pose little difficulty. By doing this, clients can be successful, and every success will strengthen their internal motivation to change. The clinician can also have the client complete the Cluttering Severity

Instrument (Bakker & Myers, 2011) (see 3.3.9). Finally a list with observed feelings and emotions should be discussed (See Appendix H). This completed list makes clients aware of their negative thoughts and feelings regarding their speech and communication overall. If therapy is in an advanced stage, the Fluency Assessment Battery and the Cluttering Severity Instrument can be administered again in order to measure the outcome of the therapy. By comparing the scores before and after therapy, the clinician is able to assess whether the feelings and thoughts of the client have improved, and whether the client's opinion is consistent with the changes in the severity of symptoms judged by a trained listener.

4.4.7 Intensity of the treatment

In order for cluttering intervention to be successful, planning an intensive program of therapy is recommended. The amount of time to be allotted to the therapy program should depend on the severity of the disorder. Self-monitoring skills take time to develop and are acquired with intensive practice (Bennett Lanouette, 2011). The period for the maintenance of the newly acquired behaviors should be expected to range from 8 to 12 weeks. The time needed for changes in speech behaviors are related to the functioning of the cerebellum and more specifically to neuroplasticity. Just as the cerebellum maintains balance, integration, and stability in the somatic-motor sphere, it may also help with balancing, integrating, and stabilizing other functions of the brain (Rapoport, van Reekum, & Mayberg, 2000).

Neuroplasticity is the brain's natural ability to reorganize itself by forming new neural pathways and connections throughout life. Neuroplasticity allows the nerve cells (neurons) in the brain to adjust their workings in response to new situations or changes in their environment to compensate for existing problems. When a stimulus is cognitively associated with reinforcement, its cortical representation is strengthened and enlarged. In some cases, cortical representations can double or triple in one or two days at the time in which a new sensory-motor behavior is first acquired, and changes are largely completed within at most a few weeks (Blake, Heiser, Caywood, & Merzenich, 2006). Exercises therefore should be practiced frequently and for short periods of time since no learned habit or skill of human beings occurs as often as speech. Most of the time, during the day, the old habits are maintained. This means the time during which the new habit is practiced is relatively limited.

An intensive training schedule is necessary for PWC to compensate for their limited self-awareness and their weak symptom awareness. Since the monitoring of PWC is weak, it is more difficult for them to establish speech control. It is also more difficult for them to acquire an internal locus of control, which is the sense that they themselves are able to influence their lives. Less intensive therapies do not provide an opportunity for the new speech pattern to be maintained. It is not enough to practice new skills only in a clinic. The new speech patterns need to be integrated into daily communication. The transfer to the new habit should be gradual. The real "practice" should take place everywhere a person speaks, e.g., at home, at work, in transit, and during sports training. Clinicians need to be honest in sharing with the client that it is difficult to control their speech quality in each and every situation, but although most clients will not be able to monitor their speech in every situation, speaking clearly is beneficial for PWC, even if it is only in a few conversational settings (Miyamoto, 2011).

4.5 Conclusion

This chapter suggested considerations for the treatment of cluttering, such as changes in social communication, problems in monitoring, priorities in the treatment of people with cluttering and stuttering, exercise hierarchy, and the intensity of the treatment. This chapter also explored how these considerations can vary, depending on applications of the four-component model of Stourneras. The following therapy goals were recommended: addressing expressive and receptive language abilities, and increasing organizational, pragmatic, word-retrieving and conversational skills. The discussion of these goals was then followed by a discussion of the development of monitoring skills at different levels of language complexity and prioritizing the verbal-motor component of cluttering. The chapter continued with an appreciation of an intensive training schedule and the significance of integrating a new pattern of speech into daily communication in order for PWC to compensate for their limited weak symptom awareness and monitoring skills. The chapter concluded with a presentation of how the time needed for changes in speech behaviors of PWC is related to neuroplasticity, which is the brain's ability to reorganize itself by forming new neural pathways and therefore to compensate for existing problems.

5

Chapter 5

Therapy planning

This chapter covers the most significant components of diagnostic therapy and intervention planning. It describes the impact that diagnostic therapy can have on a speaker. Diagnostic therapy initiates the identification stage of cluttering treatment, and assesses clients' motivation to change their speech behavior.

5.1 Introduction

In this chapter, the assessment phase is introduced, in which diagnostic therapy data is gathered and, based on that, a treatment plan is mapped out. Considering that PWC are often unaware of their symptoms, it is particularly important for clients to become aware of their cluttering symptoms and the problems they experience in communication during the assessment phase. The practice of addressing the most significant symptoms in the course of diagnostic therapy is very motivating. During this process, clinicians obtain insights into the extent to which their clients can be stimulated. The overriding question is "what works?" In order to make this determination, exercises are offered even in this early assessment phase. In this chapter, we describe the different aspects of the treatment plan. We will then focus on early transfer and stabilization, and then on some diagnostic exercises. During the diagnostic exercises, clinicians should observe the client's ability to learn about the main symptoms, and which ones are easy or difficult to improve, how quickly an exercise can help in enabling the client to recognize the symptoms (symptom awareness), how to treat symptoms by imitation of the clinician's model or by means of self-correction in focused exercises or other exercise situations. The results of the diagnostic exercises make it possible to describe a rough treatment plan (training plan). An approach that offers observable positive results increases the intrinsic motivation of the client.

5.2 Transfer and maintenance/stabilization

When it comes to cluttering, as opposed to stuttering, the effort made in performing an exercise is considered by clients to be positive (intrinsic award). Because the clients are better understood, they find their communication to be pleasant again. This offers rapid encouraging results. Due to the slow development of the internal feedback loop in PWC, the danger of a relapse is an immediate concern. Therefore, it is important to gradually reduce the frequency of therapy, thereby giving the best chances to facilitate maintenance and stabilization. Relapses can also be prevented by changing speech behavior, and especially in the case of cluttering, by transfer activities beginning in the first week. By transfer, we refer to the application of learned skills in daily communication and life in general. Effective transfer increases the chance of stabilization. Stabilization means that the learned skills have become completely habitual without a high likelihood of relapse

o   by regular control sessions;
o   by clients making deals within their environments by getting people close to them to provide feedback related to their speech; and
o   by regular self-evaluation of speech.

In this paragraph, three ways for effective transfer are discussed, starting with home assignments, followed by self-observation schemes and finally the criteria that should be met by the performance of appropriate exercises (SMART goals, see below).

5.3 SMART criteria

The results of assignments and exercises "stand or fall" depending on whether they are performed within a clear framework. The exercises therefore have to meet certain criteria. In cluttering it is very important for every exercise assignment to be described to the client as clearly as possible. SMART criteria are a useful means to reach this goal. The acronym SMART represents:

o Specific
o Measurable
o Attainable
o Realistic
o Timely

For daily use, these SMART criteria are meant to serve as guidelines. They sometimes overlap. They are also not relevant to every treatment. Such criteria are used differently in children compared to young adults. They serve as "oil" to accurately change speech behavior and should not be considered goals on their own.

If exercises do not meet the SMART criteria, the chances are high that the client will not exercise efficiently. That means that a positive result of the exercise would be unlikely; speech therapy would be perceived as a burden, and motivation would drop down. We will discuss the SMART criteria specific to cluttering below.

5.3.1 Specific

To be "specific" refers to the client's ability to evaluate precisely the goal or subgoal of each exercise. For example, the client's self-identification of a symptom is an important precondition to reach the goal of the identification stage of the treatment. Identification exercises need to be performed at home, without the assistance of the clinician. If clients are not capable of identifying the symptoms, this exercise is useless. Another example: If the syllable tapping exercise is not clear or is not successful in home assignments, the cluttering will in all likelihood remain unchanged. The goal of the assignment needs to be clear, without misunderstandings and formulated positively. So each exercise should answer the following questions: "Why?", "When?", "How?", "How long?", and "How often?"

As a general rule, the exercises should be practiced frequently and for short periods of time.

5.3.2 Measurable

The results of the performance of exercises must be measurable. This can be implemented in many different ways. The response to the question "What was the effect of the exercise?" helps the clinician to ascertain whether the client is on the right track. Furthermore, an exercise, despite a good written description, often takes on a life of its own and is not selected and not practiced the way it was intended. A clinician can control this with the question: "Please show me how you did your exercise at home." Also, the use of a recorder (on a mobile phone, voice recorder, or laptop) makes self-evaluation possible. Detailed instructions for using Praat software are provided in 3.3.7.

Quite often, at least some of the instructions for home assignments are forgotten. It is difficult to control whether a suggestion has been followed as directed and whether a goal has been reached with a desirable rate of accuracy. Using a self-observation scheme is a way to make the activities visible and measurable for both the client and the clinician.

Once again, the goal of the assignment needs to be clear and formulated positively. Here are some examples of appropriate measurements:

○ Number of errors in 100 words per minute, etc.
○ Articulatory rate in syllables per second
○ Pause duration of 0.5 -1.0 second between sentences.

5.3.3 Attainable

As clients learn to speak differently, they generally find that their speech "feels weird." It is therefore important that an exercise should be attainable to clients; otherwise, they will not do the exercises at home. The subgoal needs to be highlighted in every exercise (see example of goals in syllable tapping).

Syllable tapping
In syllable tapping, multisyllabic words are tapped at the word level. The goal of this exercise is to improve the awareness of multisyllabic words. This goal needs to be mentioned every time the exercise is assigned. If the exercise is assigned later, for practicing on the sentence level, the goal should be mentioned again, emphasizing the awareness of the reduced articulatory rate.

An assignment needs to focus on the perception of the moment. Block (2004) advocates client-focused therapy, even if this means that the clinician has to work against an evidence-based approach. Block continues by saying that the clinician should discuss the new pattern of speech, even if it does not feel natural to the client, in order to accomplish habituation to a newly acquired normally sounding speech (see 5.2). Clients who practice insufficiently should be asked exactly what they will change in the following week, in order to be encouraged to practice more frequently. "If they [clients] do not like the treatments that clinicians offer, it is irrelevant what the supporting evidence is; people will not choose to use them" (Block, 2004, p. 102). If an exercise is not yet attainable, but very much needed for the continuation of the process, the resistance of the client must be addressed, e.g., with cognitive restructuring. The exercise can be made more attainable by emphasizing the goal of the exercise again.

Change is possible. If clients have trouble focusing their attention while listening, and if they say that they are "not able to write the minutes," they may be avoiding certain behaviors. The temporary "advantage" gained by this avoidance behavior will make it impossible for clients to reach their communication goals.

5.3.4 Realistic

The exercises facilitating the selected behavior need to easily fit into the clients' daily routine. As was mentioned earlier, if the identification assignments in the beginning of the therapy were insufficient, many of the exercises will make the condition worse. If the math level in the counting backwards exercises (see below, in this chapter) is too high, the chances increase that the exercises will exhaust the client too quickly or cause the client to give up and stop doing them. So it is essential for the clinician to be "realistic" in understanding the client's potential skills. The following considerations should always be taken into account:

○ Few or no demands mean no improvement
○ Demands that are too high may lead to lack of success in therapy.
○ Taking steps that are too big may lead to disappointment.
○ Disappointment is not always caused by a lack of success in therapy, but by a client's high expectations or by the client staying at one level for too long.

Cognitive psychology defines the "internal locus of control" as the manner in which people explain their own behavior. So when people are deeply convinced that they are inevitably controlled by the condition of cluttering, it is called "external locus of control." When people have such beliefs, intervention objectives have little chance of success. On the other hand, people with a high "internal locus of control" are convinced that they can change their behavior themselves. This generally leads to a higher probability of a successful intervention outcome.

> An assignment needs to be difficult enough to be a challenge and easy enough to enable the client to reach the goal (Winkelman, 2007).

An assignment needs to be difficult enough to be a challenge and easy enough to enable the client to reach the goal (Winkelman, 2007). If a client scores negatively on both the "internal attribution" and on the "internal locus of control," addressing the cognitions of such a person is the first priority ("cognitive identification and restructuring"), before more realistic goals can be achieved. Highly related to the criteria of what goals are "realistic" are "exercise motivation" and "therapy loyalty." Many people want to learn how to draw, but only a few are willing to sit down and try. Treatment of cluttering requires the commitment of much energy in the process of change. People can visit the best clinician, but if they do not practice enough, they will not succeed in changing their speech behavior.

5.3.5 Timely

The clinician must make it absolutely clear to the client approximately how long the therapy program can take. Long-range goals can be planned over a longer period of time. Short-range goals can be planned for a shorter and specific time period, such as within a week.

Also, a clear schedule regarding the duration and frequency of therapy sessions should be set up with the client. If clients follow this schedule, the outcome of such therapy can be easily evaluated and facilitated. As mentioned before, cluttering therapy needs to be intensive (4.4.7). This is also true for the schedule of assignments. In most cases, the assignments have to be conducted frequently and for short durations of time.

Examples of time schedules for assignments are:

- o Every day, five minutes, for a week;
- o Every quarter of an hour, one minute;
- o Only in certain communicative situations, for example during telephone calls;
- o Only with a certain person;
- o In the first two minutes of every conversation;
- o When going shopping.

5.4 Home assignments

As discussed above, people speak the whole day. It is absolutely essential at the very beginning of the therapy to educate clients about their inadequate symptom awareness as one of the most serious characteristics of cluttering. It is therefore essential to convince clients to implement what they learn by practicing their exercises in their daily life. This, of course, is true for any speech and language problem, but the poor symptom awareness in cluttering increases PWC's need for practicing their exercises.

Reminding PWC of their personal responsibility to make an effort to practice is extremely important. The clinician needs to make the home assignments as attractive as possible, while discussing how the exercises can be best executed, who can be most helpful, which audio or video devices can be used, and how to best conduct the evaluation. Questions such as "What has been the effect of this exercise?" or "What makes you realize that you are learning?" can give deep insights into the importance of the home assignments.

In encouraging clients to do their exercises, memos can be used, as visual aids. Clinicians can give their clients two post-it papers to take home, telling the clients what to focus on, e.g., syllable tapping, speech rate, or melody.

The clients can stick these memos to furniture at home, photograph the "decorated" furniture, scan the photograph, and email it to the clinician. Every time clients see the memo, they are reminded about the home assignment and the points to focus on. Some other types of visual reminders:

- o   Wear a plastic bracelet indicating the technique to focus on;
- o   Put a task in a mobile phone programmed with a sound to serve as a reminder, and set the phone to repeat the sound every two hours (except overnight).
- o   Prepare minutes of the meeting with the clinician, and use colorful markings in the minutes and planning of the meeting; e.g., a yellow color means....... etc.
- o   Put 10 1-cent coins in the right pocket of your trousers. Each time you execute your exercise put one coin in the left pocket. By the end of the day all coins are supposed to be in the left pocket. This is a reminder because when you put your hand in the pocket you are like: What's that? Oh I need to practice.

As in all visual reminders, changes in color, form, or place to which the memos have been adhered make them still more memorable. Changes in the form and content of these reminders, from time to time, help to catch the attention of the client.

5.5 Self-observation schemes.

Self-observation schemes can serve as good ways to make clients aware of the differences between their old and new behaviors. Such schemes can be used during assessment and during therapy. In the assessment phase, the client should prepare schemes daily, and on some days even every hour. In the therapy phase, this can be done less often. During the therapy phase, the clinician can also choose to ask the client to pay attention to only one aspect of speech. In the self-observation schemes, the following observation goals can be given as an assignment (see Appendix K):

o   How often were the clients asked "What did you say?"
o   How often did the clients notice that they made self-corrections? In which words? Which moments? Which conversations? During which periods of time?
o   How many times did the listener respond appropriately to the story told?

As suggested above, the frequency of following through on the schemes can vary from once a day in some cases to every hour, as necessary. In the therapeutic phase, the goals just mentioned can be established less frequently, or specific exercises can be limited at times to specific goals. To keep therapy from becoming too much of a chore, the frequency of the schemes should not be too high. A variation may be, instead of following through on the schemes once a day or every hour as suggested above, it may be done once a week or three times a week, and sometimes not at all. The goal of the self-observation schemes, namely "focused attention to speech," can also be accomplished by programming a mobile phone to beep or vibrate every hour, several times a day, or in certain situations (e.g., a party or a business meeting).

5.6 Diagnostic therapy (assessment and diagnostic exercises)

An assessment plan can be written after the client has described the problem, based on the *Predictive Cluttering Inventory-revised* (see 3.1.1 and Appendix A) and the Brief Stuttering-Cluttering Questionaire (see 3.4.3 and Appendix H). The assessment should include the Fluency Assessment Battery in combination with diagnostic exercises. Information obtained by taking a case history and the results of the assessment should provide enough information about specific symptoms for each client. Amelioration of these symptoms is the goal of cluttering intervention. After the assessment, intervention should be planned and tailored to each individual client. The client's prognosis should be based on the type, number, and severity of the symptoms that need to be ameliorated. In addition, the client's ability to learn and to change contributes to the therapy outcome. A comprehensive assessment of PWC provides insight as to the approaches for cluttering intervention, including therapy style, the type of exercises, and audio-visual means.

The first sessions
Planning the first sessions varies with each client. Table 5.1 below presents an example of a plan for the first four treatment sessions. As indicated above, the feedback loop of PWC is weak. During the diagnostic exercises, therefore, strengthening the feedback loop should be the main goal. Regarding the feedback loop, Levelt (1989) suggested three levels of monitoring (see 1.6.3). The attention of PWC focuses on the third level. If monitoring skills improve at this level of the speech process, it is possible to work at the other two levels.

Table 5.1: Example of planning first assessment and diagnostic therapy sessions

Session (60 minutes) and goal	Procedures	Activity	Home assignments
1 History taking, Fluency Assessment Battery	Assess spontaneous speech, reading and SPA; Determine articulatory rate and ratio disfluencies (3.2.4). Provide information on cluttering;	Telling your name (5.4.1); Client focused reading text on cluttering (Appendix L);	Telling your name (5.4.1); Observe how often a client is asked "What did you say?" (5.6.1).
2 Evaluation session 1, and home assignments;	Summarize Fluency Assessment Battery: *Wallet story,* OMAS, Speech Situation Checklist, BCSQ	Recognize and describe difficult situations.	Inventory of job and hobby multisyllabic terminology, Speaking while tapping, every day for 5 minutes;

3 Evaluation session 2 and home assignments;	Differential diagnosis	Reading out loud, possibly while tapping (6.5.2); Counting backwards (5.4.4).	Reading out loud, every day 2 x 5 minutes; Counting backwards, one series every day.
4 Comprehensive evaluation;	Repeat assessment items and adjust the complexity level to findings. Cluttering Severity Instrument, see 3.3.9 (Bakker & Myers, 2011)	Repeat/extend exercises Inventory of possibilities to apply (built up hierarchy)	

PWC's weak monitoring skills are not necessarily obvious based on Levelt's model. All clinicians observe inadequate symptom awareness due to weak self-monitoring in their clients with cluttering. See the example below.

Example of weak self-monitoring in clients with cluttering.
The therapist records the speech of a person with cluttering. After recording the client's speech, she plays it back to the client. The client exclaims: "WOW, how did you do that!!" Only after some clients respond in the same way, the clinician realizes that clients think that in the process of playing back the recording, the clinician left her own speech unchanged while she changed the client's speech to sound fast, disfluent and/or unintelligible. It takes the clinician more than one series of playing back recordings in order to convince clients that what they hear is their own speech, unchanged, but very fast, disfluent, and/or unintelligible.

When working on the monitoring, it is important to focus clients' attention on identification, self-observation and "speech awareness." The exercises below demonstrate how to work on such monitoring skills.

5.6.1 Diagnostic exercise 1 – "Telling your name"

One excellent way to make clients aware of their symptoms at the outset of therapy is to give them an assignment, as described in the following example. The clinician should simply tell them: "Please try to answer the telephone intelligibly and fluently this week." The trouble they experience in pronouncing their name correctly increases the symptom awareness and the awareness of their own ability to start the process of change, which is referred to as improving clients' internal locus of control. Because pronouncing one's own name is more "ego bounded" than any other words, it is sometimes necessary for clients to practice pronouncing their name during the session, with or without recording and playing it back.

Note: It is our experience that the voicemail message of PWC is often not as clear and fluent as the messages of speakers with no speech problems. The assignment of recording a correct voicemail message from other people's phones can be used.

> *Two examples of the telling your name exercise*
> Michael McKenzie (fictitious name) has called himself "Myksie" his whole life. For him to change his name from two syllables to five syllables is a big step. When the clinician pronounces Michael's name in five syllables, he responds: "Yes, but I never say my name like that, it sounds weird."
> The clinician explains the goal and the topic of "adjustment." After pronouncing his name while tapping the five syllables five times in a row, Michael leaves the room with the sense of having a different name.
> In assessment session 2, it appears that this SMART goal assignment has been effective for Michael's speech and his intrinsic motivation.

The practice exercises in session 1 of telling one's own name can take some time. Many clinicians ask themselves if the diagnostic assessment should not be finalized before they start giving home assignments or exercises. In cluttering this is not always true. Svend Smith, who also used his *Accent Method* specifically in cluttering, practiced the principle that "during the treatment the diagnosis becomes clear." In other words: remaining steps in the assessment can be postponed to a point later in the program, and re-evaluation during the treatment process can be beneficial, potentially revealing various symptoms that were not evident during the initial assessment.

5.6.2 Diagnostic exercise 2 – Articulatory rate

It is necessary for PWC to adjust their articulatory rate. In most cases, this means lowering the rate. It is important to get an insight into clients' ability to learn in order to adjust their articulatory rate. During the diagnostic phase, multisyllabic words that are difficult to pronounce, such as those used in the *Screening Phonological Accuracy* (See Appendix E), can be practiced. We prefer to use words that are related to the experience of the clients, as, for example, words related to their hobby or work.

As a first step in identification of moments of cluttering during a conversation, the clinician can repeat words or sentences that were poorly pronounced or disfluent, immediately "mirroring" them, and at some point explaining the reason for this confrontational and somewhat blunt working style.

To improve clients' attitudes toward home assignments, clients can be asked to add these challenging words or phrases to their own list of words to practice. In addition to enabling the clinician to understand more about clients' intrinsic motivation to learn, this will provide the clinician with information about their clients' formulation of multisyllabic words on paper.

Example 1
In a first session, Aaron, 29, spoke about the job of his girlfriend as her being a "paro-eh-par–eh-list." Writing down and producing the word "paradontologist" was possible after we split the word into syllables: /pa/ra/don/to/lo/gist/. He then succeeded in producing the word correctly five times in a row. In the second session, he was able to pronounce the profession of his girlfriend correctly. The increased internal locus of control gave him the motivation to collect and practice words related to the jargon of his own profession.

Example 2
Giorgio, 10, thought the word "Geofy" was quite a funny word. He learned that the word "geography" consisted of four syllables. He was able to do a fast analysis of the word by writing it down with brackets in between the syllables. Repeating the word five times was interpreted by him as "cool." He also decided to analyze the word "library" the same way. The first step to a positive locus of control was set.

Taking inventory of multisyllabic words as a home assignment and tapping them (see 6.5.2) is an effective exercise at the word level. In addition, it is advisable for clients to practice the production of multisyllabic words of different levels of complexity with different speech rates. First, clients should practice pronouncing three-to-five syllable words. They should begin with words that they use daily, such as "hamburger," "computer," and "television." After this, the clients should practice with more abstract words, such as "intelligence," "correspondence," and "developmental care."

Lists of selected words of different lengths can be found on our website www.NYCSA-Center.org (Appendices B, C, and D). Such lists will assist in the decision as to what level of complexity to practice first. As a general rule, the words to be practiced should be "not too easy, not too difficult." Accordingly, clients can be assigned to write down multisyllabic words that they hear, read or use in daily life.

The level of complexity is related to phonology. If the same sound appears in two consecutive syllables, one of the sounds may be produced differently and with more effort, because of the increased chances of coarticulation. So the repeated production of "green gass" is much more difficult than the repeated production of the words "green grass." Examples of relevant exercises can be found at www.NYCSA-Center.org, and at Appendices B and C. In repeating the words at a fast rate a few times in succession, PWC are challenged to adjust their speech planning (syllable tapping) to their verbal- motor skills.

For young children, working with pictures instead of written words is a good alternative. The client can be asked to produce names at a fast rate within a sixteen square field, in a certain route, following the clinician's modelling (see Figure 5.1, Appendix A, and www.NYCSA-Center.org). In this picture the words 'guitar', 'balloon', 'football' and "backpack" are pronounced as fast as possible in different order (each line left to right; or from top to bottom, and then back up to top, down to the bottom, and then back up again, etc.), but it is important to remain intelligible and fluent. In doing this, pauses between lines are not allowed.

Some children with cluttering notice that when they speak fast, they will stumble over words, exhibit hesitations, uh-interjections and word repetitions or will not be able to recall words quickly enough from their lexicon, thereby actually losing time. A way to prove this to the child is by measuring the time with a stopwatch. As a result, children are surprised to find out that when they attempt to speak slowly, they actually spend less time than when they attempt to speak fast.

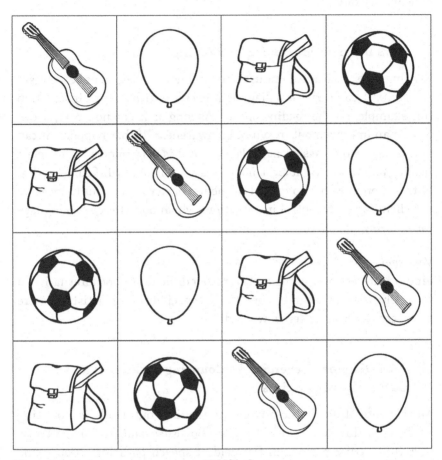

Figure 5.1: Sixteen squares, see www.NYCSA-Center.org

The implementation of syllable tapping is transferred in the therapy phase from simple to longer sentences. If working on syllable tapping in sentences is too difficult in the beginning, the reduction in rate can be attempted in multisyllabic words only. A next step can be tapping, while controlling the rhythm throughout the whole sentence.

For more examples, see www.NYCSA-Center.org, Appendices E—J. The exercises presented in this web site are used for working on the articulatory rate. Another different but suitable diagnostic exercise is "syllable tapping." This exercise is thoroughly explained in 6.5.2. When this exercise is modified for the client, a week of practice will give clinicians a good idea as to the ability of the client to reduce the articulatory rate.

5.6.3 Diagnostic exercise 3 - Reading

Reading texts, such as the one used in the Fluency Assessment Battery (see Appendix I), can serve as a diagnostic exercise with specific instruction (for example, on the reading speed). As long as it is a new text, it can lead to an improvement in symptom awareness. If that happens, it can be used as a home assignment. Note that it is very important to select reading texts at the right level, not too easy, and not too difficult. The goal of this exercise is not to make the client a better reader, but to improve the client's speech control in conditions which do not require language formulating skills.

Variation
Finding interesting reading texts is rather difficult. A good alternative to routinely used texts can be song texts, especially of rap artists, theatre texts, etc. These are often downloadable.

5.6.4 Diagnostic exercise 4 – Counting backwards and other math-related exercises

Much more difficult, compared to reading out loud, is counting backwards. This exercise was suggested by Kussmaul (1877) and Weiss (1964) in earlier periods in the field of speech pathology. Using this relatively challenging exercise as a diagnostic tool can be appropriately applied to cluttering, cluttering-stuttering and even stuttering. Counting backwards can be used in early stages of treatment, in milder forms of cluttering or cluttering-stuttering.

Counting backwards exercises (Winkelman in Mensink-Ypma, 1990)

Increase the level of intelligibility at the phrase level.

Way to do it
The client needs to count backwards out loud. The clinician needs to have not just speech skills, but also the ability to handle certain basic math computations.
An easy variation of the exercise is 20-18-16, – etc.; a more difficult variation is 100 minus 2 or minus 5, etc.; still more difficult is 100 minus 3, etc., or 300 minus 7, etc. (uneven numbers).

Possible effects
If the calculations take too much effort, the breathing can become dysrhythmic or interjections can occur, especially /uh/'. If that happens, the clinician should give the client an easier task. As clients' concentration diminishes, their intelligibility can worsen. This often occurs after doing the exercise for 40 seconds.
To get an idea of the anticipated duration of the exercise: 100 minus 2 till the client reaches 0 takes most people approximately 90 seconds; 100 minus 3 till the client reaches 1 should take approximately 60 seconds.

Additional information
In a "running" exercise, breathing regulation can be proposed. For example, the clinician can ask the client to produce three equations in one breath.

The use of math equations in the therapy of a person with cluttering has an important advantage over reading a text or telling a story. In doing math exercises, the client no longer needs to focus on grammatical constructions of pragmatics, but mental activity is still necessary. By doing this, the monitoring skills can also be trained. Another advantage of doing math exercises is that in counting backwards, emotions almost never play a role. An exception to this is when doing therapy with a very impatient client. With such a client, clinicians may find that they hit a sore spot. It is important to discuss with clients their impatience or discomfort with mathematical equations. If the counting backwards exercise is adjusted to the level of the client, after a week of practice this exercise can provide a good insight into a client's ability to learn, and to expend effort.

After exercises in counting backwards, the feedback loop can also be practiced in language formulation tasks. Monitoring during conversation is much more complicated than during counting. We will discuss this aspect later. In Table 5.2, we describe the types of attention and concentration in various speech conditions.

Table 5.2: Types of attention and concentration during various speech conditions (Winkelman, 2006)

	Thinking	Language formulation	Emotions
Reading	-	-	-
Counting backwards	+	-	-
Dialogue	+	+	+

These exercises integrate the following three processes: speech concentration, breathing regulation during speech, and activation of the feedback loop. If the counting backwards exercise is adjusted to the level of the client, after a week of practice this exercise can provide a good insight into a client's ability to learn, and the ability to put effort into effecting change. In order to increase the level of motivation of a client, it is helpful to use metaphors relevant to the client's interests or experiences. When providing therapy to a musician, a clinician can comment, "Practicing tone ladders is not music, but necessary to produce music." When providing therapy to a baseball player, the clinician can observe, "Batting practice with straight throws is not playing in game conditions, but it can help prepare the player for getting into a groove necessary to hit against major league pitching." Similarly, shooting free throws without any opposition can be helpful for a person who is interested in becoming a basketball player capable of scoring under stressful conditions.

5.7 Evaluation of the assessment (diagnostic therapy)

After the assessment is completed, a comprehensive and individualized intervention plan can be formulated. Sometimes clients are not capable of implementing diagnostic exercises into their daily routine, despite their clinician's repeated instructions. This can be a sign of resistance, which would need to be discussed with the clinician. In many cases, such a scenario may be related to the planning or scheduling of exercises in the course of the day. It is possible that simple aids, such as reminders on a computer or an alarm function on a mobile phone can help the client to plan and implement exercise schedules. Another possible reason for therapy to be ineffective may be clients' inability to identify the sensory or musical aspects of symptoms; they simply do not hear that their speech is too fast or dysrhythmic. In these cases AVF-training (see 6.5.1) is indicated. Finally, the therapy may have been initiated at an inappropriate or inconvenient time in the life of the client, for a challenging regimen of therapy. If this is the case, it is important to explore other options and to postpone the next appointment to a more convenient time in the future. The clinician can also ask such clients to record samples of their speech monthly for identification purposes.

5.8 Conclusion

Clients who were advised to consult a speech therapist often are not aware of which areas of their speech, such as poor intelligibility or fluency, need to be improved. By making clients aware of which areas of speech are in need of improvement, clinicians may educate and motivate clients to pursue the challenging journey of cluttering intervention. Clinicians should prepare their clients for the daily discipline of practicing during therapy, and should alert them to the importance of transfer of acquired new speech skills to all speaking situations.

6

Chapter 6

Therapy Exercises

6.1 Introduction

A wide variety of treatment approaches can be used in cluttering therapy. The decision of which approaches to use depends on the client's symptoms and ability to learn. It is important for the intervention tools to be compatible with the experiences of the client. We start this chapter with introductory comments about therapeutic exercises. We discuss which types of exercises should be used for the different types of cluttering. The most effective sequence of the exercises is also set forth. A number of general aspects of cluttering assessment, diagnostic therapy and intervention planning are explained. At the end of this chapter we briefly describe strategies for improving the social use of language as well as the transfer and maintenance of acquired skills.

More specifically, the treatment plan for phonological cluttering is discussed in 6.2, followed by the treatment plan for syntactic cluttering in 6.3, and the treatment plan for cluttering-stuttering in 6.4. We describe therapeutic approaches in 6.5, starting with Audio-Visual Feedback training (6.5.1), syllable tapping (6.5.2) as well as some fluency enhancing techniques (6.4). This chapter also covers a description of exercises for identification (6.5.3), auditory and syllable structure awareness (6.5.4), speech rate reduction (6.5.5), speech rhythm (6.5.6), pauses (6.5.7), and melody and prosody (6.5.8). Special attention is focused on practicing at different levels of language complexity (6.5.9) and responses to pragmatic difficulties (6.5.10). Finally, maintenance of acquired skills is presented (6.6).

A therapy plan for cluttering can be divided into four phases (see Figure 6.1). Cluttering therapy always starts with identification: becoming aware of the symptoms at the time they occur. By making clients aware of the symptoms, the effect of the poor intelligibility or disfluency on the clients and on the listeners is discussed. Such a discussion about speech behaviors may change clients' personal image of themselves as communication partners. At this time, social changes are encouraged by asking clients to modify their communication patterns during the diagnostic and therapeutic exercises. Insights into clients' speech rates will open their minds to speech rate reduction strategies (see 4.4.3 and 6.5.4 for ways to change speech behavior). After clients become aware of their speech symptoms, they can be trained to make adequate pauses and focus on prosody.

Therapy plan

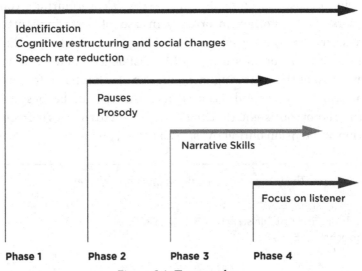

Figure 6.1: Therapy plan

■ 6.2 Treatment plan for phonological cluttering

Once the client is able to identify differences in speech rate and intelligibility, the work on slowing the articulatory rate can begin. There are two ways to slow the articulatory rate: syllable tapping (see 6.5.2) and audio-visual feedback training (AVF training, see 6.5.1). With both approaches, the client's syllable and rate awareness are addressed. The choice is determined by the clinician's knowledge of the client obtained during the diagnostic exercises and by the personal interests of the client. The clinician will, for example, choose the AVF training with youngsters and adults who love to work with computers. The benefit of syllable tapping is that it can be used at any moment during the client's speech. Once syllable awareness is achieved at different levels of linguistic complexity, the clinician may use AVF training to work on rate, rhythm, pauses and prosody.

When providing therapy for people who are not interested in working with computer feedback, there are other alternatives to accomplish their goals, utilizing more traditional methods. Another important consideration in choosing which approach to take for reducing the speech rate is whether the client's cluttering is accompanied by stuttering. It is probably best to provide AVF training for clients with cluttering-stuttering because syllable tapping creates the risk of acquiring secondary behaviors when performed incorrectly. In cases of cluttering-stuttering, AVF training has the advantage of enabling the client to visualize the duration and tension of stuttering-like disfluencies and extra pauses. The duration of the stuttering moments can also be shown to the client during visualizing. Instead of commenting that the number of stuttering moments is not consistent, the clinician can point to changes in frequency, duration and tension during the speech interruptions.

The 6 steps for treating phonological cluttering

1. identification, 6.5.3
2. auditory and syllable structure awareness, 6.5.4.
3. speech rate, 6.5.5
4. speech rhythm, 6.5.6
5. pauses, 6.5.7
6. melody and prosody, 6.5.8

In many cases of cluttering, therapy time is limited, and steps 1 and 2 have a strong impact on the performance relating to what would be accomplished in steps 3 through 6. So clinicians should be aware that it may be necessary to complete only steps 1 and 2 and there may be no need to implement steps 3 through 6 unless evaluation results show that the client needs to improve speech skills further.

6.3 Treatment plan for syntactic cluttering

After clients have proven to be capable of identifying differences in their speech rate, the training in appropriate phrasing can be initiated. During work on phrasing it is important to give clients enough time to complete language formulation, before speaking. Speaking in complete sentences begins with practice with phrases and later with combining phrases into sentences. This again is a situation where different clinicians can select different options. It is possible to work with reading texts or retelling stories, books or movies or formulating sentences by describing a picture. The choice of activities depends on the experience with the client during the diagnostic exercises. If a client is able to implement phrasing adequately, with an accurate rate, the time has come to start working on the pragmatic aspects of language.

The 7 steps for treating syntactic cluttering

1. identification, 6.5.3
2. speech rate reduction, 6.5.5
3. pauses, 6.5.7
4. language formulation, 6.5.9
5. levels of language complexity, 6.5.9
6. sharing information/pragmatics, 6.5.10
7. responses to pragmatic difficulties, 6.5.10

As was mentioned earlier, since cluttering therapy is performed within a short time frame, and because the first two steps may improve clients' communication skills to such a degree that it is possible that what steps 3 through 7 are designed to accomplish may be achieved within the first two steps, there may only be a need for the clinician to work on steps 1 and 2; nevertheless, all steps will be examined in detail later in this chapter (6.5.3 through 6.5.10).

▨ 6.4 Treatment plan for the cluttering-stuttering client

Before describing priorities in the treatment of cases of cluttering-stuttering, some background information on the topic of cluttering-stuttering will be provided.

People with cluttering and stuttering generally find that cluttering is the primary disorder (Freund, 1934). In such cases, treatment should focus on cluttering first, and if stuttering persists, treatment should then also focus on stuttering. If the therapy results in improvements, attention should increasingly focus on cluttering. Weiss (1968) recommended that the treatment of people who clutter and stutter has to be individualized, and that clinicians should prioritize the aspects of speech that are most impaired.

Freund (1966) proposed modification of the speech rate, believing that stuttering symptoms are not very pronounced in stuttering-cluttering clients, and therefore they can be ameliorated. Similarly, Daly (1986) observed that PWC do indeed make progress, but usually at a slower pace than PWS. Preus (1986) described the combination of fluency shaping and stuttering modification approaches while treating the cluttering-stuttering client. Daly (1992) reported significant gains in clients with cluttering when a synergistic and multi-dimensional perspective in treatment was implemented. Myers and Bradley (1986) introduced a widely followed synergistic perspective in treating cluttering-stuttering clients. This perspective integrates different approaches with clients who manifest various symptoms. It may be noted that these symptoms interact, and influence each other in a variety of ways. Addressing multi-faceted interactions of these symptoms can be very challenging.

According to our practice-based evidence, in combined cluttering and stuttering cases, in children with a high frequency of normal disfluencies who start to stutter, addressing stuttering should be the first priority. This is especially so in cases where stuttering-like disfluencies are observed. In adults, when the disfluencies are produced without tension, and when the client doesn't exhibit anxiety and fear of speech, the cluttering component can get first priority. In cases when adults do not manifest significant affective symptoms, priority in treatment is given to the cluttering as soon as possible. The rationale behind this is that people stumble before they fall.

> *Cluttering and stuttering, priority in treatment planning*
>
> *You stumble before you fall.*
> *So if you do not stumble, you are much less likely to fall.*
>
> In this example, cluttering is represented as stumbling,
> and stuttering as falling.

In cases where stuttering symptoms are addressed first, the cluttering symptoms should still be treated with comparable attention. If not properly treated, the cluttering symptoms will remain or worsen and may lead to a relapse of stuttering. Improving speech fluency is a common goal for clients with cluttering and stuttering.

The approach to facilitating fluency in cluttering-stuttering clients is referred to as "Flexible Fluency Search" (FFS) (Reichel, 2010). In order to elicit faster transfer, the clinician should use those fluency facilitators that least affect the naturalness of speech. While using fluency facilitators, clients need to have a sense of security and safety not only in the motoric aspect of speech, but also in their minds. In other words, no disfluencies should be anticipated; no fears should be experienced. The fluency facilitators that can be used are: slowing down the speech rate, smooth, easy onset, phrasing, initial sound prolongation, continuous phonation, abdominal-diaphragmatic breathing, varying the length of the pauses between the junctures, and, in rare cases, prolonged speech.

Once the sense of control is accomplished, at the syllable, word, and sentence levels, the client learns to feel it, enjoy it, and move ahead to the level of conversation. At this level, clients are encouraged to be independent in choosing the types of tools that work best for them, with the flexibility to adjust their tools at any specific moment in any speaking situation. By practicing enough times and in various conversational settings, they will become successful masters of the Flexible Fluency Search (FFS).

The experience of safety and ease in clients' communication in conjunction with enjoyable conversation will transform not only clients' speech but also their personal construct and sense of self-worth. It is crucial to praise and reinforce each client every time a goal is accomplished. The experience of success and fulfillment of goals will bring clients hope, pride, and courage to work on their remaining symptoms of cluttering, by various activities, such as improving speech intelligibility, and enhancing organizational, word-retrieving, and self-monitoring skills. Special attention should be focused on improving conversational abilities (turn-taking, staying on topic, and considering listeners' perspectives). A relapse in stuttering symptoms will likely occur if cluttering symptoms are not eliminated.

The cognitive, psychosocial and emotional aspects of cluttering and stuttering disorders should be addressed by using various strategies, such as role playing, negative practice, counselling about self-acceptance, assertiveness, positive self-image and coping with negative stigma. The approaches for targeting a wide range of negative cognitions and emotions may go beyond the purview of speech-language pathology by integrating advances across the following allied disciplines: cognitive-behavioral therapy, neural sciences, social sciences, positive psychology, mindfulness, and emotional intelligence (Boyle, 2011; Mayer, Salovey, & Caruso, 2000; Menzies, Onslow, Packman, & O'Brian, 2009; Ohman, 2000; Reichel, St. Louis, & van Zaalen, 2013; Reichel & St. Louis, 2011; Reichel, 2010; Reichel, 2007; Schneider, 2004; Shapiro, 2011; St. Louis, 2011; Weiss & Ramakrishna, 2006; Wilder, 1993). See 4.4.1 and 4.4.2.

Clear goals
As described earlier, in the development of the feedback loop, focused SMART goals are designed based on the complaints of the client. Below is an example also relevant to what was covered in Chapter 4.

> Lloyd, a 12-year-old boy, was given an assignment by his clinician to record his speech daily in order to determine his articulatory rate using *Praat*. Lloyd was asked to calculate fragments of 10-20 consecutive fluent syllables without pauses.
>
> The goal was to achieve a mean articulatory rate of 5.5 to 6.5 syllables per second (SPS) calculated over five attempts. In so doing, the variation between the highest and the lowest scores could not exceed 2 SPS.
>
> Lloyd entered the therapy room for the next session with a smile, and immediately started to discuss his home assignment. He calculated, on his own, that he reached his goal at least once each day and sometimes even twice a day. He thought of doing it again and to strive to reach his goal twice a day throughout that week.

▨ 6.5 Therapeutic exercises

▨ 6.5.1 Audio-Visual Feedback (AVF) training

Van Zaalen (2009) developed Audio-Visual Feedback (AVF) training to help PWC improve their poor symptom awareness. In other words, PWC do not realize that they have speech difficulties, so they believe that their speech is understandable, fluent and intelligible. How is it possible that they do not realize that their speech rate is too fast? Cluttering is like driving in a race car through New York City. Theoretically, it is possible to do it without damage, but that would require drivers to control (inhibit) their speed throughout the ride and, in all probability, not be able to see and respond to all traffic signs alongside the road and not to have a relaxed conversation with a friend sitting in the passenger seat. So how can these drivers be trained in their driving skills? Well, trainers would have to record the ride, play back the recording, discuss the traffic rules that should be obeyed, and plan improvements to be made and how to make them. Race car drivers, as so retrained, will perform every future attempt within the same general conditions in a much more controlled manner. But that is only true if the trainers take the time to praise what was done right and to make the drivers aware of what they did to make it right. This is contrary to the example of a trainer of a young talented football player who was only told what he did wrong. After a while, the young athlete in that example was completely aware of everything he was doing wrong, but had no idea about what to do correctly, how to do it, and whether he would be able to do it.

For the AVF training, positive feedback is essential. For example, the clinician may write down the successful segments of speech while recording the sample; then, when playing back this piece with the client, the clinician can say something like: "Listen, this is very clear and when we look at it, we can clearly see all syllables on the screen, you can hear every syllable of the word, and it also sounds natural; let us listen again because this is very good; yes, this is what we were hoping for; let us measure your (articulatory) rate so we know at which rate you can be really intelligible."

6.5.1.1 Rationale for the AVF training

PWC are often unaware of the speech disruptions as they occur. The fact that other people mention that PWC talk too fast, are disfluent or unintelligible is often not internalized in a manner necessary for treatment (see the four component model of cluttering, in Chapter 2). In listening to and looking at a client's speech over and over again, combined with an analysis of the rate, fluency, pause placement and duration, the client observes and hears what a listener sees and hears. Instead of arguing about the rate being too fast or the speech being disfluent, in AVF training speech is judged by an analysis using *Praat* software (see 3.3.7). Such an approach is not based on a subjective opinion but on objective analysis. As a result of this analysis, the numbers speak for themselves, as is illustrated in the example below.

Without the AVF training

Clinician: *You told me a story. What do you think about your speech rate?*
Client: *Well, I think it was okay.*
Clinician: *I cannot agree with that.*
Either:
Client: *Oh, maybe it was a little bit fast?*
Clinician: *Nice, that you agree on that. Now for the next step......*
Or
Client: *Well, but it was really slower than usual.*

In AVF training
Clinician: *You told me a story. What do you think about your rate of speech?*
Client: *Well, I think it was okay.*
Clinician: *Okay, you mean you spoke within the set limits of XX SPS?*
Client: *Yes. I think I did.*
Clinician: Let us measure it.
After measuring
Clinician: *We measured XX+2 SPS. What does that mean?*
Client: *Oops, then I spoke faster than I thought.*
Clinician: *Okay let us listen again and look at the speech output.................*

After several sessions of AVF training, clients realize that they speak too fast, are disfluent or are not adequately intelligible. In playing back and visualizing their speech on the screen, the clients' internal locus of control grows in terms of objectively analyzing their speech rate, disfluency and/or poor intelligibility. The AVF training is more effective when longer recordings are used. The longer recordings (more than two minutes) prevent clients from responding based on their memories of what they intended to say.

After the PWC become aware of their speech disruptions, AVF training focuses not on moments of disfluency or reduced intelligibility but on the moments of adequate pausing or on a normal speech rate. After making an appropriate pause, the clients' chances for the next clause being fluent are quite good. So we look for pauses that are long enough. The moment a pause is detected with the duration of 0.5 to 1.0 seconds, the clinician should listen to ascertain whether the next clause is indeed fluent or intelligible. By doing so, the clinician will be able to focus on moments of success, help clients build stronger speech control, and increase the clients' confidence and future successes. The clients learn what they can do to change their speech and how it sounds, looks and feels when their speech is accurate, fluent and intelligible. Positive audio-feedback can be given in various ways: through the recorder option of a mobile phone, an iPod, mp3 player, *Praat* software, Goldwave, Audacity, whisper phone or by a headphone (marking surround noise).

6.5.1.2 Steps in AVF training

In AVF training, different speech aspects (prosody) are practiced, such as rate, fluency, pauses, melody and loudness. This leads to the following subgoals of the identification stage of treatment:

Subgoal 1: The client will be able to accurately (min. 80% accuracy) identify the moments of *intelligibility* in recordings of running speech.

Subgoal 2: The client will be able to accurately (min. 80% accuracy) identify the *number and duration of pauses* in recordings of running speech.

Subgoal 3: The client will be able to accurately (min. 80% accuracy) identify the moments of *fluent and disfluent speech* in recordings of running speech.

Subgoal 4: The client will be able to accurately (min. 80% accuracy) identify the moments of */uh/ or other interjections* in recordings of running speech.

Subgoal 5: The client will be able to accurately (min. 80% accuracy) identify the moments of *(melodic) monotony* in recordings of running speech.

Subgoal 6: The client will be able to accurately (min. 80% accuracy) identify the moments of normal and extreme *loudness* in recordings of running speech.

The clinician should do the following:

1. Determine the goal of the recording exercises.
2. Determine how many "errors" are considered acceptable.
3. Record the speech with a digital audio recording system (software such as Audacity or Goldwave is available as freeware).
4. While recording, write down the time of significant moments on a piece of paper.
5. Open the recorded file in *Praat* software (see www.praat.org).
6. Play back a segment (maximum of 20 seconds) in which the goal set for the client will have been reached.
7. Ask the client to pay attention to specific aspects of speech production: for instance: "Are you able to hear all the syllables in this piece?" or "Please listen and count the amount of 'uh-s.'"
8. Discuss the results.
9. Repeat steps 7 and 8 with another fragment that did not go well.
10. Repeat the exercise and compare the results of the first recording to the results of the second recording.
11. Plan a home assignment.

Practical information on how to implement AVF training is described in 6.5.3.2 – 6.5.3.5.

6.5.2 Syllable tapping

Syllable tapping is an exercise which is not focused on communication. It is comparable to dry swimming, shooting at a goal or a tone ladder exercise. You practice while not being in the game, so when you are playing a game or giving a performance you can depend on the skills developed in "dry practicing." When we do an exercise in changing speech behavior, the exercise in itself or the technique is not the goal but a way to get started.

The advantage of syllable tapping is that it is very concrete and the result is directly controllable with audio-visual feedback. In addition, the client does not consider this exercise to be offensive, but realizes it is only practice. It is important to present the exercise to the client in a structured and clear way. In order for this technique to be successful, the exercises should meet the SMART criteria, especially because speech may feel unnatural to clients who practice syllable tapping, and because many of them have trouble reaching their auditory monitoring goals. The use of a metronome can be helpful in the beginning, to build a rhythmic structure; however, the metronome can lead to iatrogenic effects for some clients, e.g., speech that is too unnatural. In such instances, the exercise will be less relevant to normal conversation. In the beginning of the exercises at home, an external assessor, e.g., a parent or a partner, can listen and give feedback. But it is important for clients to develop self-monitoring skills (internal feedback loop) so that they will become more independent. Again, this exercise needs to be practiced often and for short periods of time. It is much more effective to practice for a week, three times a day, four minutes at a time, than twice a week for longer periods.

6.5.2.1 The benefits of syllable tapping

The effect of this exercise is determined by:

o   the careful transfer to the next step, which can be taken when the previous step has been performed well without correction. Depending on the client's abilities, it is possible to go one step further in one session, and sometimes after a couple of sessions;
o   the frequency with which the client exercises at home;
o   the flexibility of the client. Tapping interferes with the clinician's and client's communication which in turn forces the client to speak at a slower rate. So tapping is needed for making a change;
o   the naturalness of speech. After this exercise, "normal" speech can suddenly feel more comfortable;

○ whether the clients listen to their own audio recordings; and
○ whether PWC also have a stuttering component. If a client presents with cluttering and stuttering, syllable tapping can bring too much focus on the speech production which in turn may increase speech tension or result in secondary behaviors.

6.5.2.2 Steps in syllable tapping

1. In reading a column of monosyllabic words, the client should tap on a table with a finger upon pronouncing every word. No other body parts are supposed to move with the rhythm, especially not the head.
2. A column of two syllable words can be tapped in a rather fast mode. It is best to use the so- called spondees (two syllable words with equal stress on both syllables), such as "bureau," "maybe," "blackboard," "concept," "nervous," etc. In words with unstressed syllables, the unstressed parts seem to be deleted too frequently.
3. After practicing with two syllable words, short sentences with two or three syllable words are worked on (see the example "short sentences" below, Appendix F, and www.NYCSA-Center. org). Keep in mind that the client will omit the unstressed parts quite easily. It is therefore important to give direct feedback on these omissions. In this phase, every tap should have the same duration, in a consistent rhythm. The metronome can be useful in helping the client to maintain the rhythm. If the client does not recognize the syllables correctly, the clinician can ask the client to mark the syllables in the written text, by putting a slash between every syllable.

Variations of the exercise

○ The clinician taps syllables in a sentence, using the index finger and the middle finger. The client imitates the tapping.
○ The client taps the syllables of every word, with a different hand.
○ If this step is performed well without any errors, a transition to a regular text can be made. If clients correct themselves, this means that the exercise is understood. In this phase, every syllable gets a tap and all syllables have an equal duration.

4. The client can read a text now while tapping (see Appendices F to I and www.NYCSA-center.org). A normal speech rhythm with normal rate changes should be practiced, by tapping all syllables, including those that are unstressed. By maintaining an appropriate sequence in tapping, the rate becomes slower than it is during clients' usual speech, and more natural due to the changes in rhythm. An audio recording can show clients that their speech rate sounds natural.

5. If step 4 goes well, clients can read a text without tapping with fingers. The clients are instructed to read at a normal speech rate. At this point, the clients perceive their rate as less slow and more normal than during the previous exercises. The clients still must pay attention to the syllables. As a general rule, speaking with staccato (a consistent rhythm and stress pattern) will disappear gradually.

6. Short speech assignments are used in order to transfer a normal speech rate to reading a text and to spontaneous conversation. At first, these assignments consist of concept formulation or professional jargon. For example, credit crisis, high speed transportation, or chatting. Later, the clinician can use conversational starters for this purpose. For example: "What would you say if you would have a chance to address the whole world for one minute?"

Alternative exercise

o   After finger tapping, clients can use their toes (not visible).
o   The exercises can be more attractive by clapping or using a drum or castanets. For children, the exercise can be turned into a fun activity, by having the child speak and walk. The child can be told to put a foot on every tile and with every step produce a syllable or a rhyme or give a selected response to the clinician.
o   Turn-by-turn quiz questions can be asked by either the clinician or the client. Finger tapping can be practiced when asking and answering questions.

6.5.3 Identification – Developing feedback loop

During the whole treatment, the identification of cluttering symptoms should be a key issue. Clients should be taught how to recognize their symptoms and better understand what they are able to change (improve their locus of control). The development of the so-called internal feedback loop is often very slow. As described in 4.3, this loop consists of the elements of self-observation, self-judgement and self-correction. (See the language production model of Levelt, in 1.6.3). In training the feedback loop as a self-monitoring technique, two goals should be met:

Subgoal 1: Improvement of self-awareness at the sensory level. Rhythm, rate, timing and kinaesthetic awareness play a role;
Subgoal 2: Improvement of phonological planning (e.g., oral-motor) skills.

Often the client is only aware of the "bad" speech after the end of communication, as, for example, after completing a sentence, and noticing the frowning of a listener or even only at the end of a conversation. The feedback loop needs to be as short as possible. The AVF training can help the person with cluttering by providing feedback just after the moment of motor execution and speech production or even in real time (during production).

By using the AVF training (6.5.1), clients are able to analyze their own speech within normal (listeners) range. The most difficult aspect of changing speech behavior in cluttering is that the PWC perceive their own speech as fluent and intelligible at a normal rate. By using the AVF training, PWC have to judge their speech within the range known to be universally accepted among human listeners; the human brain is only able to process a mean of 5 syllables per second.

> The AVF-training makes it possible to correctly respond to the speech characteristics and to create a frame of reference in which the speech is intelligible and fluent.

The AVF training makes it possible to correctly respond to the speech characteristics and to create a frame of reference in which the speech is intelligible and fluent.

▓ 6.5.3.1 *The role of the environment in the identification*

The role of the environment in the identification of cluttering symptoms is rather vague because people within an immediate environment, in particular, tend to have made many comments regarding the speech behavior of PWC, without any results. The clinician has to win and maintain the client's trust so the clinician's feedback will be believed and accepted, and will lead to a positive change in the client's behavior.

It is best to start therapy by educating clients and people in their immediate environment about cluttering. In order to explain cluttering to people in an immediate environment, see Appendix L and www. NYCSA-Center.org. It is advisable to include people in the environment of the client, such as parents, partners, teachers, or a colleague as soon as possible. They can alert the child, partner or colleague to the cluttering speech behavior and so can be of help in developing symptom awareness. Such people no longer have to feel that there is nothing that can be done about the disfluent or unintelligible speech of the person with cluttering who is close to them. The best way for the people in the environment of the person with cluttering to be of assistance is by asking more often:

> "What did you say?" or "What did you mean?" or "I heard ...xxxx...
> is that what you intended to say?" or "Can you repeat what you just
> said?" or "Can you clarify what you just said?" or variations of all
> of the above.

By doing this, the listener no longer has to be resigned to interpreting the cluttered message wrongly, and the person with cluttering learns to speak at a higher level of alertness. In discussions with the client and the people in the client's environment, clear agreements will be made as to how the comments will be given. For example, confidants may make a prearranged audible or visual sign that may be used to a maximum of a designated number of times on any given day. A second agreement may be worked out to make these comments when other people are within hearing range. Finally, it is advisable to make sure that the client is confident that when a person in the environment makes a comment, this person is undoubtedly honest, caring, and constructive. So when a suggestion is made, clients will not get angry or frustrated, but will change their behavior instead.

The actions of the participating members of the immediate environment are a step toward a well-functioning feedback loop. It is important that clients are not only corrected, but are also complimented, especially when they correct their speech without any comments from members of the environment. In such a manner, internalizing monitoring will develop faster. In the process of internalizing monitoring, external sources of noise can cause confusion. In an insufficient signal-to-noise ratio, e.g., standing in front of a music source or an open window, speech can be less intelligible. A person with cluttering can be made aware of these conditions and be taught to speak louder in conditions like these. A louder voice will have a positive effect on speech intelligibility in cases where the signal-to-noise ratio interferes with the intelligibility.

6.5.3.2 Introduction to identification

It is important for PWC to learn to critically listen to their own speech. The identification stage of treatment can start by having clients listen to a recorded text. It is best to start the process of identification by having clients listen to a recording in which the clients are unaware that the recording is being made. To make recordings in this manner, the clinician can ask clients to call friends, and can then record the conversations. In general, after 40 seconds, clients are no longer fully aware and responsive to the recording and chat with their friends in a natural way. Such conversations often contain cluttering symptoms, even though the clients are hardly aware of the recording.

Listening to a recording will be more challenging when it extends for a period of several minutes or was created a couple of days earlier. In listening to longer recordings or recordings made earlier in time, the actual text tends to be a little bit vague and the speech itself has a more powerful effect on the clients as listeners.

Listening to clients' own recordings is a very effective and efficient home assignment. It is important to make sure that the home assignment meets the SMART criteria. For instance, the clients must be told very specifically how many recordings they should make; how many times a day; how long the recordings should take; and on which criteria these recordings will be evaluated. In the next session, the perception of the clients can be compared to the perception of the clinician. After the clients listen to the first playback, the identification training can be planned with various subgoals.

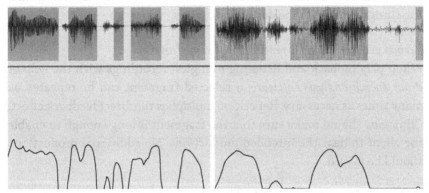

Figure 6.2A and 6.2B: Identification of intelligibility (a) syllables tapped and (b) telescoping

The word "unintelligibility" is shown in Figure 6.2A with all syllables well articulated. In Figure 6.2B not all syllables are accurately produced, i.e., bad intelligibility.

Note: Every peak refers to a vowel production. The higher the broken line is, the louder the syllable is produced.

6.5.3.3 Subgoal 1: Identification of speech intelligibility

During the session, the recorder should be stopped every time a cluttered word or phrase is heard or seen. The client should repeat the cluttered word correctly in a controlled manner. If the client does not notice the cluttered word, the clinician should imitate the word in the manner in which the client spoke. Such an approach can be rather confrontational. The clinician therefore has to clarify the goal of this imitation. It can be motivating for clients if they are able to correctly produce the whole sentence. The monitoring is not sufficiently effective if only the mispronounced word gets corrected.

In order to practice at a one-word level, the client should repeat a difficult word five times, first with pauses between words and later, without pausing. PWC with intelligibility problems experience the most trouble with low frequency words. By repeating the words many times, the word retrieval-planning-execution cycle renders the word to be familiar. When these words are used more frequently, word retrieval, planning and execution require less focus in order to be executed correctly by clients with cluttering. In addition, it is helpful to praise the client in every session for controlled and intelligible word productions. By doing this, the clinician rewards the desired behaviors.

Variation of the exercise: repeating the same fragment
When playing back and listening to digital recordings with the help of *Praat speech analysis software,* a selected fragment can be repeated as many times as necessary. Repetition multiplies the direct feedback effect. Clinicians should make sure that the fragment is long enough to enable the client to hear the intended productions. No additional productions should be played.

Variation of the exercise: mumbled speech
Poor intelligibility may also be caused by a jaw that is almost completely clammed shut, causing mumbled (or "mushy") speech due to a minimal amount of muscle or jaw activity. Such unclear and mumbled speech needs to be addressed in therapy. Frequently, speech intelligibility improves by using speech rate reduction exercises. Such exercises can be easily demonstrated. When clients open and close their mouths, while producing sounds six times faster than at the normal rate, the opening space will get smaller. A small jaw opening has a negative effect on intelligibility because the vowels can no longer be produced correctly, and consonants lose their precision.

Exercise suggestions

1. In a rigid jaw clammed speech, it is helpful to exercise with word lists and sentences that contain the /a:/ phoneme.
2. Clinicians can read a sentence out loud with a vague and unclear articulation and then they can read the same sentence with a precise articulation. Subsequently, the pronunciation of both sentences would then be discussed by the clinician and the client. The client would reflect on clear and unclear productions of the sentence. Audio recordings can be very helpful. In addition, the clinician can perform a pitch or formant analysis using *Praat,* in order to show the client an image of the differences between sentences.

Next, clients can read a text with rap lyrics out loud. After that, clients can put a cork between their teeth and read the text a second time. Finally, clients can read the same text for a third time without the cork. These clients would then be asked to reflect on differences they felt during speech production. Recordings of all three readings would then be played back. These recordings would be shown, analyzed and discussed with these clients. It is advisable to focus on syllable clarity by observing the peaks and valleys which reflect the intensity of vowels (see Figure 6.2A and 6.2B).

For more techniques to increase monitoring skills, see Myers (2011).

6.5.3.4 Subgoal 2: Identification of the number and the duration of pauses

A normal pause between phrases and between speakers (turn-taking behavior) ranges between 0.5 – 1.0 second. This is the amount of time the listener needs in order to process the message of the speaker. It is also the amount of time the speaker needs to prepare the speech plan for the next clause. During interruptions, the pause between the speaker and the listener is often shorter than 0.5 seconds. In the beginning of the treatment, most pauses will be too short and located in linguistically inappropriate places.

Exercise suggestions

1. The clinician should instruct the client to pause for 0.5 – 1.0 seconds. The clinician should also make a table. After recording, pauses are measured using Praat. Pauses of 0.0 - 0.2 seconds should be drawn in red. Pauses of 0.21 - 0.50 should be drawn in orange. Pauses of 0.5 - 1.0 should be drawn in green. Red means unacceptable; orange means almost there; green means well done.

   If the clinician tells the client that orange means not good, the chances are that almost all the attempts will not be successful. That is very demotivating. By working with the windows of opportunities as just discussed, the clinician works on increasing moments of success: *"Today you had 15 out of 20 in the almost there group. You also had 2 in the green group. Wow! I am very proud."* This is very motivating for everyone involved.

2. Identification of the places to pause can be performed with the text in which the pauses are deleted (see Appendix K and www. NYCSA-Center.org). In this exercise, the client points out where the words or phrases need to be separated by a small pause.

3. In the course of reading texts or sentences out loud, with pauses intentionally inserted by the clinician in odd places, the client can become aware of the importance of pause placement and the effect of pauses in the wrong places for the understanding of the text (see Appendix L and www.NYCSA-Center.org). For an experienced client, citations or short and funny jokes can be good material for exercises. See 6.5.8 (prosody).

4. Silent blocks can be visualized when using the spectrogram patterns in the *Praat* analysis.

5. Extra pauses, contrary to normal phrasing, can be visualized by using the "pulses." It is normal to have 4 pulse blocks within a 20 second frame (i.e., 4 clauses in 20 seconds). When a person stutters, the number of pauses can increase dramatically.

6. Normally, a person's volume of speech fluctuates from 0 to 10 dB within a phrase. When a client's volume is down for more than 10 dB within one phrase, it is considered to be a symptom of a disorder. Such a symptom is known as the night candle effect, which may be observed in people with Parkinson's disease and cluttering.

7. Melody adds to the perception of the message. Melody can be visualized by using the Intensity tab in *Praat*. On the screen a blue line is visible. If the highest score within a time frame of 10 seconds would demonstrate a difference between 80/100 – 200 Hz, then the melody range is considered to be normal. If the score is below 80 Hz (male) or 100 Hz (female), it is considered to be a monotone.

8. Melodic monotony shows the same melody pattern for every clause. Melody is not related to the meaning of the utterance.

6.5.3.5 Subgoal 3: Identification of interjections

Many PWC use interjections such as "uhm," "well," "but," "like," and "by the way." In most instances, these interjections help them gain time for language formulation (including word finding). Identification of interjections can make clients aware of their difficulties in linguistic planning. Furthermore, frequent use of interjections can adversely affect "listenability" and "intelligibility."

Tip: Clinicians should be aware that people with syntactic cluttering present with these interjections because their speech rate is not synchronous with their language formulation. Language formulation in itself is not affected in cluttering.

Exercise suggestions

1. During home recordings, the number of "uhms" is counted. At this point, it is unnecessary to set an explicit goal of reducing the number of "uhms." Keeping records prevents a decrease in motivation that might occur if such a goal is set and not reached. If this happens, clients may lose their motivation. Just making the client aware of the frequent use of "uhms," will serve as a motivator to do something about it. Only frequently occurring and strongly stressed "uhms" may interfere with communication.

Correct and incorrect breathing pauses

Sentence "A" contains correct pauses; sentence "B" contains incorrect pauses.

(_ = pause)

A. Because my Ipod is broken, _ I have tried to fix it with the help of my father's tools. My Ipod is disconnected _ and now I do not know how to connect it again.
B. Because my _Ipod is broken I have tried to fix it with the help _of my father's tools. My I_pod is disconnected and now I do not know how to connect it again.
(For more exercises, see www.NYCSA-Center.org.)

---

2. Fluent speakers generally use two or three "uhms," at the most, per minute of monologue. Before beginning the exercise, the clinician should agree with the client on how many "uhms" will be acceptable during the session. Afterwards, the "uhms" will be tallied to see whether the desired goal was reached. So if the client normally produces 10 "uhms" per minute, the clinician

might set the goal at 8 "uhms" per minute in order to enable the client to be successful.

3. An effective but challenging exercise for developing the feedback loop is to create a transcript of the client's reading of a text or a phone conversation with poor speech intelligibility. Clients with poor auditory perception should be asked to write down what they think they hear or thought they said. Writing down syllable by syllable the words that have been produced increases the clients' insight into their speech behavior. This is comparable to the transcription done based on a language sample. Transcribing is more challenging and therefore more effective if it is done the next day. It takes some practice to be able to transcribe correctly. Clients can start this assignment by transcribing a song. If a person is able to do that within a therapy session, transcribing a song or their own recordings can be designated by the clinician as a home assignment. In order to simplify this exercise, the clinician can vary assignments, e.g., limiting the number of recordings that have to be transcribed.

5. Another approach for improving auditory perception is the development of a sense for the duration of words and sentences. Clients with phonological cluttering are particularly known for their poor planning of time. For example, they may only set aside enough time for producing three syllables when five syllables need to be produced. A way to address this telescoping is by repeating words, phrases or sentences during the pauses of an audio recording. This exercise can be performed as follows: Clients read a line of a short poem. They should remain silent while listening to the sentence and then repeat the sentence in their own mind. They then read the next word, phrase or line. They continue to read the next lines in the same fashion. After about five lines, the recording should be played back and the text should be put aside. During the pauses in the recording, the clients should repeat the word, phrase or sentence. Often, the pauses prove to be too short. This exercise should be repeated until the clients have a better awareness of word and syllable duration. This improved awareness of syllable duration may assist the clients in producing pauses of appropriate duration. This exercise can be evaluated by the percentage of syllables that were accurately produced during the recorded pauses.

Variation of the exercise

6. Instead of reading a text, the client can be instructed to read a joke from a joke book, a part of a role in a theatrical play, a poem, a recipe for cooking, a song text of a rap artist, etc. (See Appendix E and www.NYCSA-Center.org.). With the help of auditory awareness exercises, clients can be trained to become more aware and skilled to listen critically. As a result, the chances of such clients experiencing moments of "overt" repairs increase, but such exercises do not necessarily lead to speech becoming more fluent. By the clients' consciously listening to their own speech, they develop their monitoring loop. Note that most clients are not likely to be aware of this weakness in auditory monitoring. Clinicians can motivate their clients by adjusting the exercises to the experiences of their clients. For example, the clinician may ask a client to transcribe a favorite song and change the words of this song, leaving the rhymes and rhythm unchanged. In fitting in the new text to the form and melody of the song, attention should be given to the language formulation and duration aspects of the speech. Also, in this assignment, the complexity level needs to be considered. Preferably, the complexity level should be difficult enough to be a challenge and easy enough to enable the client to succeed.

7. In young children, the exercise described above can be altered by singing a favorite song, but by replacing words with "lalalala." The child should be told to listen to the lalala-song, and to try to guess the name of the song. This exercise becomes more complex when other words are changed. When words of another song are used to sing the first song, the exercise becomes very challenging.

8. In line with tip 7, the clinician can also choose to clap in rhythm with the song, so the clients need to recognize the song or something they said only by the combination of these activities. If the clinician chooses 12 lines from a recording, and writes these lines down like in a Lotto game, every time the client recognizes a line associated with the clapping, the clinician should place a token onto the appropriate place on the Lotto card. When all lines will have been detected and when the Lotto card will be filled with tokens, the "game" will be over.

9. A "syllable run" is a game in which syllables are used instead of dice. When clients are able to produce a word with 5 syllables while identifying what is on a card, they are allowed to take 5 steps on the board. The longer the words the clients will come up with, the faster they will reach the final position on the board. Such a game will improve the clients' awareness of the number of syllables in various words.

10. The clinician should not assume that all adolescents or adults are skilled in counting the syllables in words or the number of words in a sentence. Clinicians should make sure that they know whether their clients are able to count the syllables accurately. The best way to do this is for the clinician to ask how many syllables are produced in a line with short, moderate and long words, e.g., *"My mom asked me to go to the nearby department store to buy us a delicious cheesecake."*

6.5.4 Auditory and syllable structure awareness

After the identification phase of the treatment, the auditory perception and the auditory discrimination for identifying interjections are addressed. This should take place not only during the sessions, but also outside the therapy room.

Exercise suggestions
The clinician should ask the client to observe other speakers as to the number of times they use interjections. It is preferable to do this exercise while watching television programs or listening to the radio. Practicing in this manner does not disturb the communication between speakers and their environment. During this exercise, it is important to specify how long and how often the clients have to do this exercise. The clinician should also make clear to the clients how they have to process their exercise data. For example, the clients can count interjections while listening to the news or when listening to a talk show.

Note: It is not advisable to ask a student to count the number of interjections used by a teacher. This would be too distracting in any classroom situation.

Variation of the exercise
As in many identification tasks, this exercise can be performed with clients' own recordings or during their daily communication, e.g, when they may be using a cell phone. The clinician should advise clients to listen several times to short excerpts of the recording.

6.5.4.1 Word structure and syllable awareness

The training of self-monitoring is nessesary when working on speech production. The main focus of speech production will be on the articulatory rate. The running of syllables into each other (i.e., "collapsing," telescoping, or overcoarticulation), is a characteristic of phonological cluttering, and occurs due to the poor adjustment of the articulatory rate. The above described exercises that help to improve syllable awareness (planning the appropriate amount of time for each syllable) are generally not sufficiently addressed. Syllable awareness can be facilitated by using syllable tapping. These exercises are also helpful in training clients to adjust their speech rate to the linguistic demands in the communicative context.

6.5.5 Speech rate reduction

PWC are not able to adjust their speech rate to language complexity. Many approaches for reducing and controlling their speech rate are available. Although clients can be taught how to slow down their speech rate, it takes an excessive amount of attention capacity to achieve this objective because most clients are not able to automatize speech rate reduction. An attempt to do so requires a conscious decision or resolve, almost like deciding to learn a second language. A distraction of any kind can interfere with clients' attempts to use their technique, to the point where another conscious commitment needs to be made to start working on the speech rate again.

Ways to slow down speech and articulatory rate:

- o   Audio feedback
- o   Audio-visual feedback
- o   Prolonging pauses

○ Tapping syllables

○ Delayed articulation

○ Feeling the movement of articulators (kinesthetic feedback)

○ Reading by breaking sentences into meaningful chunks with slash marks

○ Exaggerated rhythm

○ Exaggerated melody patterns

The methods that clinicians choose for reducing their clients' articulatory rate is determined by the clients' skills and interests, and the linguistic context of the clients' work. Clinicians should find the highest articulatory rate at which the client is still fluent and intelligible. Clients should not be asked to speak at the mean articulatory rate characteristic of the general population (5 SPS). If a client is fluent and intelligible at a rate between 6.5-7.5 SPS, then that number should be taken as a point of reference. The clinician should use a rate margin of 1 SPS between the lowest and highest rate previously mentioned. In this instance, the highest rate at which the client was still fluent and intelligible was 7.5, so the clinician should aim for 7.5 – 1.0 = 6.5 as the lowest benchmark.

A clinician should make sure that fluent and intelligible speech is produced with a natural melody (see 2.3). An improved speech rate has a positive effect on almost all symptoms of cluttering.

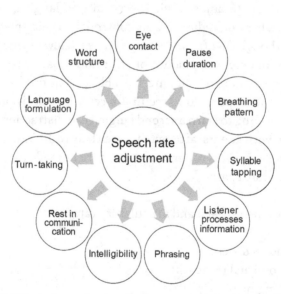

Figure 6.3: Effect of speech rate adjustment on communication behaviors.

Exercise suggestions

1. The diagnostic exercise of counting backwards can be suggested as a home assignment on a regular basis during the therapy process. For example, the exercise can serve as a warm-up and can gradually be made more complex (101 minus 3; 201 minus 4 or 502 minus 7).

2. Identification of the articulatory rate can be taught by getting clients to contrast rates that are too fast with rates that are normal, upon reviewing their own recordings. This can be done effectively with AVF training.

3. A fast speech rate can also be reduced by utilizing Delayed Auditory Feedback (DAF), Frequency Altered Auditory Feedback (FAF) or Heightened Auditory Feedback (HAF). Using these feedback options, speech can be perceived as delayed (DAF), changed in pitch (FAF) or made louder (HAF) while using headphones. Clients should be instructed to talk with their own lower/higher pitch or louder or delayed speech. If they focus more on their speech production, their rate will be significantly influenced, which will result in temporary improved speech. There is no scientific rationale for using DAF or FAF. Studies in the field of stuttering have shown that DAF has a temporary and inconsistent effect (Molt, 1996). No differential diagnosis between stuttering and cluttering-stuttering was made in the study conducted by Molt, although within groups, differences were apparent. It is possible that the group of PWS with a cluttering component was the one that temporarily improved as a result of using DAF; however, there is no clear evidence to that effect. DAF/FAF software is downloadable as Speech Monitor (Arenas, 2009). From our clinical experience, HAF is freely accessible to everyone, and can be very effective temporarily for PWC. We therefore advise clinicians to use HAF, which can be installed by using a "whisper phone," a head phone and microphone set, builders' headphones, DAF software and setting the delay on zero, or by covering their ears with their hands. As described in Appendix L, we even advise clinicians to use HAF for testing children and adolescents. Choosing HAF for telephone conversations, for example, can yield satisfying effects for some clients.

4. The clinician can also provide direct feedback to clients by showing them a "rate indicator" board with a green and an orange side. In a conversation with clients, the clinician can show them the green side of the board as long as their speech rate is within acceptable limits, and as long as they speak fluently or intelligibly. The minute clients start to telescope or use word and/or phrase repetitions, the clinician can alert clients to their errors by using the orange side of the indicator. The benefit of this color indicator approach is that every time the clinician shows clients a color, the clients have to interpret the meaning of the color and act upon it. In our experience, we have noticed that after using this rate indicator in a couple of conversations, clients started to anticipate the orange indicator, and therefore corrected themselves before the clinician was able to turn on the indicator. This was a sign of the clients' auditory feedback loop doing its important work.

Variation to the exercise

5. By imposing a penalty for speeding, the clinician makes clients aware of their fast rate, and "forces" them to adjust this rate (St. Louis et al., 2003). This speeding penalty can be imposed in the form of a token on a table, a yellow card, or an extra home assignment.

6. Give the client the following assignment with *Praat*:
The clinician should ask clients to set a goal for their speech rate, and then to tell a story, which can be recorded with *Praat*. The clients should be asked to guess what their speech rate was. Is it above, below or within limits of the goal they set for their speech rate? The clinician should control this by measuring the rate. This exercise should also be practiced when the clients think that they are speaking at their desired speech rate. The clinician should record all the data in an Excel or Access file. Clinicians should tell their clients to "strive for the borders to get closer and closer."

6.5.6 Speech rhythm

Speech rate and speech rhythm are not the same concepts (see 2.2.7). A change in the speech rate has a direct influence on the speech rhythm, and vice versa. Depending on the client, the clinician has to determine whether working on the speech rhythm should be a priority. PWC are often not aware that every word has a duration of its own and that not all syllables have the same duration. In case an unnatural speech rhythm results from working on syllable tapping, it is wise to focus attention on the speech rhythm.

Exercises suggestions
During exercises on speech rate reduction, attention can be given to the speech rhythm. If the speech rhythm cannot be differentiated from the speech rate, focus on pauses or stress patterns may be good options.

Variation to the exercise
Practicing rhythm can be combined with exercises facilitating exaggerated facial expressions and mimics.

6.5.7 Pauses

Pauses in speech are of tremendous importance, both in the production and understanding of speech. In order to be able to monitor speech at the sentence level, a speaker needs sufficient pause time between sentences.

Pauses between sentences allow for normal breathing patterns. Appropriate pausing provides enough time to plan the structure of a new speech plan. Pauses are also needed for listeners' understanding of speech. If the pause is too long, listeners can get the impression that the speaker stopped talking; when pauses are too short, listeners may not have enough time to process what was just told to them. Both problems in pausing can result in miscommunication. Pause duration is correlated to speech rate: the faster the speech rate, the shorter the pause duration. Normal pausing is usually an indication of a normal speech rate.

A normal pause has a duration of 0.5 – 1.0 second in most languages. Pause duration between sentences is usually equal to pause duration between speakers (turn-taking behavior). The counting backwards exercise is good training for more complex "natural" pauses for thinking. Another way of working on pause duration is to ask clients to tap twice with their index fingers on the table. Tapping twice takes 0.5 – 1.0 second for most people. But the exercise that works best is one that measures pause duration with the AVF training (6.5.1). In particular, appropriate pausing should be addressed in therapy. Clients derive no significant benefit from practicing appropriate pause lengths if they do not have an opportunity to listen to the effect the exercises have on their speech. So we advise clinicians to use the AVF training, ascertain whether the pauses in the recordings are of appropriate duration, and listen to the sentence or clause followed by the pause that is to be measured.

> *Example of working on pause duration in conversation during AVF training*
> *Let us look for a good pause.... I hear a pause that I guess is long enough......Let us measure it........Yes......This pause is 0.7 seconds.......That must have an effect on the next line........I guess it will be fluent and intelligible....Let us listen..........*
> *(listening).....What do you hear?.......... Fluency and intelligibility!.....So when you made an appropriate pause, the result was fluency and intelligibility. Good for you.*

Measuring one pause within a sample is not enough. Clinicians should ideally ask their clients to measure five pauses within a recording, and to write down the duration of the pause in an Excel or Access table. Clinicians should make sure that the pauses are made by their clients between sentences or clauses and not within a clause. For the home assignments, clinicians should ask their clients to make five measurements in a recording twice each day. The clinicians should ask their clients to assign a color to each range; for example, green upon reaching the goal (e.g., 0.5 -1.0 seconds); orange approaching the goal (e.g., 0.3 -0.49 seconds) and red not close enough to the goal (e.g., 0 -0.29 seconds). The reason for such an approach is clear. Clients tend to build on their successful experiences. Initially, the chances of the clients' having pauses of a normal duration are small. The clients will not experience a sense of success if only the normal pauses will be praised, and the chances of producing them are very limited. When clients speak at a fast rate, pauses are likely to be short (shorter than 0.5 seconds). If clients are praised even if pauses are longer than the clients normally make them, but still are not long enough, successful experiences will encourage the clients to try harder to produce longer pauses.

6.5.8 Melody and prosody

Stress patterns, pauses, and intonation determine whether a text is easy to listen to and understand. Many PWC speak in a monotonous manner, which can manifest itself in two ways: by speaking at the same pitch or in the same melody pattern. In monotony all words and syllables have approximately the same pitch. Some PWC speak in a melodic monotone. In these cases, all sentences have approximately the same melodic pattern (see 2.2.6).

Exercise suggestions

1. For some clients, short jokes or brief excerpts from plays are very appropriate. Reading interesting news items out loud on the Internet for friends, family or colleagues will ensure that clients will practice within the communicational context.

2. In Figure 6.4, intonation patterns are practiced at the sentence level. Clinicians should read a sentence out loud and follow the intonation points in the pattern with their index finger. The client should then imitate this modeling in the rest of the sentences on the form. Then the client should be instructed to compose a number of sentences and add intonation points.

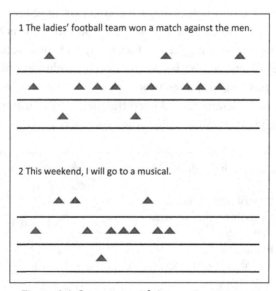

Figure 6.4: Sentences with intonation patterns

Variation to the exercise

○ Clinicians can work with the support of a musical instrument.
○ Clinicians can work with fairy tales or children's story books. These kinds of books will encourage clients to use melody within a communication setting.

6.5.9 Levels of language complexity

If the PWC are capable of sufficiently identifying their symptoms, and their attention is given to the appropriate characteristics of speech, then the clinician can work on language formulation skills. Clients should be encouraged to focus intensely because good concentration improves clients' ability to monitor their speech performance during complex language formulation tasks. Exercises facilitating higher language complexity for increased time periods should be assigned. Focused attention is considered to be a controlled process. Controlled processes are activities that are intentional, controllable, effortful and implemented in the presence of conscious awareness (Bargh, 1994; Johnson & Hasher, 1987; Kahneman & Treisman, 1984; Logan & Cowan, 1984). Such conscious awareness uses a segment of the attention capacity that would otherwise be used for other processes, such as language formulation. Too much focus on speech production can have a negative effect on language formulation in linguistically complex conditions, while too much focus on language formulation can have a negative effect on speech production. In order to reduce the discrepancies between speech production and language formulation, training language production in more complex conditions can be helpful. Clinicians should keep the hierarchy of different levels of language complexity in mind in planning assessment and therapy exercises.

The hierarchy of different levels of language complexity

1. Describing
2. Describing fun pictures
3. Explaining
4. Exploring
5. 1-4, above, with abstract words
6. Arguing
7. Convincing

Level 1 Describing:
The clinician should ask clients to imagine a picture, and to describe it to another person who does not see the image. In the beginning, no restrictions should be imposed. After some time, when a client is able to do this exercise fluently and intelligibly, the clinician should present the client with some taboo words (words that cannot be used) in the process of describing the image.

Variation to the exercise

o   While formulating language, speakers should not only focus on what they say or how they express themselves, but they also need to be able to draw on their memory. When the clinician asks clients to look at a busy picture for a couple of minutes before formulating a description of what they saw, their attention is partially diverted from their memory.
o   Clients should be asked to retell daily experiences to the clinician or partner. If the result is not satisfying enough, the clinician can ask the clients, instead, to retell minor news items from the Internet or to describe family pictures (see 4.12.7).

Level 2 Describing fun pictures
Description exercises can be made more difficult by the use of "fun photos" containing bizarre details.

Variation to the exercise

o   When a client describes a photograph, and the clinician has to choose the correct photo from a number of similar photos, the process of making this choice comes at the expense of the listener's attention, attention that is focused on the knowledge of the listener, and the memory of the client.
o   Formulation of minor visual changes, such as identifying four differences in the presented pictures, is more difficult than simply formulating what the client sees. The clinician can use different computer games, such as Mirror Magic (Zylom, 2012) or Playhouse Group (2012). The client has to be asked to describe the differences in clearly produced full sentences. Because the game is not the goal but a procedure to achieve a goal, it is best for clinicians not to give this exercise as a home assignment. If

the game is presented as a home assignment, the chances of the child only playing the game and not describing it are too high.

Level 3 Explaining
The clinician should ask clients to explain the functional procedures for operating machines. It is essential to mention all steps in the procedures. In order to do this, a part of the clients' attention capacity is allocated to memory, part to focusing on the listener, and part to language formulation, so less attention capacity is left for correct speech production.

Variation to the exercise
When the clinician asks a client to describe details of a graduation in school or work processes, a higher level of complexity is expected.

Level 4 Exploring
In the earlier exercises, the clinician just asked clients to describe what they observed or did. In this next level of formulation, the clinician should ask the client to present new ideas. E.g., "You could also...." Or "If you change this, it is also possible..."

Variation to the exercise

o The clinician may ask the client not only to describe new ideas as presented above, but also to explain why this would or would not be possible.
o The clinician may ask the client not only to describe new ideas, as presented above, but also to explain what is necessary to make each idea possible.

Level 5 Abstract words in 1-4
Using concrete words in the exercises is much easier than doing these exercises with abstract words such as "disappointment", "vague," "impossible," etc.

Processing abstract words requires additional efforts on the part of the listener, so the client needs to really focus on the listener's perspective in order to know whether the message is understood.

Level 6 Arguing
Performing complex linguistic tasks, such as arguing, pleading, advocating, and reasoning requires a great deal of effort and skills in order to be effective. Clients need to make various arguments to be convincing. Explaining why they make the choices requires strong language formulation skills. If clients do not have these skills, the complexity of the exercise will affect the clients' fluency or intelligibility. The clinician should set up an exercise program at a gradually increasing level of language complexity until clients are able to argue while remaining fluent and intelligible.

Variation to the exercise
After the clinician conducts exercises that facilitate arguing and reasoning on non-emotional topics, the clinician may choose to work with emotional topics, such as arguing whether or not it is a good idea to spend money on developing countries.

Level 7 Convincing
In level 6, arguing is not focused on the ideas or beliefs of the listener. In this final step of language formulation, the beliefs and ideas of the listener should be taken into account by the client. So attention capacity is divided between many variables of interpersonal communication.

Variation to the exercise
After exercising the convincing step on non-emotional topics, the clinician should then choose to work with emotional topics, for instance, argue whether or not it is a good idea to make it mandatory for a therapist/adult to spend time working without pay for the chronically sick or the elderly.

6.5.10 Pragmatics

Different aspects of communication were discussed within the communicative component (4.4.4). The negative effects of cluttering on communication were also addressed, such as inadequate turn-taking behavior, or the inability of the client to relate to the listener's perspective. Such inadequate use of language should be addressed in therapy. The pragmatic rules do not really need to be explained to clients, but the clients should become aware of such rules and should use them correctly. For instance, it can be important for one client to practice how to appropriately start or end a conversation, while another client may need to learn how to respond to a facial expression of a listener who does not understand or follow the speaker. Therefore, pragmatic goals should be included in planning cluttering intervention.

6.6 Maintenance of acquired skills

When clients have improved their skills and have reached their goals in different speaking situations, they should focus on preventing the possibility of a relapse. It is therefore important to conduct follow-up evaluations on a regular basis. This can be done by scheduling appointments with the clinician at appropriate time intervals. The frequency of such follow-up evaluations should decrease as time goes on. Clients need to develop various tools to enable them to efficiently practice newly acquired speech behaviors. The best way to do this is with AVF training with recorded conversations. A mobile phone can be programmed to give a scheduled signal to remind the client to set aside time for practice. The use of an observation list helps to ensure that the control moment has as much impact as needed (Appendix K). Clinicians should advise their clients to evaluate each new recording the day after it was recorded. If this does not lead to satisfactory results within a week, clients should be advised to restart their training. If this additional training does not lead to satisfactory results within two weeks, the client should be advised to contact the clinician. Maintenance of acquired skills should begin at the first session by practicing within a communicative context and should continue after the therapy is concluded, preferably for up to two years

6.7 Conclusion

This chapter has set forth a program of cluttering therapy, using many suggested and alternative exercises. Training in self-awareness is of the highest priority. The acquired pattern of speech should become the client's habitual way of talking, which should become automatic and effortless. Frequent and short home exercises facilitating gradual habituation to the new speech pattern are essential in cluttering intervention.

APPENDICES

APPENDICES

Appendix	Title
A	Predictive Cluttering Inventory-Revised (PCI-r)
B	Analysis of Spontaneous Speech, Reading and Retelling
C	Mean Articulatory Rate
D	Retelling a Memorized Story: "The Wallet Story"
E	Screening Phonological Accuracy (SPA)
F	Protocol for Differential Diagnosis of Fluency Disorders
G	Oral-Motor Assessment Scale (OMAS)
H	Brief Cluttering and Stuttering Questionnaire (BCSQ)
I	Reading Text for Adult Readers

Additional Appendices

Appendix	Title
J	Assignments for Video Case of Baruti
K	Self-Evaluation of Speech
L	Cluttering Statement
M	Personal Stories of People with Cluttering and Stuttering
N	Reading Passages
O	Speech Situation Checklist for Cluttering

APPENDIX A

Predictive Cluttering Inventory-Revised (PCI-r)

PREDICTIVE CLUTTERING INVENTORY (PCI)-revised
Original by Daly and Cantrell (2006);
revised version by van Zaalen et al (2009)

INSTRUCTIONS to SLP:

Ask the client to speak for 2-3 minutes about an experience during the holidays last year. This task is meant to be a monologue, rather than a dialogue. If the client starts to sum up, ask him/her to explain the rules of a sports activity or a certain procedure.

Please respond to each section below. Circle the number you believe is the most descriptive of this client's cluttering during the evaluation. Count the scores of the *italicized* items in each section.

	5 Always	4 Almost always	3 Frequent	2 Some times	1 Almost never	0 Never
Section 1: Speech-motor						
1 *Lack of pauses between words and phrases*						
2 *Repetition of multi-syllablic words and phrases*						
3 *Irregular speech rate; speaks in spurts or bursts*						
4 *Telescopes or condenses words*						
5 *Initial loud voice trailing off to unintelligible murmur*						
6 *Oral diadochokinetic coordination below expected normed levels*						
7 *Rapid rate (tachylalia)*						
8 *Co-existence of excessive disfluencies and stuttering*						
9 *Speech rate progressively increases (festinating)*						
10 *Poor planning skills; misjudges effective use of time*						
Total *italicized* items section 1						
11 Little or no excessive effort observed during disfluencies						
12 Poor planning skills for pauses (place and duration)						
13 Articulation errors						

Section 2: Language planning						
14 Disorganized language increases as topic becomes more complex						
15 Poor language formulation; poor story-telling; sequencing problems						
16 Language is disorganized; confused wording; word-finding problems						
17 Many revisions; interjections; filler words						
18 Inappropriate topic introduction, maintenance, or termination						
19 Improper linguistic structure; poor grammar; syntax errors						
20 Variable prosody; irregular melody or stress pattern						
Section 3: Attentiveness						
21 Does not recognize or respond to listener's visual or verbal feedback						
22 Does not repair or correct communication breakdowns						
23 Lack of awareness of own communication errors or problems						
24 Speech better under pressure (improves short-term with concentration)						
25 Distractible; poor concentration						
26 Attention span problems						
27 Seems to verbalize before adequate thought formulation						
28 Little or no anxiety regarding speaking; unconcerned						

Section 4: Motor planning (describe these symptoms compared to age level norms)							
29 Clumsy and uncoordinated; motor activities accelerated or impulsive							
30 Writing includes omission or transposition of letters, syllables, or words							
31 Poor motor control for writing (messy)							
32 Compulsive talker; verbose; tangential; word-finding problems							
33 Poor social communication skills; inappropriate turn-taking; interruptions							

Interpretation

Section one: > 24 points in *italicized* items => possible cluttering
Section two: *italicized* items provide information on linguistic component in cluttering
Section three and four provide additional information about client's communicative skills

APPENDIX B

Analysis of Spontaneous Speech, Reading and Retelling

Purpose:

By means of the *Assessment Form for Analysis of Spontaneous Speech, Reading and Retelling*, clinicians will be able to get more knowledge about the normal and stuttering-like disfluencies and the ratio of disfluencies. The form is filled in for all three speech tasks separately. A comparison of the results in the different speech tasks gives the clinician insight into the influence of linguistic complexity on speech output.

Assessment:

The client will be asked to say something spontaneously, read a story, and retell a story. These assessment tasks will be audio and video recorded. When clinicians proceed to fill in the form, they should start at a random moment of speech. They differentiate between normal and stuttering-like disfluencies during the speech sample analysis. Clinicians should only count normal disfluencies, such as multisyllabic word repetitions, interjections, and revisions.

Analysis and interpretation:

The sentences the client produces will be scored based on the types of normal disfluencies.

Example	Summary
The client says: *I can't can't go on on holiday tomrow*	6 Stutter free words

I	can't	go	on	holiday	tomorrow	2 Normal disfluencies
___	WR	___	WR	___	T	1 extra characteristic consistent with cluttering

Normal disfluencies (NDF)

Normal disfluencies can be categorized as follows:

word repetition (WR)	Repetition of a word in a relaxed manner in a calm rate.
part word repetition (PWR)	Repetition of a part of a word in a relaxed manner in a calm rate. Example: "dif-different."
interjection (Int.)	Insert a word or phrase which is inconsistent with the grammar or linguistic structure. Example: "You know" or "uuh."
revision (Rev.)	A reformulation of an utterance. Example: "I'm going, I went to school."
phrase repetition (PR)	A repetition of a part of a sentence. Example: "I went, I went, I went to school."
Total number of normal disfluencies (NDF)	The total will be determined by the sum of the normal disfluencies mentioned above.

Stuttering-like disfluencies

Stuttering-like disfluencies can be categorized as follows:

tense word repetitions (tWR)	Repetition of a word in a tense manner in a rapid or dysrhythmic rate.
tense part-word repetitions (tPWR)	Repetition of a part of a word in a tense manner in a rapid or dysrhythmic rate. Example: "dif-different."
prolongations (Pro.)	The continuation of a sound at the articulation place. Example: "ffffffffffffish."

blocks (Block)	The stream of breath stalls during the production of a sound. The sound can no longer be produced. This results in a very powerful production of the sound. Example: "......Book."
Stuttering-like disfluencies (SDF)	The total will be determined by the sum of the stuttering-like disfluencies mentioned above.

Example						Summary
The client says: *I ca-ca-ca-can't go on on hhhhhhholiday tomorrow*						2 Stuttered words
I	can't	go	on	holiday	tomorrow	1 Normal disfluency
___	/ tPWR	___	WR	/ Pro	T	1 extra characteristic consistent with cluttering

Ratio of disfluencies

The ratio of disfluencies (RDF) will be determined by dividing the percentage of normal disfluencies by the percentage of stuttering-like disfluencies.

> *Norms for the ratio of disfluencies (RDF)*
>
> o RDF < 1.0   indicates stuttering
> o RDF 1.0 – 3.0   indicates cluttering-stuttering
> o RDF > 3.0   indicates cluttering
>
> These norms are based on the research of van Zaalen et al., 2009b, 2009c)

Interpretation

Normally people adjust their speech rate to more complex linguistic tasks and thereby prevent a higher frequency of disfluencies. If people are not able to adjust their speech rate to the complexity of the task, a more complex task will provoke more normal disfluencies. Stuttering-like disfluencies are known to increase in more complex syntactic structures as well.

See Assessment Form on next page.

Assessment Form: Percentage of Normal and Stuttering-like Disfluencies

Name:
Date:
Age:
Task: □ Spontaneous speech □ Retelling □ Reading

										Type	Number
										WR	
										pWR	
										PR	
										Int	
										Rev	
										NDF	
										tWR	
										PRO	
										Block	
										SDF	
Comments on secondary behavior ○ Visible: ○ Auditory: ○ Avoidance:										RATIO: NDF SDF	

APPENDIX C

Mean Articulatory Rate

Purpose

The assessment of the articulatory rate is crucial in determining whether the speaker has the obligatory symptom of an excessively high and/or an excessively variable articulatory rate. Only if this obligatory symptom is present can cluttering be diagnosed.

Assessment

The articulatory rate will be determined by analyzing samples of fluent speech from the audio recordings of spontaneous speech, reading and retelling.

Analysis

Five measurements of the articulatory rate will be taken randomly from each digital audio recording.

The articulatory rate measurements should be perfomed on at least 10 and at most 20 syllables of fluent speech. Utterances with nonfluent speech, pauses or interjections should not be included in the analysis. These disturbances have unwanted effects on the reliability of the measurements.

The measurements will be performed by using the speech analysis software Praat (Boersma & Weenink, 2014).

Form for Assessment of Articulatory Rate

Name:

Date:

Age:

Measurement	Spontaneous speech sample	Retelling	Reading
1.			
2.			
3.			
4.			
5.			
Mean Articulatory Rate			
Variation within speech condition			
Variation between speech conditions			

Interpretation

Norms for the articulatory rate at different ages	Articulatory Rate variation (ARV)
Syllables Per Second (SPS) Mean Articulatory Rate spontaneous speech o Children > 5.2 SPS o Adolescents > 5.6 SPS o Adults > 5.4 SPS	Adequate rate variation: 1.0 < VAR < 3.3 SPS Cluttering: VAR < 1.0 between speech tasks and/or VAR > 3.3 SPS within speech task

If the variation within the same speech condition, between the highest and the lowest measurement, is more than 3.3 SPS, the articulatory rate is considered to be too variable. If the variation between different speech conditions is 1.0 SPS or less, then the variation is too rigid. So inadequate adjustment of the articulatory rate to the speech condition or language complexity is indicative of cluttering.

Retelling a Memorized Story: "The Wallet Story"

Purpose:

While a client is retelling a memorized story, the clinician can observe to what extent the client is able to convey a message that someone else has already formulated.

Instruction:

The clinician should tell the client: "I will read you a story. After I have finished reading the story, please retell back to me the same story as completely as possible. I am not allowed to help you with it."

The Wallet story:

It was a rainy day in November. A woman drove to the supermarket in her brand new car. She invited three girlfriends to dinner that night, and had promised them that she would prepare something Italian. That was her speciality. While she was shopping, her wallet fell from her pocketbook, but she did not notice it. Her shopping cart was already loaded. When she arrived at the cashier, she could not pay for her groceries. The cashier was willing to watch her shopping cart for a while. The woman put her groceries aside, and went home. The windshield wipers of her car moved rapidly from side to side. All the traffic lights she encountered were red, of course. She was terribly fed up! Just when she opened the door to her house, the phone started ringing. A little boy told her he had found her wallet. The woman was very relieved. The end.

Scoring Form for "The Wallet Story" (van Zaalen, Wijnen, & Dejonckere 2009)

Name					
Date					
Age					
Main issues	Side issues	Story	Client's Response	Syntax not correct	DF
1		It was a rainy day in November.			
2		A woman drove to the supermarket in her brand new car.			
3		She invited three girlfriends to dinner that night,			
	1	and had promised them that she would prepare something Italian.			
	2	That was her speciality.			
4		While she was shopping,			
5		her wallet fell from her pocketbook,			
6		but she did not notice it.			
	3	Her shopping cart was already loaded.			
7		When she arrived at the cashier, she could not pay for her groceries.			
	4	The cashier was willing to watch her shopping cart for a while.			
	5	The woman put her groceries aside,			
8		and went home.			
	6	The windshield wipers of her car moved rapidly from side to side.			

Main issues	Side issues	Story	Client's Response	Syntax not correct	DF
	7	All the traffic lights she encountered were red, of course.			
	8	She was terribly fed up!			
9		Just when she opened the door to her house,			
10		the phone started ringing.			
11		A little boy told her			
12		he had found her wallet.			
	9	The woman was very relieved.			
13		That was the story.			

Of the 13 main issues the client retold ... ... main issues (almost) completely.

Of the 9 side issues the client retold ... ... side issues (almost) completely.

The proportion of main issues to side issues is ... ... : ... ...

Total number of grammatically correct sentences: ... ...

Total number of sentences with the incorrect use of structure: ... ...

Mistakes in linguistics: ... ...

Mistakes in syntax: ... ...

Analysis:

1. Transcribe the story told by the client.
2. Determine story components (main issues, side issues and noise).
3. Determine the correct use of syntax (% correct; % false).
4. Determine type of dysfluencies.
5. Determine the percentage of dysfluencies and the ratio of dysfluencies.

Screening Phonological Accuracy (SPA)

Purpose

This assessment can provide insight into speech-motor skills at the word level in test conditions. Of ten test words, only the three boldfaced words are analyzed as to accuracy, smooth flow and articulatory rate.

Instruction:

The clinician should tell the client: "Please look at these words for up to 5 seconds. Then I will cover the words and ask you to repeat the words 3 times in consecutive syllable strings, in a fast but still intelligible manner and without pauses."

Words:

Previously unpublished encounters – Distinctive sounds – Clinical management perspective – **Possible probabilities** – Epidemiological data – Screaming and shrieking audience – **Impracticable communicative implications** – Hierarchically organized behavior – Most favored nation clause – **Compromised alternative condemnation** – Frequently used devices – Delayed auditory feedback.

Scoring

The most important feature to observe is the consistency in the production of the sequence. In other words, whether production 1 is similar to production 2, and to production 3. If not, it indicates planning or phonological encoding problems. Productions are judged regarding accuracy, smooth flow and rate. When analyzing word accuracy, possible sound distortion or errors in voicing are described. Errors in smooth flow can include extra pauses, telescoping, disrhythmic flow and problems in sequencing. Errors are scored for every instance of the error. So an expression can contain several errors. The mean amount of errors per attempt of three repetitions is used in the table to refer to norm data in the table directly below.

Screening Phonological Accuracy
Dutch version: van Zaalen, 2009;
English version: van Zaalen, Cook, Elings and Howell, 2011

Name:
Age:
Date:

Word set	Accuracy Distortion/ voicing			Pausing			Smooth Flow Telescoping			Flow		Sequencing			Rate in SPS
Possible Probabilities	0	1-2	3+	0	1-2	3+	0	1-2	3+	yes	no	0	1-2	3+	Sec. A
Error score	0	1	3	0	1	3	0	1	3	0	1	0	1	3	
Impracticable communicative implications	0	1-2	3+	0	1-2	3+	0	1-2	3+	yes	no	0	1-2	3+	Sec. B
Error score	0	1	3	0	1	3	0	1	3	0	1	0	1	3	
Compromised alternative condemnation	0	1-2	3+	0	1-2	3+	0	1-2	3+	yes	no	0	1-2	3+	Sec. C
Error score	0	1	3	0	1	3	0	1	3	0	1	0	1	3	
Overall score															A+B+C= Sec

For an explanation to all items in the Screening Phonological Accuracy we refer to the website that is linked to this book: www.NYCSA-Center.org.

NORM TABLE for Screening Phonological Accuracy					
N=356	Mean	-0.5 SD	-1.0 SD	- 1.5 SD	- 2.0 SD
Accuracy	0.42 (.94)	0.89	1.36	1.83	2.30
Pausing & Telescoping	0.92 (1.70)	1.77	2.62	3.47	4.32
Flow	0.99 (1.28)	1.63	2.27	2.91	3.55
Sequencing	1.20 (1.70)	2.05	2.90	3.75	4.60
Smooth Flow	3.03 (3.17)	4.62	6.20	7.79	9.37
Rate	5.40 (1.2)	6.00	6.60	7.20	7.80
Total score	8.82 (4.1)		12.9		17.0
Severity scores	3.8 - 8.8 no disorder 8.9 - 12.9 very mild disorder 3.0 - 17.0 mild disorder 17.0 - 21.1 average disorder 21.2 - 25.2 severe disorder > 25.3 very severe disorder				

APPENDIX F

Protocol for Differential Diagnosis of Fluency Disorders

Protocol for Differential Diagnosis of Fluency Disorders Y. van Zaalen (2009)				
Communication feature	Description			
	Cluttering	Stuttering	Learning difficulties	ADHD
1. Mean articulatory rate	Rapid and/or irregular	Slow to moderate	Normal	Normal to fast
2. Ratio of disfluencies (NSLDs to SLDs) in monologue or retelling a story	High in favor of NDFs	High in favor of SLDs	High in favor of NDFs	High in favor of NDFs
3. Pauses	Too few/ short, or in linguistically inappropriate places	Accurate, too many and too long	Many	Too short, in normal places
4. Adjustment rate to language complexity	No	Yes	Yes	No
5. Errors in word structure	Possible	No	Possible	Possible
6. Possible cause of errors in sentence structures	Sentence formulation under stress in fast rate	Avoiding behavior	Sentence formulation under-developed	Absent
7. Attention makes speech:	Better	Worse	Better	Better

Communication feature	Description			
	Cluttering	Stuttering	Learning difficulties	ADHD
8. Relaxation makes speech:	Worse	Better	Better	Better
9. Speaking a foreign language is:	Better	Personal	Worse	Better
10. Reading out loud from a known text is:	Worse	Worse in cases of sound fear	Better	Worse
11. Reading out loud from an unknown text is:	Better	Better	Worse	Worse
12. Communication or speech fear:	Possible	Absent	Absent	Absent
13. Awareness of symptoms	Mostly not	Mostly	Mostly not	Present
14. Awareness of speech disorder	Often	Mostly	Absent	
15. Word fear mainly in case of:	Multisyllable words	Possible initial bilabials or vowels	Absent	Absent
16. Sound fear of	Absent	Possible initial bilabials or vowels	Absent	Absent

Oral-Motor Assessment Scale (OMAS)

Purpose:

Van Zaalen et al. (2009b) found no correlation between accuracy, smooth flow, and rate scores in oral-motor control and speech-motor control at the word level. If it turns out that in the articulation screening the client makes more word structure errors than normal, the OMAS can be used to rule out weak oral-motor skills as the cause of word structure errors. The OMAS cannot be used as a differential diagnostic instrument for cluttering and other disorders of fluency.

Assessment:

During this test, the following three syllable sets will be evaluated:

- puh
- tuhkuh
- puhtuhkuh

The clinician should model the syllable sets. The client must produce the sets at least 10 times in a row, at a rapid rate. The assessment should be audio recorded and should be evaluated as to accuracy, equability and rate.

Analysis and interpretation:

By means of the Norm Table, the scores can be interpreted and a determination can be made as to whether there are any oral-motor problems which cause word structure errors.

Scoring Form for the Oral-Motor Assessment Scale						
Name:						
Date:						
Age:						
	Accuracy		Smooth flow			Rate
Syllable set	Distortion errors	Voicing errors	Coarticulation errors	Equability	Sequencing errors	
Puh	0 1-2 3+	0 1-2 3+	0 1-2 3+	yes no	yes no	X 0.5 1.0 1.5 2.0
Error score	0 1 2	0 1 2	0 1 2	0 1	0 1	0 1 3 5 6
Tuhkuh	0 1-2 3+	0 1-2 3+	0 1-2 3+	yes no	0 1-2 3+	X 0.5 1.0 1.5 2.0
Error score	0 1 2	0 1 2	0 1 2	0 1	0 1 3	0 1 3 5 6
Puhtuhkuh	0 1-2 3+	0 1-2 3+	0 1-2 3+	yes no	0 1-2 3+	X 0.5 1.0 1.5 2.0
Error score	0 1 2	0 1 2	0 1 2	0 1	0 1 3	0 1 3 5 6
Total error score						
Overall error score:						
Conclusion:						

Analysis and interpretation

If the score deviates > 1.5 SD from the norm, it can be concluded that the oral –motor control is below the age appropriate level. If a weak score on OMAS is accompanied by word structure errors or phonetic defects, then training of oral -motor skills is recommended.

Norm Table OMAS based on Riley (1985) & van Zaalen (2009)						
	Age	Mean	- 0.5 SD	-1.0 SD	-1.5 SD	- 2.0 SD
Puh	8	2.1	2.3	2.5	2.7	2.8
	9	2.0	2.2	2.4	2.6	2.7
	10-11	1.8	2.0	2.2	2.4	2.5
	12	1.7	1.9	2.0	2.2	2.3
	13+	1.6	1.9	2.0	2.1	2.3
Tuhkuh	8	4.8	5.5	6.1	6.5	7.5
	9-10	4.4	5.0	5.5	6.0	6.6
	11-12	3.8	4.3	4.7	5.1	5.5
	13+	3.4	3.9	4.3	4.7	5.1
Puhtuhkuh	8	8.3	9.3	10.3	11.3	12.3
	9	7.7	8.7	9.7	10.7	11.7
	10	7.1	7.9	8.6	9.4	10.1
	11-12	6.5	7.2	8.0	7.9	9.6
	13+	5.7	6.4	7.2	8.0	8.7
Total points per category						
Accuracy	8-11	1.11	1.19	1.26	1.34	1.41
	13+	0.81	0.83	0.86	0.88	0.91
Smooth Flow	8-11	2.34	3.21	4.08	4.95	5.82
	13+	1.98	2.34	3.21	4.08	4.95
Rate	8-11	0.85	1.55	2.31	3.04	3.77
	13+	0.84	1.52	2.30	2.98	3.76
Total	8-11	0-6	7	8	9	10
	13+	0-5	6	7	8	9

Brief Cluttering and Stuttering Questionnaire (BCSQ)

Purpose

When clients present with cluttering and stuttering at the same time, their personal experiences influence how the two disorders impact on communication skills, fear and avoidance behavior. Although some symptoms are easier to treat in therapy than others, priorities in treatment should be based on the clients' complaints. In other words, zoom in to the complaints and zoom out to the client. Responses to this brief questionnaire provide insights into the impact of stuttering and cluttering on the lives of clients.

Instructions

When clinicians have clients complete the questionnaire, the interview should be flexible enough to allow clients to elaborate on one question with a response to a question that appears later in the questionnaire, so the interview is meant to be semi-structured. We therefore advise clinicians to make recordings of this part of the assessment so clinicians can fully focus on active listening.

As the clients respond to the questions, the clinician should invite them to elaborate by responding to follow-up questions such as: Can you expand on this? Can you tell me more? Can you give an example?

1. At what ages, respectively, were you diagnosed with cluttering and stuttering?
2. Did the diagnosis of cluttering bring about changes in your life? If so, please describe them.
3. Which disorder is more negatively stigmatized? Cluttering or stuttering?
4. Do you find that the symptoms of cluttering and stuttering influence each other? If so, how are they interrelated?
5. Which disorder affects you more, emotionally? Cluttering or stuttering?
6. What interferes more with your communication? Planning and formulating thoughts or fast and unclear speech?
7. Do you speak more than one language? If so, which languages do you speak? Which language is primary? Which language (primary or secondary) is affected more by cluttering and which by stuttering?
8. Which disorder is easier than the other to manage as a result of speech therapy? Cluttering or stuttering?
9. Do you believe that addressing cognitive and emotional aspects in cluttering therapy is as important as addressing them during stuttering therapy?
10. As a person with cluttering and stuttering, what progress do you expect to make, assuming you will consistently adhere to your speech therapy program?" ("Outstanding," "Good," "Fair," or "Poor"?)

Reading text for adult readers

The Secret of Happiness

Happiness has a magical attraction for humanity. Some seek bread, some seek wealth, and some seek fame, but all seek happiness. Most of us bend our efforts, more or less, to finding it and bringing it home. Unfortunately, only a few succeed. Most people do not understand where happiness can be found and naturally cannot obtain it. Some who succeed in finding happiness do not know how to nourish, develop, and preserve it. Consequently, it vanishes. It is easy to smile and be happy under pleasant conditions, but it takes a real optimist to see and find pleasure in life under adversity. That is the art of living. To know how to live is, after all, the best knowledge. A good way to find happiness is simply to be good, to be kind, and to develop in oneself an empathetic and optimistic view of things in the world, of its creatures, and fellow human beings. It is the pleasant feeling of kindness which makes a person happy. The more a person develops this feeling, the more such a person is sure of acquiring happiness.

Kindness is a general term. A noble character acquires happiness through the opportunity of making someone else happy. It is only that kind of kindness that will lead to happiness. When people develop a kindly opinion, a kindly thought, looking upon their environment through the light of kindness, they attract that power of electric magnetism – kindness. It forms an orbit of pleasantness and happiness around them. It develops in them a dynamo producing kindness with radiating power to influence their surroundings, thus creating a kind and happy atmosphere.

To acquire the quality of kindness, which is a mental faculty, simply follow the method of physical acquirement – exercise. Athletes develop their muscles, their physical strength by practice. The same rule may apply to the mental qualities of kindness and happiness. People who practice kindness become kind and happy. There is no kind word or kind deed which does not have an effect, a return. Kindness is soft, flexible, springlike. Like a rubber ball, when one throws it at another, it bounces – it returns to oneself. Nothing wasted. Indeed, how badly our world needs kindness to make it happy! It is starved; it is as thirsty as the vegetation and the flowers in the dry desert anxiously awaiting a drop of moisture for the sustenance of life. What a pity! What a waste! How many beautiful flowers fade! How many worthy lives are wasted merely for the lack of a little dew, for a few drops of rain, or refreshing water, for a kind word, for a kind deed! A little water is not very much, but how much it does mean to the one who really needs it! It may mean the person's life. An act of kindness has a marvelous effect. It transforms the donor to the recipient. In consequence, it is not an expenditure, but it is an investment with an immediate return of high yield.

(Modified excerpt from *The Secret of Happiness* by David Miller, 1937).

APPENDIX J

Assignments for video case of Baruti

Go to www.NYSCSA.org and look at all video recordings of Baruti. After watching the recordings, please complete the assignments below.

a) The clinician should look at the recording of Baruti's spontaneous speech for a maximum of five minutes and fill in the first ten items of the Predictive Cluttering Inventory-revised (see Appendix A).

b) The clinician should listen to one of the recordings without looking at the video. The clinician should then write down what in her opinion is the most disturbing aspect of Baruti's communication.

c) The clinician should look at the recordings of spontaneous speech, retelling and reading at a different time and should fill in the Assessment Form (see Appendix B). The clinician should determine the percentage of normal disfluencies, percentage of stuttering-like disfluencies and the ratio of disfluencies. In addition, the clinician should determine the percentage of correct sentence structures and story components. The clinician should then discuss the effect of the speech condition on fluency and intelligibility.

d) The clinician should determine Baruti's mean articulatory rate and his mean articulatory rate variation within and between the speech conditions. The clinician should use the form Mean

Articulatory Rate (Appendix C), and then consider how to interpret the rate within and between conditions.

e) The clinician should look at the recording of Oral-Motor Assessment Scale and fill in the scoring form of the Oral-Motor Assessment Scale (see Appendix G). The clinician should then write conclusions based on these findings.

f) The clinician should look at the two recordings of the Screening Phonological Accuracy, and fill in the SPA scoring form (see Appendix E). Based on these video recordings, the clinician should record general conclusions about Baruti's phonological encoding skills and whether these skills differ in various speech conditions.

g) The clinician should listen to the BCSQ- interview and transcribe what Baruti said. Based on his language sample, the clinician should describe the impact of both disorders on Baruti's communication skills, experiences and beliefs. The clinician should write an abstract of the interview.

h) Based on all of the clinician's findings on Baruti's video recordings, the clinician should fill in the Diagnostic Protocol and finalize the differential diagnostics. The clinician should then explain the diagnostic decisions arrived at.

i) The clinician should complete the Cluttering Severity Instrument and determine the level of severity and the type of cluttering. The clinician should then compare her findings with the findings of the experts.

Self Evaluation of Speech

Awareness of excessively fast speech

Date	Topic	Speech rate (in relation to formulation)			
		Too fast	*Fast*	*Moderate*	*Did not notice*

Awareness of interjections

Date	Topic	Number of interjections per minute

APPENDIX L

Cluttering Statement

My Speech Therapist
83-24 Cluttering Street
Disfluency Town

CLUTTERING STATEMENT

Place & Date: - -

With this statement I declare that ....(name), born .... (birth date) and living in .... (place) has been diagnosed with cluttering.

Cluttering is a disorder of fluency that can lead to unintelligible or very disfluent speech, sometimes in combination with language formulation problems. These symptoms occur at an uncontrollably fast rate of speech.

The problems that occur in cluttering increase with time pressure. If the person with cluttering is able to focus and has enough time to formulate verbal and written speech tasks, this will lead to improved performance.

It is also advisable to provide special accommodations for students with cluttering, as is done for students with dyslexia, e.g., headphones while taking reading tests, audio support while taking reading comprehension tests. Some people with cluttering can be helped by using a feedback device during oral testing.

Digitally signed in .... (Place) .... (Date) ....

The clinician
(Name) ....
Then send to parents.

Personal stories of people with cluttering and stuttering

(The first three stories are excerpted with permission from *The Stuttering Home Page*, Minnesota State University, Mankato www. mnsu.edu/*comdis/kuster/*)

Tanya

For many years, I was struggling with my communication problems as a student, as a teacher, and as a mother. A year ago, I searched the National Institute for Literacy Learning Disabilities listserv, where I started looking for an explanation of my speech difficulties which I had managed to "cover up" for so long. I extensively described my experiences with my speech "...I could not pull out the word "RESPECT" every time I needed it or why I tried to hurry up and finish my statements before I was ... interrupted." Why couldn't my frustrated teacher get any words out of me after the command to sit on my hands, while I was answering? Why could I not slow down with my speech, and just had to spit it out?" I got quite a few responses; however, the real answer came from an unexpected source – a speech pathologist who was evidently following our thread discussing issues relating to adults with learning disabilities, and who responded to one of my cries for help. She asked if I knew anything about cluttering and stuttering, and shared the ICA's website to assist me in my quest. A few days later, I hurried to inform her, "According to all the materials I've read so far, I am a clutterer..." Very soon, we were constantly communicating on-line and on the phone. I was trying to catch up with the fireballs of her questions concerning the additional details I was sharing with her, which prompted the possibility of the coexisting issues, "Does your sound come out with tension? Does your unclear speech make you frustrated? ... Do you have an SLP in your town?" I was very surprised to find out that my hand movements were a secondary behavior which originally helped me to get through the word and that my feelings associated with my speech had an explanation. During our discussions, I kept revisiting my life experiences and reassessing the knowledge of myself. Our dialogue was unstoppable. Soon, she knew a lot more about me than people who surrounded me daily. My mind started filling up with the long-forgotten memories: my mom's effort to exclude the fill-ups in my speech; the lessons in piano and singing, when I had to use a metronome to slow me down; acting lessons, during which the sound production was addressed by putting marble balls in the mouth. Later, when I was exposed to the necessity of doing multiple presentations during my teaching career, I had to learn how to overcome blocks by playing them down as the intended pauses, or slapping my hand, by concentrating on the positive faces in the audience. I also had to learn how to overcome the wish to never open my mouth again after running sentences in an unknown direction and not looking smart. Delegating my speech controls to my students (they were my time keepers and reminded me to "hit a space bar" when needed) happened to be one of my "saving grace" tools. Through my discussions with [the speech pathologist referred to above], we discovered that my college course in Phonetics contained exercises also used in a speech pathology field. I started using these exercises again and found that by doing so, my speech started improving. There were two major components of our communication which helped tremendously in sorting things out: A very knowledgeable specialist, and a supportive ICA community with the availability of the resources on the website. Finding out my diagnosis and discussing my options made the whole experience invigorating. I felt such a sense of relief in knowing that what I had been experiencing was not my imagination; the problems were real; and they could be helped.

Charlene

Stuttering was never a big part of my life until I entered the world of adulthood and started to work in corporate America. Experiencing the stigma associated with stuttering was much harder than I had expected it to be. It began to set in every time I had a block and as a result I felt my personality change just to conform to the stuttering demon I had trapped inside. There were instances where my blocks would cause me to want to rip out my throat out of pure frustration. For years, I plastered on a fake smile to the world and hid the sadness in my eyes. Fluent speakers do not know that every pitied look or disgusted glance hurt ten times more than if I had been stabbed. Finally, after a few months at my second job, the anger gave me the determination to seek out the aid of a speech therapist. My first session with [my speech pathologist] was like letting the dam break free and letting the water run free. I remember crying, which I had always held inside, and telling her my story, and from then on, I began to feel healed. Every insulting look and smirk that I encountered once I got better slid off my back like water sliding off the waterproof feathers of a duck. My stuttering was minimized from a block every sentence to one block every two weeks. Once the issue of stuttering was resolved, another issue came to the forefront - cluttering. There were instances when my thoughts raced faster than my mouth could catch up. The competition usually resulted in a jumbled mass of words exiting my mouth, leaving both recipient and myself perplexed. Unlike stuttering, I was not ashamed about this problem. Instead, I shrugged it off as if a pesky bug, but it became an apparent problem when it became more frequent and when I would intend to say a word, but something completely different would come out. I always attributed this sort of mental dyslexia as normal, yet I had never heard another person jumble sentences into one verbal mass the way I did. I knew there was a problem, but denial is always easier to accept than the truth. It was a slow healing process, which I had to overcome. Between my second and third jobs, I was fluent for two years, with some minor relapses at times. I was hired for my third job as a fluent speaker, but the stress of the job and my personal life began to bear down on me and distracted me from thinking about the possibility of a relapse and practicing to maintain control of my speech. This led to a resumption of my stuttering and cluttering and brought on my current relapse with the same onslaught of emotions that attacked me in the past; however this time, I knew how to stop it from affecting me mentally. Now I began to work on my speech, practicing every other night, which helped decrease my blocks. To this day, the sadness has slowly crept out of my eyes again, but I am still working on regaining my natural smile rather than the mask. By practicing, I am able to bring myself to a higher foothold, a step closer to my freedom of speech. Despite my increase in blocks compared to when I had been down to about one every two weeks, I am 100 miles ahead of where I had been before I attended speech therapy.

Baruti

My name is Baruti Smith. In order to accomplish, one must have the attitude to do it. This is what I have learned over the years of overcoming my cluttering and stuttering. In my early years, especially in the stage in my life when I was in the 3rd grade, my speech problem first hit me. It was evident in the way my peers interacted with me. I began to make progress in this area when I made it my goal to be naturally accepted by other people without receiving sympathy. In the 7th grade I wasn't afraid to speak despite my speech issue. Let me add there is always frustration and an angry feeling that is a result of a speech impairment. I began to have success in my high school years, when I went to [a speech pathologist at a university clinic] for speech therapy and was diagnosed with cluttering and stuttering. First I thought it was a recipe for a lifetime of defeat and misunderstanding. I couldn't read normally either. I overcame my stuttering for good. I took it step by step; from phrases to simple sentences to paragraphs, etc. Since then I don't stutter at all. As a result of my speech therapy, my cluttering was mostly corrected as well. It cleared up so that it seemed like I had never stuttered or cluttered in the first place. I would make speeches in my speech therapist's classes; none of the students in the classroom realized that I had a cluttering or even a speech issue. After one and a half years of clear speech, after the completion of my therapy, my speech gradually got worse and I suffered a relapse of my cluttering. I'm not as bad as before, but at the same time I am not back to where I ought to be yet. So I can say I have tasted victory over cluttering for one and a half years, and then lost it. After a five-year break, I have now resumed speech therapy again. My present focus is on my cluttering. My philosophy is the better the mindset for success, the earlier one will get past one's troubles. I just want to encourage others to follow my lead in correcting speech issues. It is important to have ultimate confidence in yourself. As long as people work on their speech and maintain an attitude that they can overcome their cluttering and stuttering, they will be successful and accomplished!

From "People with Cluttering and Stuttering Have Room for Success" by Tatyana Exum, Charlene Absalon, Baruti Smith and Isabella K. Reichel http://www.mnsu.edu/comdis/ica1/papers/exumc.html

---

This account is based on the experiences of a client of one of the authors. This client agreed to share his experiences with the use of an assumed name.

Michael

Michael, a 32-year-old successful accountant, sought treatment to address his unusual complaints of long duration. Although he had no speech or language disorders during regular communication, he encountered difficulties speaking when praying in a congregational setting and in front of small groups, including saying grace at festive meals with his family members. Michael stated that during such speaking situations, his speech rate escalated, resulting in fast and unclear speech, collapsing of syllables, lack of pauses and fear that people would not understand him. His frustration grew when his wife and his children wondered why no one in the family could understand what he was saying and offered ideas to make his speech clearer. As time went on, Michael developed anxiety when anticipating a call to recite blessings publicly in front of the congregation he attends. He silently prayed that his name would not be chosen. He exhibited some symptoms of hyper-arousal typical for people with anxiety, such as heart palpitations, muscle tension and inadequate pauses to catch his breath during speaking. He went to a few speech pathologists, including some at a college speech clinic, and was invariably told that his condition was simply an abnormally fast speech rate at certain times, and he was assured that if only he would get used to speaking more slowly, all his problems would be resolved. Michael desperately tried to follow their advice, but without success. His anxiety, fear of embarrassment, low self-esteem, and negative beliefs about his speech gradually became unbearable, so he continued his search for help. Eventually he was seen by a clinician who explained Michael's speech symptoms as those characteristic of the fluency disorder of cluttering, which in his case only occurred during the public recitation of prayers that are viewed as automatic tasks where no programming and formulating ideas are required. Visibly relieved and excited, Michael embraced a new opportunity to try a treatment that required a commitment to change and adherence to a rigid schedule of exercises. Therapy addressed not only behavioral but also cognitive and affective aspects of cluttering. Bringing awareness of his symptoms gave him hope for recovery and motivation to practice. His speech intelligibility was addressed by working on grammatically appropriate breath group locations and duration which also contributed to the slowing down of his speech rate. The natural flow of his speech was facilitated by improving his speech rhythm and adequate intonational patterns. The clinician's strategies for reducing Michael's emotional arousal included discussing his negative beliefs, and implementing cognitive- behavioral and emotional intelligence concepts to address distorted thoughts about anticipated audiences' reactions. After eight sessions, Michael was happy to observe that his speech rate and intelligibility during prayers at home were completely normalized and that his cardiac and respiratory symptoms and muscle tension during congregational prayers almost disappeared.

Anjea Ray, a speech-language pathologist who was diagnosed with cluttering, is a co-author of an article that includes her story, which appears below:

Reichel, I. K., & Ray, A. (2008). The ICA adopts the cluttering orphan. *Perspectives on Fluency and Fluency Disorders, 18*, (2), 84-86.

Many individuals who stutter become SLPs to help others who suffer from the same condition. These SLPs enter the field armed with a much more personal understanding of the disorder that they wish to treat in others. But how often do SLPs enter the field unaware of their own speech difficulties and disfluencies? I have always been dubbed a "fast talker," and others have asked me to repeat myself or to slow down. My mother advised people that they would "just have to learn to listen faster," because she believed that my speaking patterns mirrored my outgoing, bubbly personality. As my family was habituated to my speech, they never thought anything errant about it. I never did, either, until I began my graduate studies in communication disorders to become an SLP. I consistently received positive feedback for my clinical work, but every one of my supervisors, in addition to the other faculty members, commented on my rate of speech. I thought I was speaking more slowly after these persistent reminders, but apparently my perception and that of my supervisors, fellow student clinicians, and clients did not match. It wasn't until my fluency professor told me that I needed to "stop this cluttering business to truly succeed as a speech-language pathologist" that I realized it was a real problem. He had labeled my speech and I didn't know what that label meant or its potential implications for my future career path. After some research, a phone call to Dr. Kenneth St. Louis, some self-analysis, and more consultations with my fluency professor and supervisors, I acknowledged and accepted that I was indeed a clutterer. I became extremely self-conscious as I began to notice more and more disfluencies in my speech—repetition of words/syllables, omission of sounds within words, abrupt/abnormal pauses, poor verbal organization, and "rushes" of speech (an incoherent, poorly articulated gibberish that only my closest friends can understand within a known context) formed with incomplete sentences without transitions. As my awareness increased, so did my stress from clinical rotations, my ongoing frustration with my inability to break the speech patterns, and my mounting fear of being ineffective as a SLP working with cognitively and linguistically impaired populations and their families. The awareness of how my cluttered speech would affect my success as a clinician spurred my interest in the disorder—in particular, its management. My professor advised me to take a behavioral approach—to think about moving slowly, rather than talking slowly, and to feel each sound as I produced it. That has probably helped the most, coupled with Dr. St. Louis' advice about practicing reading aloud (and in particular, poetry) while recording myself and analyzing my own speech to better understand the patterns specific to my speech. I try to organize my thoughts in my head before I express them, in an effort to keep the ideas linear, clear, and concise; this skill is critical for SLPs in general, but arguably more so for me as I work with the elderly in a nursing home.

APPENDIX N

Reading Passages

My Grandfather

You wish to know all about my grandfather. Well, he is nearly 93 years old, yet he still thinks as swiftly as ever. He dresses himself in an ancient, black frock coat, usually minus several buttons. A long, flowing beard clings to his chin, giving those who observe him a pronounced feeling of the utmost respect. When he speaks his voice is just a bit cracked and quivers a trifle. Twice each day he plays skillfully and with zest upon a small organ. Except in the winter when the snow or ice prevents, he slowly takes a short walk in the open air each day. We have often urged him to walk more and smoke less but he always answers, "Banana oil!" Grandfather likes to be modern in his language.

The Rainbow

When the sunlight strikes raindrops in the air, they act like a prism and form a rainbow. A rainbow is the division of white light into many beautiful colors. These take the shape of a large, round arch, with its path high above and its two ends apparently beyond the horizon. There is, according to legend, a boiling pot of gold at one end. People look, but no one ever finds it. When a man looks for something beyond his reach, his friends say he is looking for the pot of gold at the end of the rainbow.

Limpy

Limpy is a fuzzy, yellow, baby duck. He belongs to a fisherman. The fisherman lives in a little house by the bay. Every morning children go swimming in the bay. About 10:00, Limpy waddles out to the road to wait for the children. When he hears them coming he begins a loud, excited quacking. The children always bring bread or corn for Limpy. He will nip at their fingers or peck at their bare toes until he is fed. Limpy never follows the children down to the shore. He likes to swim in his own little pond. It is much safer.

Speech Situation Checklist for Cluttering (Adapted from Brutten & Shoemaker, 1974)

Goal

With the help of the Speech Situation Checklist, the client will become aware of the level of complexity of diverse speaking situations. If clients start to practice new skills in their daily life situations, these levels of complexity have to be taken into account. The list developed for people with stuttering is adjusted for people with cluttering. In the column of disturbed speech, attention is given to poor intelligibility, fast or irregular rate, pauses in the linguistically inappropriate places, and the production of an excessive number of normal disfluencies. Normative data for the questionnaire are only available for stuttering (Behavior Assessment Battery, 2007)

Procedure

Ask the client to complete the table. Provide the following instructions:

1. First fill in the right column, "disturbed speech."
2. Temporarily cover over the right column so you cannot see it.
3. Fill in the left column, "emotional response," a day later.
4. Compare the scores.

Tip Compute a separate mean score each time. For example: talking on the phone is dependent on the topic or the person. Compute a mean score.

Scores:

1. not at all
2. a little bit
3. pretty much
4. a lot
5. very much

SPEECH SITUATION CHECKLIST (Adapted from Brutten & Shoemaker, 1974)		
Name: Date:		
Situation	Emotional response	Disturbed speech
1 having a telephone conversation		
2 talking to a stranger		
3 giving one's own name or introducing oneself		
4 talking to a small child		
5 producing a word or sentence that gave difficulties earlier		
6 ordering in a restaurant		
7 talking to an animal		
8 asking to be forwarded on the phone to a certain person		
9 having a conversation with a good friend		
10 having an argument with parents or a partner		
11 talking to a sales person		
12 participating in a group conversation		
13 receiving criticism		
14 meeting someone for the first time		
15 talking after being criticized		

16 talking after being misunderstood		
17 saying hello		
18 reading an unknown text out loud		
19 responding to a certain question		
20 being interviewed for a job		
21 asking for information		
22 trying to convince other people		
23 talking through skype or facetime		
24 giving instructions		
25 talking after drinking some alcohol		
26 talking with a hairstylist		
27 trying to impress someone		
28 speaking when depressed		
29 talking to teachers or authorities		
30 making an appointment		
31 asking a question in a classroom or office meeting		
32 answering questions about one's speech		
33 repeating an answer		
34 talking when at home		
35 introducing a friend to a friend		
36 giving one's personal data (name, address, etc.)		
37 talking when tired		
38 buying a ticket to a certain destination		
39 presenting in front of a big group		
40 presenting in front of a small group		
41 presenting without preparation		
42 being rushed during speech		
43 explaining important issues to friends		
44 talking in a bar		
45 talking after a sporting event		
46 talking while playing a computer game		
47 telling a joke		

REFERENCES

References of literature on cluttering and related topics.

Abwender, D. A., Como, P. G., Kurlan, R., Parry, K., Fett, K. A., Cui, L., Plumb S., & Deeley C. (1996). School problems in Tourette's syndrome. *Archives of Neurology. 53*(6), 509-511.

Abwender, D. A., Trinidad, K., Jones, K. R., Como, P. G., Hymes, E. (1998). *Brain & Language, 62,* 455-464.

Al-Khaledi, M., Lincoln, M., McCabe, P., Packman, A., & Alshatti, T. (2009). The attitudes, knowledge and beliefs of Arab parents in Kuwait about stuttering. *Journal of Fluency Disorders, 34*(1):44-59.

Alm, P. (2004). Stuttering and the basal ganglia circuits: A critical review of possible relations. *Journal of Fluency Disorders, 29,* 123-133.

Alm, P. (2007). *On the causal mechanisms of stuttering.* PhD thesis, University of Lund: Sweden.

Alm, P. (July 2008). *Fluency disorders: A discussion of possible causes and mechanisms, from a neuroscience perspective.* Presentation Oxford Dysfluency Congress.

Alm, P. (2011). Cluttering: A neurological perspective. In D. Ward & K. Scaler Scott (Eds.), *Cluttering: A handbook of research, intervention and education* (pp. 3—28). East Sussex: Psychology Press.

American Speech-Language-Hearing Association (2008). *Cluttering: A pathology lost but found* [Convention mini seminar audio-tape Tape #1150]. Available from 800-747-8069.

Arenas (2009). DAF/FAF-software download Speech Monitor (rickarenas@yahoo.com).

Arndt, J., & Healey, E. C. (2001). Concomitant disorders in school-age children who stutter. *Language, Speech and Hearing Services in Schools, 32,* 68-78.

Bakker, K. (1996) Cluttering: Current scientific status and emerging research and clinical needs. *Journal of Fluency Disorders, 21,* 359-366.

Bakker, K. (2007). *Objectifying measures of cluttered speech.* First World Conference on Cluttering, Katarino, Bulgaria.

Bakker, K., Myers F.L. (2010). Recent developments in the Cluttering Severity Instrument (CSI). Paper presented at the International Cluttering Online Conference, Minnesota State University, Mankato., Retrieved on June 12, 2010 from http://www.mnsu.edu/comdis/ica1/papers/bakker1c.html

Bakker, K., Bos, C., & Finn, P. (1999). Counting syllables or words: Implications for speech rate determination. Paper presented at the Annual Convention of the American Speech-Language-Hearing Association: San Francisco, CA.

Bakker, K., Bos, C., St. Louis, K. O., Myers, F. L., & Raphael, L. J. (1999). *Articulation rates and spectrographic characteristics of cluttered speech.* Paper presented at the Annual Convention of the American Speech-Language-Hearing Association, San Francisco, CA.

Bakker, K., & Lawson, S. (2006). Manual measurement of talking time: Reliability, validity and accuracy. *Annual National Convention of the American Speech Language and Hearing Association,* Miami Beach, FL.

Bakker, K., Myers, F. L., Raphael, L. J., & St. Louis, K. O. (2011). A preliminary comparison of speech rate, self-evaluation, and disfluency of people who speak exceptionally fast, clutter, or speak normally. In D. Ward & K. Scaler Scott (Eds.), *Cluttering: A handbook of research, intervention and education* (pp. 45-65). East Sussex: Psychology Press.

Bakker, K., Raphael, L. J., Myers, F. L., & St. Louis, K. O. (2000). *Acoustic and perceptual-phonetic analyses of cluttered and noncluttered speech.* Paper presented at the Annual Convention of the American Speech-Language-Hearing Association: Washington, D.C.

Bakker, K., St. Louis, K. O., Myers, F., & Raphael, L. (2005). A freeware software tool for determining aspects of cluttering severity. *Annual*

National Convention of the American Speech Language and Hearing Association, San Diego, CA

Bakker, K., St. Louis, K. O., Myers, F., Adams, C., Bennet-Launette, E., Filatova, Y., Kissagizlis, P., Kuster, P., Launette, D., Reichel, I. K., Rhein, D., Simonska, M., van Zaalen-op't Hof, Y., & Ward, D. (2008, November). Providing world-wide cluttering education: Accomplishments of the International Cluttering Association. Poster session. American Speech-Language-Hearing Association convention. Chicago, IL.

Bargh, J. A. (1994). The Four Horsemen of automaticity: Awareness, efficiency, intention, and control in social cognition. In R. S. Wyer, Jr. & T. K. Srull (Eds.), Handbook of social cognition (2nd ed., pp. 1-40). Hillsdale, NJ: Erlbaum.

Barnes, E., Long, S., Martin, G.E., Berni, M.C., Mandulak, K. C., & Sideris, J. (2009). Phonological Accuracy and Intelligibility in Connected Speech of Boys With Fragile X Syndrome or Down Syndrome. Journal of Speech, Language, and Hearing Research, 52, pp 1048–1061.

Bar-On, R. (2000). Emotional and social intelligence: Insights from the emotional quotient inventory. In R. Bar-On & J. D. A. Parker (Eds.), *The handbook of emotional intelligence* (363 --388). San Francisco: Jossey-Bass.

Bauer, H. (1980). Speech and voice disorders seen in the oral clinic (author's translation). *HNO 28*, 171-174.

Baumgartner, J. (1999). Acquired psychogenic stuttering. In: R.F. Curlee (Ed.), *Stuttering and related disorders of stuttering and related disorders of fluency (pp. 269-288).* New York: Thieme.

Bazin, D. (1717). Speech and its disorders. Basel, in Luchsinger, R. (1951). Remarks to the history of phoniatrics in the Eighteenth Century. Folia Phoniatrica, III (in German).

Becker, K. P., & Grundmann, K. (1970). Investigation on incidence and symptomatology of cluttering. *Folia Phoniatrica 22*, 261-271.

Belser, R. C., & Sudhalter, V. (2001). Conversational characteristics of children with fragile X syndrome: Repetitive speech. *American Journal on Mental Retardation*, 106, 28-38.

Bennett, E. M. (2006). *Working with people who stutter: A lifespan approach.* Upper Saddle River, NJ: Pearson Merrill Prentice Hall.

Bennett Lanouette, E. (2011). Intervention strategies for cluttering disorders. In D. Ward & K. Scaler Scott (Eds.), *Cluttering: A handbook of research, intervention and education* (175-197). East Sussex: Psychology Press.

Bezemer, B.W., Bouwen, J., & Winkelman, C. (2006). *Stotteren van theorie naar therapie.* Bussum: Uitgeverij Coutinho.

Blake, D. T., Heiser, M. A., Caywood, M., & Merzenich, M. M. (2006). Experience-dependent adult cortical plasticity requires cognitive association between sensation and reward. *Neuron, 52*, 371-381.

Bloch, A. (1994). *Murphy's law.* Utrecht: Bruna.

Block, S. (2004). The evidence base for the treatment of stuttering. In S. Reilly, J. Douglas, & J. Oates (Eds.), *Evidence based practice in speech pathology.* London: Whurr.

Blokker, M., Vos, S., & van Wingerden, K. (2010). Normale niet-vloeiendheden in adolsecenten met dyslexie. Bachelor Thesis, Hogeschool Utrecht.

Blomgren, M., Nagarajan, S. S., Lee, J. N., Li, T., & Alvord, L., e.a. (2003). Preliminary results of a functional MRI study of brain activation patterns in stuttering and nonstuttering speakers during a lexical access task. *Journal of Fluency Disorders 28*, 337-356.

Blood, G. W., Ridenour Jr., V. J., Qualls, C. D., & Hammer, C. S.W. (2003). Co-occurring disorders in children who stutter. *Journal of Communication Disorders, 36*, 427-448.

Blood, G., & Seider, R. (1981). The concomitant problems of young stutterers. *Journal of Speech and Hearing Research, 46*, 31-33.

Blood, I., & Tellis, G. (2000). Auditory processing and cluttering in young children. *Perceptual and Motor Skills, 90*, 631-639.

Boehme, G. (1976). *Angewandte Phoniatrie. III. Stotter-Syndrom. Polter-Syndrom.* (Applied phoniatrics: III. Stuttering. Cluttering). *HNO, Wegweiser fuer die fachaerztliche Praxis, 24* (12), 431-438.

Boersma, P., & Weenink, D. (2007). *Praat: doing phonetics by computer* (Version 4.4.26) [Computer program].

Boersma, P., & Weenink, D. (2012). Praat: doing phonetics by computer. Software package, retrieved August 2, 2013 from www.praat.org.

Boey, R. (2000). *Stotteren detecteren and meten.* Leuven-Apeldoorn: Uitgeverij Garant.

van Borsel, J. (2011). Cluttering and Down syndrome. In D. Ward & K. Scaler Scott (Eds.), *Cluttering: A handbook of research, intervention and education* (90-99). East Sussex: Psychology Press.

van Borsel, J., Dhooge, I., Verhoye, K., Derde, K., & Curfs, L. (1999). Communication problems in Turner syndrome: A sample survey. *Journal of Communication Disorders, 32*, 435-446.

van Borsel, J., Dor, O., & Rondal, J. (2008). Speech fluency in fragile-X syndrome. Clinical Linguistics and Phonetics, 22, 1-11

van Borsel J., Goethals, L., & Vanryckeghem, M. (2004). Disfluency in Tourette syndrome: Observational study in three cases. *Folia Phoniatrica et Logopaedica Journal of Communication Disorders, 33*(3) 227-240.

van Borsel, J., & Tetnowski, J. A. (2007) Fluency disorders in genetic syndromes. *Journal of Fluency Disorders, 32* (4), 279-296.

van Borsel, J., & Vandermeulen, A. (2008). Cluttering in Down syndrome. Folia Phoniatrica et Logopaedica, 60, 312-317.

van Borsel, J., & Vanryckeghem, M. (2000). Dysfluency and phonic tics in Tourette syndrome: A case report. Journal of Communication Disorders, 33(3), 227-240.

Bothe, A. K. (2008) Identification of children's stuttered and nonstuttered speech by highly experienced judges: Binary judgments and comparisons with disfluency-types definitions. Journal of Speech, Language, and Hearing Research, 51(4), 867-78.

Boyle, M. P. (2011). Mindfulness training in stuttering therapy: A tutorial for speech-language pathologists. Journal of Fluency Disorders, 36(2), 122-129.

Bradford, D. (1963). Studies in Tachyphemia: A framework of therapeusis for articulation therapy with tachyphemia and/or general language disability. Logo 6, 59-65.

Bradford, D. (1970). Cluttering. Folia Phoniatrica, 22, 272-279.

Brady, John P. (1993). Treatment of Cluttering. New England Journal of Medicine, 329 (11), 813-814.

Bray, M. (2003). Monica Bray's survey looks at dysfluency in Down's syndrome and at the success or otherwise of different treatment approaches. British Stammering Association. Retrieved at http://www.stammering.org/downs_survey.html.

Bretherton-Furness, J., & Ward, D. (2012). Lexical access, story re-telling and sequencing skills in adults who clutter and those who do not. Journal of Fluency Disorders, 37(4), 214-224.

Brutten, G. (1979). Vragenlijst spreeksituaties. In: P. Janssen (Ed.) (1992), Gedragstherapie bij stotteren. Utrecht: Bohn Stafleu van Loghum.

Brutten, G., & Shoemaker, D. (1974). Speech Situation checklist. In the Southern Illinois Checklist. Carbondale, IL: Southern Illinois University.

Brutten, G., & Vanryckeghem, M. (2003). *Behavior Assessment Battery: A multi-dimensional and evidence -based approach to diagnostic and therapeutic decision making for adults who stutter.* Organization for the Integration of Handicapped People, Belgium & Acco Publishers: Netherlands.

Bubenickova, M. (1981). Speech reeducation in cluttering. *Psycholgia a Patopsychologia Dieta, 16*(1), 57-61.

Cabanas, R. (1978). Diagnostico diferential temprano entre tartamudez y tartaleo. *Importancia clinica* (Early Differential Diagnosis of Stuttering and Cluttering. Clinical Significance). *Revista Cubana Pediatrica, 50* (1), 65-71.

Campbell, J. G., & Hill, D. (1987). *Systematic Disfluency analysis.* Paper presented at the annual convention of the American Speech Language and Hearing Association: New Orleans.

Campbell, J. G., & Hill, D. (1994). *Systematic Disfluency Analysis.* Evanston, IL: Northwestern University.

Carlo, E. J. (2006). *Speech rate of non-stuttering Spanish speaking adults.* Second World Congress on Fluency Disorders. Proceedings, 111-117.

Carroll, D. (1996). *A study of the effectiveness of an adaptation of melodic intonation therapy in increasing the communicative speech of young children with Down syndrome.* McGill University. www.musictherapyworld.de/ modules/archive/dissertations/pdfs/MA_DC.pdf.

Chaloku, C. I., Ghazi, M. A., Foord, E. E., & Lebrun, Y. (1997). Subcortical structures and non-volitional verbal behaviour. *Journal of Neurolinguistics, 10,* 313-323.

Chmelova, A., Kujalová, V., Sedláčková, E., & Zelený, A. (1975). Neurohumorale Reaktionen bei Stotterern und Poltern

(Neurohumoral reactions in stutterers and clutterers). *Folia Phoniatrica, 27* (4): 283-286.

Colombat de Isère, M. (1849). Les maladies de la voix et les vices de la parole. Journal de Réadaptation ` Médicale, 23(1–2), 54–60.

Conture, E. D., & Curlee, R. F. (Eds.) (2007). *Stuttering and related disorders* (3rd ed.). New York / Stuttgart: Thieme.

Coppens-Hofman, M. C., Terband, H. R., Maassen, B. A., van Schrojenstein Lantman – de Valk, H.M., van Zaalen-op't Hof, Y., & Snik, A. F. (2013). Dysfluencies in the speech of adults with intellectual disabilities and reported speech difficulties. *Journal of Communication Disorders, 46*(5-6), 484-94.

Cosyns, M., van Zaalen, Y., Mortier, G., Janssens, S., Amez, A., van Damme, J., & van Borsel, J. (2013). Disfluency: It is not always stuttering. Clinical Genetics. For retrieval, as first published online, http://onlinelibrary.wiley.com/journal/10.1111/%28ISSN%291399-0004

Curlee, R. (1996). Cluttering: Data in search of understanding. *Journal of Fluency Disorders, 21*, 367-372.

Curlee, R. F., & Conture, E. G. (2007). *Stuttering and related disorders of fluency* (3rd ed.). New York, Stuttgart: Thieme.

Craig, A. (1996). Long-term effects of intensive treatment for a client with both a cluttering and stuttering disorder. *Journal of Fluency Disorders, 21*, 329-336.

Dalton, P., & Hardcastle, W. (1993) *Disorders of fluency and their effects on communication. (2nd ed.)*. London: Whurr.

Daly, D. (1986). The Clutterer. In K. St. Louis (Ed.), *The Atypical Stutterer: Principles and Practice of Rehabilitation (pp. 155-192)*. New York: Academic Press.

Daly, D. A. (1988). *The freedom of fluency*. East Moline, IL: LinguiSystems.

Daly, D. (1992). Helping the clutterer: Therapy considerations. In: F. Myers & K. St. Louis (Eds.), *Cluttering: A Clinical Perspective* (pp. 107-124). Leicester, England: FAR Communications (reissued in 1996 by San Diego, CA: Singular).

Daly, D. A. (1993). Cluttering: Another fluency syndrome. In: R. Curlee (Ed.), *Stuttering and Related Disorders of Fluency* . New York: Thieme Medical Publishers, Inc.

Daly, D. (1993a). Cluttering: The orphan of speech-language pathology. *American Journal of Speech-Language Pathology 2*(2), 6-8.

Daly, D. (1993b). Cluttering: A Language-Based Syndrome. Treatment strategies for the cluttering syndrome: Planning your work and working your plan. *The Clinical Connection*, 4-9.

Daly, D.A. (1994). Speech cluttering. *JAMA 272*(7), 565.

Daly, D. (1996). *The source for stuttering and cluttering.* East Moline, IL: LinguiSystems.

Daly, D. (2008). Cluttering: A language-based syndrome. Audio-tape. Clinical Connection, 708 Pendleton Street, Alexandria, VA 22314.

Daly, D. (2008). *Proceedings of the Oxford Dysfluency conference*, DVD.

Daly, D. A., & Burnett-Stolnack, M. (1995). Cluttering: A language based syndrome (audio cassette tape). Alexandria, VA: *The Clinical Connection*.

Daly, D. A., & Burnett-Stolnack, M. (1995). Identification of and treatment planning for cluttering clients: Two practical tools. *The Clinical Connection, 8*, 1-5.

Daly, D., & Burnett, M. (1996). Cluttering: Assessment, Treatment planning, and case study illustration. *Journal of Fluency Disorders, 21*, 239-244.

Daly, D. A., & Burnett, M. L. (1999). Cluttering: Traditional views and new perspectives. In: R. F. Curlee (Ed.) *Stuttering and Disorders of Fluency* (pp. 222-254) (2d ed). New York: Thieme.

Daly, D. A., & Cantrell, R. P. (2006). *Cluttering characteristics identified as diagnostically significant by 60 fluency experts.* Second World Congress on Fluency Disorders. Proceedings.

Daly, D. A., Myers, F. L., & St. Louis, K. O. (1992). Cluttering: A pathology lost but found. *Paper presented at the annual convention of the American Speech-Language-Hearing Association*, San Antonio, TX.

Damsté, P. H. (1984). *Stotteren.* Utrecht: Bohn, Scheltema en Holkema (in Dutch).

Damsté, P.H. (1990). *Stotteren* (4ᵉ druk.). Utrecht/Antwerpen: Bohn, Scheltema en Holkema (in Dutch).

Dannenbauer, F. M. (1999). *Grammatik.* In G. Baumgartner & J. Fussenich (Hrsg) *Sprachtherapie mit Kindern* (pp. 105-161). Munchen: Basel, E. Reinhardt.

Dauer, K., & Tetnowski, J. A. (2005). Stuttering and Moya-Moya Disease. *Perspectives in Fluency Disorders, 15* (2), 3-7.

de Andrade, C. R., & de Oliveira Martins, V. (2009). Fluency variation in adolescents. *Clinical Linguistics & Phonetics, 21,* 771-782.

de Andrade, C. R. F., & de Oliveira Martins, V. (2009). Speech fluency variation in elderly. *Pro-Fono Revista de Atualizacao Cientifica, 22*(1), 13-18.

Defloor, T., van Borsel, J., & Curfs, L. (2000). Speech fluency in Prader-Willi syndrome. *Journal of Fluency Disorders, 25,* 85-98.

DeFusco, E. M., & Menken, M. (1979). Symptomatic cluttering in adults. *Brain and Language, 8*(1), 25-33.

De Hirsch, K. (1961). Studies in Tachyphemia: Diagnosis of developmental language disorders. *Logos, 4*, 3-9.

De Hirsch, K. (1970). Stuttering and cluttering: Developmental aspects of dysrhythmic speech. *Folia Phoniatrica, 22*, 311-324.

De Hirsch, K. (1975). Cluttering and stuttering. *Bulletin of the Orton Society, 25*, 57-68.

De Hirsch, K., & Jansky, J. (1980). Patterning and organizational deficits in children with language and learning disabilities. *Bulletin of the Orton Society, 30*, 227-239.

De Nil, L. F., Jokel, R., & E. Rochon, E. (2007). Etiology, symptomatology, and treatment of neurogenic stuttering. In: E. G. Conture and R. F. Curlee (Eds.), *Stuttering and related disorders of fluency* (pp. 326-343). York: Thieme Medical.

De Nil, L. F., Sasisekaran, J., Van Lieshout, P. H. H. M., & Sandor, P. (2005). Speech disfluencies in individuals with Tourette syndrome. *Journal of Psychosomatic Research,*58(1):97-102.

Devenny, D., & Silverman, W. (1990). Speech dysfluency and manual specialization in Down's syndrome. *Journal of Mental Deficiency Research, 34*, 253-260.

Dewar, A., Dewar, A. D., & Barnes, H. E. (1976). Patterning and organizational deficits in children with masking in stammering and cluttering. *British Journal of Disorders of Communication, 11*(1), 19-26.

Diedrich, W. M. (1984). Cluttering: Its Diagnosis. In: H. Winitz (Ed), *Treating Articulation Disorders: For Clinicians by Clinicians*. Baltimore: University Park Press.

Dinger, T., Smit, M., & Winkelman, C. (2008). *Expressiever en gemakkelijker spreken*. Bussum: Uitgeverij Coutinho.

Drayna, D. (2011). Possible genetic factors in cluttering. In D. Ward & K. Scaler Scott (Eds.), *Cluttering: A handbook of research, intervention and education* (pp. 29—33). East Sussex: Psychology Press.

Eggers, K. (August, 2010). What is normal dysfluency and why measure it? Paper presented at 28th World Congress of the International Association of Logopedics and Phoniatrics, Athens, Greece.

Einarsdóttir, J., & Ingham, R. (2009). Accuracy of parent identification of stuttering occurrence. *International Journal of Language & Communication Disorders, 44*(6), 847–863.

Eisenson, J. (1986). Dysfluency disorders: Cluttering and stuttering. In: A. Goldstein, L. Krasner, & S. Garfield (Eds.). *Language and Speech Disorders in Children*. New York: Pergamon Press, pp. 57-75.

Eldridge, K. A. (2007) *Phonological Complexity and Speech Disfluency in Young Children*. Doctoral Dissertation, University of Pittsburgh.

Erickson, R. L., (1969). Assessing communication attitudes among stutterers. *Journal of Speech and Hearing Research, 12*, 711–724.

Exum, T., Absalon, C., Smith, B., & Reichel, I. K. (2010). People with cluttering and stuttering have room for success. International Cluttering Online Conference, 2010 [Minnesota State University, Mankato].

Filatova, Y.O. (2005). *Cluttering*. Moscow: Prometey (in Russian).

Filatova, Y. O., Belyakova, L. I. (2012). Central stuttering and cluttering mechanisms: Multiparadigmal analysis. Seminar. The 7th World Congress on Fluency Disorders, International Fluency Association. Tours, France.

Florenskaya, J. A. (1934). A question about functional speech disorders. Paraphazia and tachylalia. Contemporary Psychoneurology, 4. (in Russian)

Fox, P.T. (2003). Brain imaging in stuttering: Where next? *Journal of Fluency Disorders, 28,* 265–272.

Freund, H. (1952). Studies in the interrelationship between stuttering and cluttering. *Folia Phoniatrica, 4,* 146-168.

Freund, H. (1966). Psychopathology and the problems of stuttering. Springfield, IL: Charles C. Thomas.

Freund, H. (1970). Observations on tachylalia. *Folia Phoniatrica, 22,* 280-288.

Froeschels, E. (1946). Cluttering. *Journal of Speech Disorders, 11,* 31-36.

Froeschels, E. (1955). Contribution to the relationship between stuttering and cluttering. *Logopaedic and Phoniatrie, 4,* 1-6.

Garnett, E. O., Adams, C. F., Montgomery, A. A., St. Louis, K. O., & den Ouden, D. B. (2012). Phonological encoding in cluttering. Poster presented at the 7th World Congress on Fluency Disorders, International Fluency Association. Tours, France.

Geerts, G., & Heestermans, H. (2005). *Van Dale: Groot Woordenboek der Nederlandse Taal,* 3 Delen (12th ed.). Utrecht: Van Dale Lexicografie.

Georgieva, D. (2004). Professional awareness of cluttering: A comparative study (Part Two). In H.-G. Bosshardt, J. S. Yaruss, & H. F. Peters (Eds.), *Fluency disorders: Theory, research, treatment, and self-help: Proceedings of the Fourth World Congress on Fluency Disorders* (pp. 630--634). International Fluency Association: Katarino, Bulgaria.

Georgieva, D. (2010). Understanding cluttering: Eastern European traditions vs. Western European and North American traditions. In K. Bakker, L. Raphael, & F. Myers (Eds.), *Proceedings of the First International Conference on Cluttering* (pp. 230—243). International Cluttering Association: Katorino, Bulgaria.

Georgieva, D., & Miliev, D. (1996). Differential diagnosis of cluttering and stuttering in Bulgaria. *Journal of Fluency Disorders, 21,* 249-260.

German, D. J. (1979). Word finding skills in children with learning disabilities. *Journal of Learning Disabilities, 12*, 43-48.

German, D. J. (1984). Diagnosis of word-finding disorders in children with learning disabilities. *Journal of Learning Disabilities, 17*, 353-358.

German, D. J. (1992). Word-finding skills in children and adolescents. *Topics in Language Disorders, 12*, 43-48.

Gettinger, M., & Koscik, R. (2001). Psychological services for children with disabilities. In J. N. Hughes & A. M. LaGreca (Eds.), *Handbook of psychological services for children and adolescents*. New York: Oxford Press.

Gillberg, J. (1992). Subgroups in autism: Are there behavioural phenotypes typical of underlying medical conditions? *Journal of Intellectual Disability Research, 36*(3), 201–214.

Giraud, A. L., von Gudenberg, A. W., Euler, H. A., Lanfermann, H., & Preibisch, C. (2008). Severity of dysfluency correlates with basal ganglia activity in persistent developmental stuttering. *Brain and Language, 104*, 190–199.

Goldstein, A. (2007). Dysfluency disorders: Cluttering and stuttering. In: L. Krasner & S. Garfield (Eds.), Language and speech disorders in children (pp. 57–75). New York: Pergamon Press.

Green, T. (1999). The Cluttering problem. A short review and a critical comment. *Logopedics Phonology Vocology, 24*, 145-153.

Gregory, H. (1995) Analysis and commentary. *Language, Speech, and Hearing Services in Schools, 26*, 19-25

Gregory, H. H. (1995). Analysis and commentary. *Language, Speech and Hearing Services in Schools, 26*(2), 196-200.

Gregory, H. H., Campbell, J. H., & Hill, D. G. (2003). Differential evaluation of stuttering problems. In: H. H. Gregory, *Stuttering therapy: Rationale and procedures (pp. 80-141)*. Boston: Allyn & Bacon.

Grewel, F. (1970). Cluttering and its problems. *Folia Phoniatrica, 22,* 301-310.

Grinfeld, D., & Amir, O. (2006). Articulation rate in children and adolescents: Hebrew speakers. *Second World Congress on Fluency Disorders. Proceedings,* pp. 125-129.

Guitar, B. (2006). *Stuttering an integrated approach to its nature and treatment (3rd ed.).* Baltimore: Lippincott/ Williams & Wilkins.

Gutzman, H. (1893). *Vorlesungen über die Störungen der Sprache und ihre Heilung.* Berlijn: Kornfeld.

Hall, K. D., Amir, O., & Yairi, E. (1999). A longitudinal investigation of speaking rate in preschool children who stutter. *Journal of Speech Language and Hearing Research, 42,* 1367-1377.

Hanson, D. M., Jackson, A. W. 3d, & Hagerman, R. J. (1986). Speech disturbances (cluttering) in mildly impaired males with the Martin-Bell/fragile X syndrome. *Am J Med Genet* (3L4), 23(1-2), 195-206.

Hartinger, M., & Mooshammer, C. (2008). Articulatory variability in cluttering. *Folia Phoniatrica et Logopaedica, 60,* 64-72.

Hartinger, M., & Pepe, D. (2003). *An articulatory and acoustic study of cluttering.* 15th ICPhS, Barcelona: 3245-3248 (pdf-file).

Van Hartingsveldt, M., Cup, E., & Corstens-Mignot, M. (2006/2010). *Korte Observatie Ergotherapie Kleuters.* Nijmegen: Ergoboek.

Hashimoto, R., Taguchi, T., Kano, M., Hanyu, S., Tanaka, Y., Nishiwaza, M., & Nakano, I. (1999). A case report of dementia with cluttering-like speech disorder and apraxia. *Rinsho Shinkeigaku, 39,* 520-526.

Hayden, D.A. (1994). Differential diagnosis of motor speech dysfunction in children. Developmental apraxia of speech: Assessment. *Clinics in Communication Disorders, 4*(2), 118–147, 162–174.

Healey, E. C., & Reid, R. (2003). ADHD and stuttering: A tutorial. *Journal of Fluency Disorders, 28*(2), 79-94.

Healey, E. C., Scott Trautman, L., & Susca, M. (2004). Clinical applications of a multidimensional approach for the assessment and treatment of stuttering. *Contemporary Issues in Communication Disorders, 31*, 40-48.

van Heeswijk, E., van Zaalen, Y., & de Jong, N.H. (in review). Silent pauses in cluttered speech. *Stem, spraak-en taalpathologie.*

Heitmann, R., Asbjørnsen, A., & Helland, T. (2004). Attentional functions in speech fluency disorders. *Logopedics, Phoniatrics, Vocology, 29*(3), 119-27.

Helm, K. (1997). *A perceptual, acoustic-phonetic, and linguistic analysis of cluttering.* Unpublished master's thesis. Southwest Missouri State University, Springfield, MO.

Howell, P. (2008). Assessment of Some Contemporary Theories of Stuttering That Apply to Spontaneous Speech. *Contemp Issues Commun Sci Disord, 31*, 122–139.

Howell, P., & Au-Yeung J. (2002). The EXPLAN theory of fluency control and the diagnosis of stuttering. In: E. Fava (Ed.), *Current Issues in Linguistic Theory series: Pathology and therapy of speech disorders* (pp. 77-94). Amsterdam: John Benjamins.

Howell, P., & Davis, S. (2011). The epidemiology of cluttering with stuttering. In D. Ward & K. Scaler Scott (Eds.), *Cluttering: A handbook of research, intervention and education* (pp. 69-89). East Sussex: Psychology Press.

Howell, P., & Dworzynski, K. (2005). Planning and execution processes in speech control by fluent speakers and speakers who stutter. *Journal of Fluency Disorders, 30*(4), 343–354.

Hunt, J. (1861). *Stammering and stuttering; Their nature and treatment* (1ST ed.). London: Longmans, Green & Co., Ltd.

Hutchinson, J. M., & Burke, K. W. (1973). An investigation of the effects of temporal alterations in auditory feedback upon stutterers and clutterers, *Journal of Communication Disorders, 6*, 193-205.

Janse, E., Sely, F., & Sittig, E. (2000). *Verstaanbaarheid na sterke tijdscompressie: natuurlijke vs. Synthetische spraak.* The day of Phonetics, Proceedings 1-2.

Janssen, P. (1985). *Gedragstherapie bij stotteren.* Utrecht, Bohn, Scheltema, & Holkema.

Jerome, L. (2003). Some observations on the phenomenology of thought disorder; a neglected sign in attention-deficit hyperactivity disorder. *Journal of the Canadian Academy of Child and Adolescent Psychiatry 12*(3), 92--93

Johnson, M. K., & Hasher, L. (1987). Human learning and memory. In M. R. Rosenzweig & L. W. Porter (Eds.), *Annual Review of Psychology* (pp. 631- 668). Palo Alto, CA: Annual Reviews.

Juste, F., Sassi, F. C., & de Andrade, C. R. (2006). Typology of speech disruptions and grammatical classes in stuttering and fluent children. *Pro Fono, 18*(2), 129-40.

Kahneman, D., & Treisman, A. (1984). Changing views of attention and automaticity. In R. Parasuraman, D.R. Davies, & J. Beatty (Eds.), *Variants of attention* (pp. 29-61). New York: Academic Press.

Kalinowski, J., Armson, J., & Stuart, A. (1995). Effect of normal and fast articulatory rates on stuttering frequency. *Journal of Fluency Disorders, 20*(3), 293-302.

Katz-Bernstein, N. (1986). Poltern – Therapieeinsatz für Kinder. *Vierteljahresschrift für Heilpädagogik und ihre Nachbargebiete, 55*, 413-426.

Katz-Bernstein, N. (1988). Arbeit mit Eltern polternder Kinder. *Der Sprachheilpädagoge, 20*, 32-40.

Kehoe, T.D. (1999). *Stuttering: Science, Therapy & Practice*. Boulder, CO: Casa Futura Technologies.

Kelly, E. M. (1994). Speech rates and turn-taking behaviors of children who stutter and their fathers. *Journal of Speech and Hearing Research, 37*, 1284-1294.

Kelly, E., & Conture, G. (1992). Speaking rates, response time latencies, and interrupting behaviors of young stutterers, nonstutterers and their mothers. *Journal of Speech and Hearing Research, 35*, 1256-1267.

Kent, R. D. (1984). Stammering as a temporal programming disorder. In R. F. Curlee & W. Perkins (Eds.), *Nature and treatment of stammering: New directions* (pp. 283-301). San Diego, CA: College Hill Press.

Kidron, M., Scaler Scott, K., Lozier., J. L., & Cino, D. (2012a). The consumer perspective of teens and adults with cluttering. Poster. The 7th World Congress on Fluency Disorders, International Fluency Association. Tours, France.

Kidron, M., Scaler Scott, K., Lozier, J. (2012b). Working memory in relation to children's cluttering symptoms in 3 speaking contexts. Poster. The 7th World Congress on Fluency Disorders, International Fluency Association. Tours, France.

Kochergina, V. S. (1969). Bradylalia, tachylalia, dysfluency. In S. S. Lyapidevsky (Ed.), *Speech impairment in children and adolescents* (pp. 213—226). Moscow: Prosveshtenie. (In Russian.)

Korrelboom, K., & ten Broeke, E. (2004). Geïntegreerde cognitieve gedragstherapie. Bussum: Uitgeverij Coutinho.

Kussmaul, A. (1877). *Speech disorders. In Cyclopedia of the practice of medicine*, XIV (pp. 581—875). New York: William Wood & Co.

Langevin, M., & Boberg, E. (1996). Results of intensive stuttering therapy with adults who clutter and stutter. *Journal of Fluency Disorders, 21*, 315-328.

Langová, J., & Morávek, M. (1964). Some results of experimental examinations among stutterers and clutterers. *Folia Phoniatrica, 16*, 290—296.

Langová, J., & Morávek, M. (1970). Some problems of cluttering. *Folia Phoniatrica, 22*, 325-326.

Lanoutte, E. B. (2011). Intervention strategies for cluttering disorders. In D. Ward & K. Scaler Scott (Eds.), *Cluttering: A handbook of research, intervention and education* (pp. 175-197). East Sussex: Psychology Press.

Lastovka, M. (1976). *Tetanicka pohotovost u koktavych a brebtavych* (Tetanic susceptibility in stutterers and clutterers). *Ceskolovenska Otolaryngologie, 25*(1), 36-40.

Lebrun, Y. (1996). Cluttering after brain damage, *Journal of Fluency Disorders, 21*, 289-296.

Lees, R. M., Boyle, B. E., & Woolfson, L. (1996). Is cluttering a motor disorder? *Journal of Fluency Disorders, 21*, 281-288.

Levelt, W. J .M. (1983). Monitoring and self-repair in speech. *Cognition, 14*, 41-104.

Levelt, W. J. M. (1989). *Speaking: From intention to articulation.* Cambridge, MA: MIT Press.

Levelt, W. J. M. (1992). Assessing words in speech production: Stages, processes and representations. *Cognition, 42*, 1-22.

Levelt, W. J. M. (1993). Lexical selection, or how to bridge the major rift in language processing. In F. Beckmann, G. Heyer, & W. de Gruyter (Eds.), *Theorie und Praxis des Lexikons* (pp. 164-172). Berlin: Walter De Gruyter.

Levelt, W. J. M. (1999). A theory of lexical access in speech production. *Behavioral and Brain Sciences, 22*, 1–38.

Logan, K. J., & Conture, E. G. (1995). Length, grammatical complexity, and rate differences in stuttered and fluent conversational utterances of children who stutter. *Journal of Fluency Disorders, 20*, 35-61.

Logan, K., & Cowan, W. B. (1984). On the ability to inhibit thought and action: A theory of an act of control. *Psychological Review, 91*(3), 295-327.

Logan, K., & LaSalle, L. (1999). Grammatical characteristics of children's conversational utterances that contain disfluency clusters. *Journal of Speech, Language, and Hearing Research, 42*, 80–91.

Luchsinger, R. (1951). Remarks to the history of phoniatrics in the Eighteenth Century, *Folia Phoniatrica, III*, 178-183.

Luchsinger, R. (1955). About Cluttering, the so-called "stutter with cluttering component" and its relations to aphasia. *Folia Phoniatrica* 7, 12-43.

Luchsinger, R. (1963). *Poltern*. Berlin-Charlottenburg: Manhold Verlag (in German).

Luchsinger, R., & Arnold, G. E. (1965). Cluttering: Tachyphemia. In: *Voice-Speech-Language, clinical communicology: Its physiology and pathology* (pp. 598-618). Belmont, CA: Wadsworth,.

Luchsinger, R., & Arnold, G. E. (1970). *Handbuch der Stimm – und Sprachheilkunde*. Wien, New York: Springer—Verlag.

Marks, C. J. (1978). *Identification of Cluttering Behavior among Children Who Stutter*. Dissertation, Lehigh University.

Marriner, N. A., & Sanson-Fisher, R. W. (1977). A behavioral approach to cluttering: A case study, *Australian Journal of Human Communication Disorders, 5*, 134-141.

Mayer, J. D., Salovey, P., & Caruso, D. R. (2000). Models of emotional intelligence. In R. J. Sternberg (Ed.). *Handbook of intelligence* (pp. 396—420). New York: Cambridge University Press.

McNeil, M. (2002). Clinical characteristics of apraxia of speech: Model/ behavior coherence. *Proceedings of the 2002 Childhood Apraxia of Speech Research Symposium.* An experimental psycholinguistic study.

Meixner, F. (1992). Poltern aus entwicklungsspychologischer Sicht. In M. Grohnfeldt (Hrsg.), *Störungen der Redefähigkeit (Handbuch der Sprachtherapie 5,* S (pp. 468-490). Berlin: Spiess.

Mensink–Ypma, M. (1990). *Broddelen and leerstoornissen,* Houten/ Antwerpen: Bohn Stafleu van Loghum.

Menzies, R.G., Onslow, M., Packman, A., & O'Brian, S. (2009). Cognitive behavior therapy for adults who stutter: A tutorial for speech-language pathologists. *Journal of Fluency Disorders, 3,* 187- 200.

Merzenich, M. M., Nelson, R. J., Stryker, M. P., Cynader, M. S., Schoppmann, A., & Zook, J. M. (1984). Somatosensory Cortical Map Changes Following Digit Amputation in Adult Monkeys. *Journal of Comparative Neurology, 224,* 591-605.

Messer, D., & Dockrell, J. E. (2006). Children's Naming and Word-Finding Difficulties: Descriptions and Explanations, *Journal of Speech Language Hearing Research, 49*(2), 309-324.

Miller, David (1937). *The secret of happiness.* New York: Committee of David Miller Foundation.

Missulovin, L. (2002). *Patomorphoz of stuttering; Change in picture of the onset and development of stuttering – Specifics of the correctional work.* St. Petersburg: Souz (in Russian).

Miyamoto, S. (2011). Assessment and intervention of Japanese children exhibiting possible cluttering. In D. Ward & K. Scaler Scott (Eds.), *Cluttering: A handbook of research, intervention and education* (pp. 198-210). East Sussex: Psychology Press.

Miyamoto, S., Hayasaka, K., & Shapiro, D. (2007). An Examination of the Checklist for Possible Cluttering in Japan. In J. Au-Yeung & M.

Leahy (Eds.), *Research, treatment, and self-help in fluency disorders: New horizons:* (pp. 279 –283). International Fluency Association.

Molt, L. (1996). An examination of various aspects of auditory processing in clutterers. *Journal of Fluency Disorders, 21,* 215-226.

Moolenaar-Bijl, A. (1972). *Iets over vertraagde spraakontwikkeling en broddelen. Logopedie Foniatrie, 44,* 21-25.

Morávek, M., & Langová, J. (1962). Some electrophysiological findings among stutterers and clutterers. *Folia Phoniatrica, 14,* 305-316.

Mowrer, D. (1987). Reported use of a Japanese accent to promote fluency. *Journal Of Fluency Disorders, 1,* 19-39.

Mullet, C. F. (1971). 'An Arte to Make the Dumbe Speake, the Deafe to Heare': A Seventeenth- Century goal. *Journal of the History of Medicine and Allied Sciences, 26,* 123—140.

Mussafia, M. (1970). Various aspects of cluttering. *Folia Phoniatrica, 22,* 337-346.

Myers, F. (1996a). Annotations of research and clinical perspectives on cluttering since 1964. *Journal of Fluency Disorders, 21,* 187-200.

Myers, F. (1996b). Cluttering: A matter of perspective. *Journal of Fluency Disorders, 21,* 175-186.

Myers F. (2011). Treatment of cluttering: A cognitive-behavioral approach centered on rate control. In D. Ward & K. Scaler Scott (Eds.), *Cluttering: A handbook of research, intervention and education* (pp. 152-174). East Sussex: Psychology Press.

Myers, F. L., & Bradley, C. L. (1992). Clinical management of cluttering from a synergistic framework. In F. L. Myers & K. O. St. Louis (Eds.), *Cluttering: A clinical perspective* (pp. 85-105). Kibworth, Great Britain: Far Communications. (Reissued in 1996 by Singular, San Diego, CA.)

Myers, F., & St. Louis, K. O. (1992). *Cluttering: A Clinical Perspective*. Leicester, England: Far Communications. (Reissued in 1996 by Singular, San Diego, CA.)

Myers, F., & St. Louis, K. O. (1996). Two youths who clutter, but is that the only similarity? *Journal of Fluency Disorders, 21*, 297-304.

Myers, F. L., & St. Louis, K. O. (2007). *Cluttering* [DVD]. Nashville, TN: The Stuttering Foundation.

Myers, F. L., St. Louis, K. O., Bakker, K., Raphael, L. J., Wiig, E. K., Katz, J., Daly, D. A., & Kent, R. D. (2002, November). *Putting cluttering on the map: Looking ahead*. Seminar presented at the annual convention of the American Speech-Language-Hearing Association, Atlanta, GA.

Myers, F.L., St. Louis, K. O., Bakker, K., Raphael, L. J., Wiig, E. K., Katz, J., Daly, D. A., & Kent, R. D. (2002, November) *Putting cluttering on the map: Looking back*. Seminar presented at the annual convention of the American Speech-Language-Hearing Association, Atlanta, GA.

Myers, F. L., Stueber, K. A., & St. Louis, K. O. (1997) *Clustering of disfluencies in cluttering*. Poster presented at the Annual Convention of the American Speech-Language-Hearing Association, Boston, MA.

NCLD: National Center for Learning Disabilities (2002). *LD basics and fast facts*. Retrieved June 3, 2002, from www.ncld.org/info/index.cfm.

Nelson, L. (1996). Critical review of the special edition on cluttering. *Journal of Fluency Disorders, 21*, 345-348.

Neumann, K., Euler, H.A., von Gudenberg, A.W., Giraud, A, L., Lanfermann, H., Gall, V., & Preibisch, C. (2003). The nature and treatment of stuttering as revealed by fMRI. A within- and between-group comparison. *Journal of Fluency Disorders, 28*, 381-410.

Ohman, R. (2000). Fear and anxiety: Evolutionary, cognitive, and clinical perspectives. In M. Lewis & J. M. Haviland-Jones (Eds.), *Handbook of emotions* (2nd ed.) (pp.573–593). New York: Guilford Press.

Olsthoorn, N. M. (2007). Relationships between grammatical encoding and decoding. An experimental psycholinguistic study. Ph.D. Thesis, Leiden University. Netherlands.

Op 't Hof, J., & Uys, I. (1974). A clinical delineation of tachyphemia (cluttering): A case of dominant inheritance. *South African Medical Journal, 48*, 1624-1628.

Otto, F. M., & Yairi, E. (1975). An analysis of the speech dysfluencies in Down's syndrome and in normally intelligent subjects. *Journal of Fluency Disorders, 1*, 26-32.

Parks, G. R. (1993) (Interview with David A. Daly). Cluttering: A language based syndrome. *The Clinical Connection, 6*, 4-7.

Perelló, J. (1970). Tachyphemia – A clinical contribution. *Folio Phoniatrica, 22*, 381—382.

Pindzola, R. H., Jenkins, M. M., & Lokken, K. J. (1989). Speaking Rates of Young Children. *Language, Speech, and Hearing Services in Schools, 20*, 133-138.

Pireira, M. M. de B., Rossi, J. P., & Van Borsel, J. (2008). Public awareness and knowledge of stuttering in Rio de Janeiro. *Journal of Fluency Disorders, 33*, 24--31.

Pitluk, N. (1982). Aspects of the expressive language of cluttering and stuttering school children. *South African Journal of Communication Disorders, 29*, 77-84.

Playhouse group (2012). http://www.online-games-zone.com/pages/pnc/find-the-difference.php, retrieved October 21, 2012.

Postma, A., & Kolk, H. M. J. (1993). The covert repair hypothesis: Prearticulatory repair processes in normal and stuttered dysfluencies. *Journal of Speech and Hearing Research, 36*, 472-487.

Preibisch, C., Neumann, K., Raab, O., Euler, H. A., von Gudenberg, A. W., Lanfermann, H., & Giraud, A.L. (2003a). Evidence for compensation for stuttering by the right frontal operculum. *NeuroImage, 20,* 1356–1364.

Preibisch, C., Raab, O., Neumann, K., Euler, H.A., von Gudenberg, A.W., Gall, V., Lanfermann, H., & Zanella, F. (2003b). Event-related fMRI for the suppression of speech associated artifacts in stuttering. *NeuroImage, 19,* 1076–1084.

Preus, A. (1981). *Identifying Subgroups of Stuttering.* Oslo, Norway: Universitetsforlaget.

Preus, A. (1987). The cluttering type of stutterer. *Nordisk tidsskrft for logopedi og foniatr, 12,* 3-19.

Preus, A. (1989). Stammebehandling. *Nordisk tidsskrift for logopedi of foniatri, 14.*

Preus, A. (1992). Cluttering or stuttering: Related, different or antagonistic disorders. In F.L. Myers and K. O. St. Louis (Eds.), *Cluttering: A clinical perspective.* Kibworth: Far communications.

Preus, A. (1996). Cluttering upgraded. *Journal of Fluency Disorders, 21,* 349-358.

Prior, M. (1996). *Understanding Specific Learning Difficulties.* UK: Psychology Press, Hove.

Quesal, B. (2004). *Fluency and Fluency Disorders.* Stuttering course. Downloaded June 1, 2007. (www.mnsu.edu/comdis/kuster/StutteringCourseSyllabi/Quesal.html).

Raphael, L. J., Bakker, K., Myers, F. L., St. Louis, K. O., & Mac Roy, M. (2001). *Articulatory/acoustic features of DDKs in cluttered, tachylalic, and normal speech.* Paper presented at the Annual Convention of the American Speech-Language-Hearing Association, New Orleans, LA.

Rapoport, M., van Reekum, R., & Mayberg, M. D. (2000). The role of the cerebellum in cognition and behavior: A selective review. *The Journal of Neuropsychiatry and Clinical Neurosciences, 12,* 193-198.

Reichel, I. K. (2007). Emotional intelligence and stuttering intervention. 10th International Stuttering Awareness Day Online Conference, Minnesota State University, Mankato. For retrieval, http://www. mnsu.edu/comdis/isad10/papers/reichel10.html

Reichel, I. K. (2008). Speech upon presenting Deso Weiss award to Dr. Kenneth O. St. Louis. *The Bulgarian Journal of Communication Disorders 2*(2), 84-86.

Reichel, I. K. (2010). Treating the person who clutters and stutters. In K. Bakker, L. Raphael, & F. Myers, F. (Eds), *Proceedings of the First World Conference on Cluttering,* Katarino, Bulgaria, 2007 (pp. 99 -108).

Reichel, I. K. (July, 2011). Cluttering: Questions, Answers, Myths and Facts. Workshop. 28th Annual Conference of the National Stuttering Association, Fort Worth, Texas.

Reichel, I. K. (July, 2014). Cluttering management: Global challenges and successes. Seminar. 2nd World Conference on Cluttering. International Cluttering Association, Eindhoven, Netherlands.

Reichel, I., Ademola, G. S., Bakhtiar, M., Barrett, E., Bona, J., Busto-Marolt, L., Nanjaya, N. C., Diaz, C., Haj-Tas, M., Lilian, D., Makauskiene, M., Miyamoto, S., Shah, M., Touzet, B. B., Yasin, S. Frontiers of cluttering across continents: Research, clinical practices, self-help and professional preparation. *Perspectives on Global issues in Communication Sciences and Related Disorders 4*(2), 42-50.

Reichel, I. K., Bakker, K., & Myers, F. (2010) The worldwide panorama of cluttering: Non-Western countries. International Cluttering Online Conference, 2010. Minnesota State University, Mankato. For retrieval, http://www.mnsu.edu/comdis/ica1/papers/reichel1c.html

Reichel, I., Cook, S., Howell, P., Schnell, A., & van Zaalen, Y. (July 2014). Prevalence of cluttering: Pilot studies in three European countries. Poster. International Cluttering Association 2nd World Conference on Cluttering, Eindhoven, the Netherlands.

Reichel, I., & Draguns, J. (2011). International perspectives on perceiving, identifying, and managing cluttering. In D. Ward & K. Scaler Scott

(Eds.), *Cluttering: A handbook of research, intervention and education* (pp. 263-279). East Sussex: Psychology Press.

Reichel, I. K., & Ray, A. (2008). The ICA adopts the cluttering orphan. Perspectives on Fluency and Fluency Disorders, *American Speech-Language Hearing Association, 18*(2), 84-86.

Reichel, I. K., Scaler Scott, K., Myers, F., Bakker, K., van Zaalen, Y., de Touzet, B., Busto, L. M., Diaz, C. L., Lajos, P., Makauskiene, V., Miyamoto, S., Bona, J., Haj-Tas, M. A., Bakhtiar, M., Lilian, D., Shah, E., Barrett, H., Nanjaya, N., Kambanga, J. B., Yasin, S. A., & Ademola, G. S. (May, 2011). The rise of global collaboration in exploring cluttering. The 9th World Congress of People Who Stutter, International Stuttering Association. Buenos Aires, Argentina.

Reichel, I. K., Scaler Scott, K., & van Zaalen, Y. (November, 2012). Tribute to international partnership in research and education in cluttering. Seminar. American Speech-Language-Hearing Association Convention, Atlanta.

Reichel, I. K., Scaler Scott, K., van Zaalen, Y., van Borsel, J., Leahy, M., Ward, D., Sonsterud, H., Adams, C., St. Louis, K. O., & Ademola, G. (August, 2009). ICA seminar: Global Perspectives on Cluttering: Research, Assessment and Treatment. Sixth World Congress on Fluency Disorders, International Fluency Association. Rio de Janeiro, Brazil.

Reichel, I., Scaler Scott, K., van Zaalen, Y., St. Louis, K. O., Van Borsel, J., Leahy, M., Ward, D., Sonsterud, H., Adams, C., Ademola, G. (2013). ICA International mosaic on cluttering: Historic origins, research, assessment, and treatment. *Perspectives on Global issues in Communication Sciences and Related Disorders., 3 (1)*, 5-13.

Reichel, I., Scaler Scott, K., van Zaalen, Y., Touzet, B., Myers, F., Bakker, K., Miyamoto, S., Lajos, P., Makauskiene, V., Bona, J., Haj-Tas, M., Marolt, L. B., Diaz, C., Ademola, G. S., Bakhtiar, M., Lilian, D., Shah, E., Barrett, H., Nanjaya, N., Kambanga, J. B., Yasin, S. (July, 2012). International Cluttering Association forum: Outcomes of 5 Years of Successful Collaboration. Seminar. 7th World Congress on Fluency Disorders, International Fluency Association. Tours, France.

Reichel, I., & St. Louis, K. O. (2007). Mitigating negative stereotyping of stuttering in a fluency disorders class. In J. Au-Yeung & M. Leahy (Eds.), *Research, treatment, and self-help in fluency disorders: New horizons* (pp. 236 –244). International Fluency Association.

Reichel, I., St. Louis, K. O., & van Zaalen, Y. (September, 2013). Emotional intelligence training for speech- language pathologists. Seminar. 4th International Congress on Emotional Intelligence. New York, USA

Renfrew, C. (1997). *The Renfrew language scales: Bus story test, a test of narrative speech*, Speechmark.

Rieber, R. W., Breskin, S., & Jaffe, J. (1972). Pause time and phonation time in stuttering and cluttering. *Journal of Psycholinguistic Research, 1*, 149-154.

Rieder, K., & Rumler, A. (1990). Poltern. In H. Aschenbrenner & K. Rieder (Hrsg.) Sprachheilpëdagogische Praxis (2. überarb. und erw. Aufl., S 129). Wien: Jugend und Volk.

Riley, G. D. (1981). Stuttering Prediction Instrument for young children (SPI). Austin, TX: PRO-ED.

Riley, G.D. (2008). *Stuttering severity instrument for children and adults SSI-4* (3rd Ed.). Austin, TX: PRO-ED.

Riley, G. D., & Riley, J. (1985). *Oral Motor Assessment and treatment: Improving syllable production*. Austin: PRO-ED.

van Riper, C. (1970). Stuttering and cluttering. *Folia Phoniatrica, 22*, 347-353.

van Riper, C. (1982). *The nature of stuttering*. Englewood Cliffs, NJ: Prentice Hall.

Rondal, J. A. (2001). Language in mental retardation: Individual and syndromic differences, and neurogenitic variation. *Swiss Journal of Psychology, 60*, 161-178.

Sasisekaran, J., de Nil, L., Smyth, R., & Johnson, C. (2006). Phonological encoding in the silent speech of persons who stutter. *Journal of Fluency disorders, 31*, 1-21.

Scaler Scott, K. (2008). A comparison of disfluency and language in matched children with Asberger's disorder, children who stutter, and controls during an expository discourse task. Doctoral dissertation, University of Louisiana at Lafayette.

Scaler Scott, K. (2011). Cluttering and autism spectrum disorders. In D. Ward & K. Scaler Scott (Eds.), *Cluttering: A handbook of research, intervention and education* (pp. 115-133). East Sussex: Psychology Press.

Scaler Scott, K., (2012). Treatment techniques for children, teens, and adults with cluttering. Seminar presented at the 7th World Congress on Fluency Disorders, International Fluency Association. Tours, France.

Scaler Scott, K., & St. Louis, K. O. (2011). Self-help and support groups for people with cluttering. In D. Ward & K. Scaler Scott (Eds.), *Cluttering: A handbook of research, intervention and education* (pp. 211-229). East Sussex: Psychology Press.

Scaler Scott, K., Tetnowski, J. A., Roussel, N. C., & Flaitz, J.F. (2010). Impact of a pausing treatment strategy upon the speech of a clutterer-stutterer. In K. Bakker, L. Raphael, & F. Myers (Eds.), Proceedings of the First World Conference on Cluttering, Katarino, Bulgaria, pp 132-140.

Scaler Scott, K., & Ward, D. (2013). *Managing Cluttering: A comprehensive guidebook of activities*. Austin, TX: PRO-ED.

Scharfenaker, S., & Stackhouse, T. (2012). Strategies for day-to-day-life, National Fragile X Foundation, http://www.fragilex.org/2012/support-and-resources/strategies-for-day-to-day-life/.

Schlanger, B. B., & Gottsleben, R. H. (1957). Analysis of speech defects among the institutionalized mentally retarded. *Journal of Speech and Hearing Disorders, 22*, 98-103.

Schneider, D. J. (2004). *The psychology of stereotyping*. New York/London: Guilford.

Schnell, A., Abbink, M., & van Zaalen, Y. (2013). Poltern prevalence in Deutschland. Bachelor's thesis, Zuyd University of Applied Sciences, Netherlands.

Scott, K. S., Grossman, H. L., Abendroth, K. J., Tetnowski, J. A., & Damico, J. S. (2007). *Asperger syndrome and attention deficit disorder: Clinical disfluency analysis*. Proceedings of the Fifth World Congress on Fluency and Fluency Disorders in Dublin, Ireland.

Scripture, E. W. (1912). *Stuttering and lisping*, New York: Macmillan.

Seeman, M. (1965). *Sprachstorungen bei Kindern*. Berlin: Volk und Gesundheit, Berlin.

Seeman, M. (1970). Relation between motorics of speech and general motor ability in clutterers. *Folia Phoniatrica, 22*, 376-380.

Seeman, M. (1974). *Sprachstorungen bei Kindern*. Berlin: VEB Verlag Volk und Gesundheit.

Seeman, M., & Novak, A. (1963). *Ueber die Motorik bei poltern. Folia Phoniatrica, 15*, 170-176.

Shapiro, D. (2011). *Stuttering intervention: A collaborative journey to fluency freedom* (2d ed.). Austin, TX: PRO-ED.

Sheehan, J. G. (1975). Conflict theory and avoidance-reduction therapy. In J. Eisenson (Ed.), *Stuttering: A symposium*. New York: Harper and Row.

Shepherd, G. (1960). Studies in Tachyphemia: II. Phonetic description of cluttered speech. *Logos, 3*, 73-81.

Shields, L. (2010). Treating cluttered speech in a child with autism: Case study. Presentation at the Annual Convention of the American Speech-Language-Hearing Association, Philadelphia.

Shklovsky, V. M. (1994). Stuttering. Moscow (in Russian)

Shriberg, L. D. (2003). Diagnostic markers for child speech-sound disorders: Introductory comments. *Clinical Linguistics and Phonetics, 17*(7), 501-505.

Sick, U. (2004). *Poltern, Theoretische Grundlagen, Diagnostik, Therapie.* Stuttgart: Thieme.

Silverman, F. H. (1996). Cluttering (Tachyphemia). In F. H. Silverman, *Stuttering and Other Fluency Disorders* (pp. 211-219). Needham Heights, MA: Allyn and Bacon.

Simkins, L. (1973) Cluttering. In B. B. Lahey (Ed.), *The modification of language behavior* (pp. 178-217). Springfield, IL: Charles C. Thomas.

Smith, A., Goffman, L., Zelaznik. H. N., Ying, G., & McGillem, C. (1995). Spatiotemporal stability and patterning of speech movement sequences. Experimental Brain Research, 104, 493–501.

Sønsterud, H., Andrup, G. (2012). Motor control and speech - Is there a connection? Neuromotor examination of four individuals who clutter. Seminar. The 7th World Congress on Fluency Disorders, International Fluency Association. Tours, France.

Sønsterud, H., Heitmann, R. R., Kvenseth, H., & St. Louis, K. O. (2012). Public attitudes toward cluttering and/or stuttering in three regions of Norway. Poster. The 7th World Congress on Fluency Disorders, International Fluency Association. Tours, France.

Stang, H. M. (1984). *Glichkeiten der Behandlung polternder Kinder. Die Sprachheilarbeit, 29,* 255-264.

Stansfield, J. (1990). Prevalence of stuttering and cluttering in adults with mental handicaps. *J Ment Defic Res 34* (Pt 4), 287-307.

Starkweather, C. W. (1987). *Fluency and stuttering*. Englewood Cliffs, NJ: Prentice-Hall.

St. Louis, K.O. (Ed.) (1986). *The Atypical stutterer: Principles and practices of rehabilitation*. Orlando, FL: Academic Press.

St. Louis, K.O. (1991). A successful approach to cluttering. In L. Rustin (Guest Ed.). Clinical focus: Dysfluency. *Human Communication 1*, 20-21.

St. Louis, K. O. (1992). On defining cluttering. In F. L. Myers & K. O. St. Louis (Eds.), *Cluttering: A clinical perspective* (pp. 37-53). Kibworth, Great Britain: Far Communications. Reissued in 1996 by Singular, San Diego, CA.

St. Louis, K. O. (1996a). A tabular summary of cluttering subjects in the special edition. *Journal of Fluency Disorders, 21*, 337-344.

St. Louis, K. O. (1996b). Purpose and Organization of the Special Edition on Cluttering. *Journal of Fluency Disorders, 21*, 171-174.

St. Louis, K. O. (Ed.) (1996c). Research and opinion on cluttering: State of the art and science (Special Edition), *Journal of Fluency Disorders, 21*, 171-173.

St. Louis, K. O. (1998). *Cluttering: Some guidelines*. Memphis, TN: Stuttering Foundation of America. (Brochure: On-line at www.stuttersfa.org/brochures/br_clutt.htm).

St. Louis, K. O. (2000). Cluttering. In C. R. Reynolds & E. Fletcher-Jantzen (Eds.). *Encyclopedia of special education*. New York: John Wiley & Sons.

St. Louis, K. O. (2001). *Living with stuttering: Stories, basics, resources, and hope*. Morgantown, WV: Populore.

St. Louis, K. O. (2011). International project on attitudes toward human attributes (IPATHA). Morgantown, WV: Populore., retrieved at http://www.stutteringattitudes.com

St. Louis, K. O., & Daly, D. (1995). Cluttering: Past, present and future. In C. W. Starkweather & H. F. M. Peters (Eds.), *Stuttering: Proceedings of the First World Congress on fluency disorders*. The International Fluency Association, pp. 659-662.

St. Louis, K. O., Filatova, Y., Coşkun, M., Topbaş, S., Ozdemir, S., Georgieva, D., McCaffrey, E., & George, R. D. (2010). Identification of cluttering and stuttering by the public in four countries. *International Journal of Speech-Language Pathology, 12*, 508-519.

St. Louis, K. O., Filatova, Y., Coşkun, M., Topbaş, S., Ozdemir, S., Georgieva, D., McCaffrey, E., & George, R. D. (2011). Public attitudes toward cluttering. In E. L. Simon (Ed.), *Psychology of stereotypes* (pp. 81-113). Hauppauge, NY: Nova Science Publishers.

St. Louis, K.O., & Hinzman, A. R. (1986). Studies of cluttering: Perceptions of cluttering by speech-language pathologists and educators. *Journal of Fluency Disorders, 11*, 131-149.

St. Louis, K. O., Hinzman, A. R., & Hull, F. M. (1985). Studies of cluttering: Disfluency and language measures in young possible clutterers and stutterers. *Journal of Fluency Disorders, 10*, 151-172.

St. Louis, K. O., & McCaffrey, E. (November 2005). *Public Awareness of Cluttering and Stuttering: Preliminary Results*. Poster Presented at the 2005 ASHA Convention, San Diego, CA.

St. Louis, K.O., & Myers, F. L. (1995). Clinical management of cluttering, *Language, Speech, and Hearing Services in the Schools, 26*, 187-194.

St. Louis, K.O., and Myers, F. L. (1997). Management of cluttering and related fluency disorders. In R. Curlee & G. Siegel (Eds.), *Nature and Treatment of Stuttering: New Directions* (pp. 313-332). New York: Allyn & Bacon.

St. Louis, K. O., & Myers, F. L. (1998). A synopsis of cluttering and its treatment. Paper presented at the International Stuttering Awareness Day On-Line Conference. www.mankato.msus.edu/dept/comdis/isad/isadcon.html.

St. Louis, K. O., Myers, F. L., Bakker, K., & Raphael, L. J. (2007). In E. Conture & R. Curlee (Eds.), *Stuttering and Other Fluency Disorders* (3rd ed.). Philadelphia, PA: Thieme Medical.

St. Louis, K., Myers, F., Cassidy, L., Michael, A., Penrod, S., Litton, B., Olivera, J., and Brodsky, E. (1996). Efficacy of delayed auditory feedback for treating cluttering: Two case studies. *Journal of Fluency Disorders 21*, 305-314.

St. Louis, K. O., Myers F. L., Faragasso K., Townsend, P. S., & Gallaher, A. J. (2004). Perceptual aspects of cluttered speech. *Journal of Fluency Disorders, 29*, 213-235.

St. Louis, K. O., Raphael, L. J., Myers, F. L., and Bakker, K. (2003). Cluttering Updated. *The ASHA Leader, 18*, 4-5, 20-22.

St. Louis, K. O., & Rustin, L. (1992). Professional awareness of cluttering. In F. L. Myers & K. O. St. Louis (eds.), *Cluttering: A clinical perspective* (pp. 23-35). Leicester: Far Communications. Reissued: San Diego, CA: Singular, 1996.

St. Louis, K. O., & Schulte, K. (2011). Defining cluttering: The lowest common denominator. In D. Ward & K. Scaler Scott (Eds.), *Cluttering: A handbook of research, intervention and education* (pp. 233-253). East Sussex: Psychology Press.

St. Louis, K. O., Sønsterud, H., Heitmann, R. R., Kvenseth, H., Flobakk, C., & Helmen, L. N. (2012). Identification of cluttering and/or stuttering by the public in three regions of Norway. Seminar. The 7th World Congress on Fluency Disorders, International Fluency Association. Tours, France.

Stourneras, E. F. (1980). *Stotteren bij kinderen*. In C. H. Waar (Ed.), *Stem-, Spraak- en Taalstoornissen bij kinderen* (pp. 65-95). Alphen a/d Rijn: Stafleu's Wetenschappelijke Uitgeversmaatschappij.

Sturm, J. S., & Seery, C. H. (2007). Speech and articulatory rates of school-age children in conversation and narrative contexts, University of

Wisconsin–Milwaukee. *Language, Speech, and Hearing Services in Schools, 38,* 47-59.

Teigland, A. (1996). A study of pragmatic skills of clutterers and normal speakers, *Journal of Fluency Disorders, 21,* 201-214.

Tetnowski, J. A., & Douglass, J. (2011). Cluttering in the academic curriculum. In D. Ward & K. Scaler Scott (Eds.), *Cluttering: A handbook of research, intervention and education* (pp. 280-296). East Sussex: Psychology Press (2011).

Thacker, A., & Austen, S. (1996). Cluttered Communication in a Deafened Adult with Autistic Features, *Journal of Fluency Disorders, 21,* 271-279.

Thacker, R., & De Nil, L. (1996). Neurogenic cluttering. *Journal of Fluency Disorders, 21,* 227-238.

Tiger, R. J., Irvine, T. L., & Reis, R. P. (1980). Cluttering as a complex of learning disabilities. *Language, Speech and Hearing Services in Schools, 11,* 3-14.

Verhoeven, J., Pauw, G., & Kloots, H. (2004). Speech rate in a pluricentric language: A comparison between Dutch in Belgium and the Netherlands. *Language and Speech, 47,* 297-308.

Voelker, C. H. (1935). The Prevention of Cluttering, *The English Journal, 24,* 808-810.

Volker, G., & Giraud, A. L. (2005). Cortical plasticity associated with stuttering therapy. *Journal of Fluency Disorders, 30,* 23–39.

Vygotsky, L. (1986). *Thought and language* (rev. ed.). Cambridge, MA: The MIT Press.

Walker, J. F., Archibald, L. M. D., Chemiak, S. A., & Fish, V. G. (1992). Articulation rate in 3 and 5 year old children. *Journal of Speech and Hearing Research, 35,* 4-13.

Wallen, M., Bonney M. A, & Lennox, L. (1996). Handwriting speed test. *Australian Occupational Therapy Journal, 53*, 141.

Ward, D. (2004). Cluttering, speech rate and linguistic deficit: Case report. In A. Packman, A. Meltzer, & H. F. M. Peters (Eds.), *Theory, research and therapy in fluency disorders* (pp. 511-516). Proceedings of the 4th World Congress on Fluency Disorders, Montreal, Canada, Nijmegen: Nijmegen University Press.

Ward, D. (2006). *Stuttering and cluttering, Framework for understanding and treatment.* East Sussex: Psychology Press.

Ward, D. (2010). Stuttering and normal nonfluency: Cluttering spectrum behaviour as a functional descriptor of abnormal nonfluency. In Proceedings of the First World Conference on Cluttering, May 12-14, 2007, Katarino: Bulgaria.

Ward, D. (2011a). Scope and constraint in the diagnosis of cluttering: Combining two perspectives. In D. Ward, & K. Scaler Scott (Eds.), *Cluttering: A handbook of research, intervention and education.* 254-263. East Sussex: Psychology Press.

Ward, D. (2011b). Motor speech control and cluttering. In D. Ward, & K. Scaler Scott (Eds.), *Cluttering: A handbook of research, intervention and education* (pp. 34-44)..East Sussex: Psychology Press.

Ward, D., & Scaler Scott, K. (2011). *Cluttering: A handbook of research, intervention and education.* East Sussex: Psychology Press.

Watkins, K. E., Smith, S. M., Davis, S., & Howell, P. (2008). Structural and functional abnormalities of the motor system in developmental stuttering. *Brain, 131*, 50-59.

Watzlawick, P., Bavin, J. H., & Jackson, D. D. (1970). *De pragmatische aspecten van de menselijke communicatie.* Deventer: Van Loghum Slaterus.

Weiss, D. A. (1964). *Cluttering.* Englewood Cliffs, NJ: Prentice-Hall.

Weiss, D. A. (1967). Similarities and differences between stuttering and cluttering. *Folia Phoniatrica, 19*, 98-104.

Weiss, D. A. (1968). Cluttering: Central language imbalance. *Pediatric Clinics of North America,* 15, 705-720.

Weiss, M. G., & Ramakrishna, J. (2006). Stigma interventions and research for international health. *The Lancet, 367*, 536-538.

WHO (2007). *International Classification of Functioning, Disability and Health (ICF).* www.who.int/classifications/icf/en.

Wigg, E. H., & Semel, E. M. (1984). *Language Assessment and Intervention for the Learning Disabled* (2nd ed.), Columbus, OH: Charles E. Merrill.

Wilder, D. (1993). Affect, arousal, and stereotyping. In D. M. Mackie & D. L. Hamilton (Eds.), *Affect, cognition, and stereotyping: Interactive processes in group perception* (pp. 87–109). San Diego: Academic Press / Harcourt Brace, Jovanovich.

Williams, D., & Wener, D. L. (1996). Cluttering and stuttering exhibited in a young professional. *Journal of Fluency Disorders,* 21, 261-270.

Winkelman, C. L. (1990). Broddelen. In W. M. Mensink-Ypma, *Broddelen en Leerstoornissen.* Utrecht: Bohn, Scheltema & Holkema.

Winkelman, C. L. (1993). Broddelen, een verborgen stoornis. *Logopedie en foniatrie,* 6, 175-179.

Winkelman, C. L. (2006). Terugrekenoefening. In B. W. Bezemer, J. Bouwen, & C. Winkelman, *Stotteren van theorie naar therapie* (pp. 320-321). Bussum: Uitgeverij Coutinho.

Wolk, L. (1986). Cluttering: A diagnostic case report. *British Journal of Disorders of Communication,* 2, 199-207.

Woolf, G. (1967). The assessment of stuttering as struggle, avoidance and expectancy. *British Journal of Disorders of Communication,* 2, 158-171.

Wright, L., & Ayre, A. (2000). *WASSP: the Wright and Ayre stuttering selfrating profile.* Bicester: Winslow.

Yairi, E., & Ambrose, N. (2005). *Early Childhood Stuttering.* Austin: Pro Ed.

Yaruss, S., Logan, K., & Conture, E. (1994). Speaking rate and diadochokinetic abilities of children who stutter. *Journal of Fluency Disorders, 19,* 221-222.

Yaruss, S., & Quesal, R. (2010). Overall assessment of the speaker's experience of stuttering: Documenting multiple outcomes in stuttering treatment. *Journal of Fluency Disorders, 31,* 90-115.

van Zaalen, Y. (2007). Articulatory rate and accuracy in stuttering and cluttering. Proceedings of the First World Conference on Cluttering. Katarino, Bulgaria, 199-205

van Zaalen, Y. (2007). Differential diagnostic between cluttering and stuttering. Implications for treatment. Paper presented at the 27th World Congress of the International Association of Logopedics and Phoniatrics, Denmark, Goteborg.

van Zaalen, Y. (May, 2008a). Differential diagnostics in cluttering, stuttering and learning disabilities. Kolloquium, Universität Aachen, Germany.

van Zaalen, Y. (May, 2008b). Putting cluttering on the map. Workshop presented at the University of Blagoevgrad, Bulgaria.

van Zaalen, Y. (2009). *Cluttering identified. Differential diagnostics between cluttering, stuttering, and learning disability.* Ph.D. thesis, Utrecht, Zuidam.

van Zaalen, Y. (2010). Assessment of reading and writing: Consequences for speech therapy in fluency disorders. Paper presented at the ECSF, 2010, Antwerp, Belgium.

van Zaalen, Y. (2010). Cluttering: A Language based Fluency Disorder. Paper and seminar presented at Intensive Programme, Belgium, KHBO, Brugge.

van Zaalen Y. (2010). Cluttering and stuttering: Disfluency, reading, and writing. Paper presented at the European Symposium on Fluency Disorders, Antwerp, Belgium.

van Zaalen Y. (2010). The defective language automation hypothesis in cluttering. Paper presented at the European Symposium on Fluency Disorders, Antwerp, Belgium.

van Zaalen, Y. (2010). Is cluttering a language based fluency disorder?, Proceedings of the 2010 IALP Conference in Athens, pp. 492-498.

van Zaalen, Y. (2010). Speech motor control on word level. Paper presented at 7th CPLOL Congress, Ljubljana, Slovenia.

van Zaalen, Y. (2010). *Stotteren en broddelen: Niet-vloeiendheid, lezen en schrivjven.* Paper presented at the Simea Congress, 2010, Lunteren.

van Zaalen, Y. (2011). Differential diagnostics between cluttering and stuttering, how to do it. Workshop presented at the 9th Oxford Disfluency Conference, Oxford, United Kingdom.

van Zaalen, Y., (2012). Is cluttering a language based fluency disorder? Proceedings of the International Conference on Stuttering, pp. 29-35. Rome, Italy

van Zaalen, Y. (2012). Cluttering understood. Paper presented at the ECSF Conference on Fluency Disorders, Antwerp, Belgium.

van Zaalen, Y. (2012). Differential diagnostics between cluttering and stuttering; How you do it. Seminar. The 7th World Congress on Fluency Disorders, International Fluency Association. Tours, France.

van Zaalen, Y., Abbink, M., & Dejonckere, P. (2012). *Is broddelen een op taal gebaseerde vloeiendheidsstoornis? Tijdschrift Logopedie Vlaamse Vereniging van Logopedisten.*

van Zaalen, Y., & Bochane, M. (2007). "The Wallet story," Paper presented at the 27th World Congress of the International Association of Logopedics and Phoniatrics, Denmark, Goteborg Proceedings, p. 85.

van Zaalen, Y., Cook, S., Elings, J., & Howell, P. (2011). Screening Phonological Accuracy, effects of articulatory rate on phonological encoding. Poster presented at the 2011 Speech Motor Conference, Groningen, the Netherlands.

van Zaalen, Y., Deckers, S., Dirven, C., Kaiser, C., van Kemenade, P., & Terhoeve, A. (2012). Prevalence of cluttering in a school-aged population. Seminar. The 7th World Congress on Fluency Disorders, International Fluency Association. Tours, France.

van Zaalen, Y., & Dejonckere, P. H. (2010). Cluttering a language based fluency disorder. Paper presented at the first online conference on cluttering.

van Zaalen, Y., & van Heeswijk, E. (2012). Linguistic disfluencies in persons with cluttering. Paper presented at the ECSF Conference on Fluency Disorders, Antwerp, Belgium.

van Zaalen, Y., & van Heeswijk, E. (2012). Linguistic fluency in narration of persons with cluttering. Paper presented at the 2012 European CPLOL Congress, The Hague, The Netherlands.

van Zaalen, Y., & van Heeswijk, E. (2012). Linguistic fluency in narrative tasks of persons with cluttering. Seminar. The 7th World Congress on Fluency Disorders, International Fluency Association. Tours, France.

van Zaalen, Y., van Heeswijk, E., & Reichel, I. Linguistic fluency in narrative tasks of persons with cluttering (in preparation).

van Zaalen, Y., Myers, F., Ward, D., & Bennet, E. (2008). The cluttering assessment protocol. Retrieved at http://associations.missouristate.edu/ICA/.

van Zaalen, Y., & Reichel, I. K. (2011). Assessment of the cluttering component in stuttering, One Day Workshop presented at Touro College, New York, USA.

van Zaalen, Y., & Reichel, I. K. (2011). The cluttering component in stuttering. Workshop presented at the 9th World Congress of People

Who Stutter. International Stuttering Association. Buenos Aires, Argentina.

van Zaalen, Y., & Reichel, I. K. (May 2014). Prevalence of Cluttering in European adolescents and young adults. Poster. Touro Research Day, New York, USA.

van Zaalen, Y., & Reichel, I. (2014) Cluttering treatment: Theoretical considerations and intervention planning. *Perspectives on Global issues in Communication Sciences and Related Disorders* 4(2), 57-62.

van Zaalen, Y., & Reichel, I. (2013). Qu'est-ce que le bredouillement? Pistes pour l'intervention orthophonique. Reeducation Orthophonique. 256, 119—153 (in French).

van Zaalen, Y., & van Wanseele, B. (2012). Cluttering and Parkinson: Kinematic similarities and differences. Paper presented at the European CPLOL Congress, the Hague, Netherlands.

van Zaalen, Y., van Wanseele, B., Vos, A., van Hoeve, F., & Scheepens, L. (2012). Cluttering and Parkinson: Kinematic similarities and differences. Poster. The 7th World Congress on Fluency Disorders, International Fluency Association. Tours, France.

van Zaalen, Y., Ward, D., Nederveen, A. J., Lameris, J. L., Wijnen, F., & Dejonckere, P. H. (2009). Cluttering and stuttering: Different disorders and differing functional neurologies. Paper presented at the 6th World Congress on Fluency Disorders, Rio de Janeiro

van Zaalen, Y., Wijnen, F., & Dejonckere, P. H. (2009a). A test of speech motor control on word level productions: The SPA Test (Dutch: Screening Pittige Articulatie) - *International Journal of Speech and Language Pathology, 11*(1), 26-33.

van Zaalen, Y., Wijnen, F., & Dejonckere, P. H. (2009b). Language planning disturbances in children who clutter or have learning disabilities, *International Journal of Speech and Language Pathology, 11*(6), 496-508.

van Zaalen, Y., Wijnen, F., & Dejonckere, P. H. (2009c). Differential diagnostics between cluttering and stuttering. *Journal of Fluency Disorders, 34*(3), 137-154.

van Zaalen, Y., Wijnen, F., & Dejonckere, P. H. (2009d). The Predictive Cluttering Inventory- Dutch revised, part two. *Journal of Fluency Disorders, 34*(3), 147-154.

van Zaalen, Y., Wijnen, F., & Dejonckere, P. H. (2011a). Cluttering and learning disability. In D. Ward & K. Scaler Scott (Eds.), *Cluttering: A handbook of research, intervention and education* (pp. 100-14). East Sussex, Psychology Press.

van Zaalen, Y., Wijnen, F., & Dejonckere, P. H. (2011b). Cluttering Assessment: Rationale, tasks and interpretation. In D. Ward & K. Scaler Scott (Eds.), *Cluttering, A handbook of research, intervention and education* (pp. 137-51). East Sussex: Psychology Press.

van Zaalen, Y., & Winkelman, C. (2009). *Broddelen, een (on) begrepen stoornis. Bussum: Coutinho.*

Zajac, D. J., Harris, A. A., Roberts, J. E., & Martin, G. E. (2009). Direct Magnitude Estimation of Articulation Rate in Boys With Fragile X Syndrome. *Journal of Speech, Language, and Hearing Research, 52,* 1370–1379.

Zemlin, W. R., Daniloff, R. G., & Shriner, T. H. (1968). Difficulty of listening to time-compressed speech. *Journal of Speech and Hearing Research 11,* 875-881.

Zonneveld, W., Quené, H. & Heeren, W.F.L. (2011). *Sound and sounds, Studies presented to M. E. H. (Bert) Schouten on the occasion of his 65th birthday.* Utrecht: UiL-OTS, pp. 161-171.

Zylom (2012). Mirror magic.www.zylom.com/nl/gratis-online-spelletjes/ zoek-en-vind-spellen classic games/

INDEX

A

ABCD. *See* Arizona Battery for
Communication Disorders of
Dementia test
ACC. *See* Anterior cingulate cortex
Accent Method, 138
Acoustic phonetic processing, 37
ADD, 90, 108–9
ADHD. *See* Attention deficit
hyperactivity disorder
Adolescence, 22–25, 61, 69, 80
Adolescents
cluttering, 20
self-image development, 60–61
speech rate, 24
stuttering, 17
Adults
reading text, 211–12
speech rate reduction, 24
Age
articulatory rate in the elderly, 25
speech rates and, 62
Alertness, 161
Analysis of disfluencies, 191–94
Analogue communication, 123
Anterior cingulate cortex (ACC), 21
Antidepressants, 68
AR. *See* Articulatory rate
Arizona Battery for Communication
Disorders of Dementia test
(ABCD), 83
Articulation, 6, 21, 35, 41, 76–77,
103, 106, 121, 164, 172
Articulator, 37
Articulatory rate (AR), 12–13, 37,
77, 173
assessment form, 196
determination, 13–15

diagnostic exercise, 139–42
elderly, 25
speech rate, versus, 46
syllables per second in children, 23
versus speech rate, 46
Articulatory variability,104
ASDs. *See* Autism spectrum disorders
Assessment, 16, 65–71, 73–79, 91
Assessment form(s)
analysis of spontaneous speech,
reading and retelling,
191–94
articulatory rate, 196
Brief Cluttering and Stuttering
Questionnaire, (BCSQ)
209–10
percentage of normal
and stuttering-like
disfluencies, 194
protocol for differential
diagnosis of fluency
disorders, 204–5
retelling a story, 199–200
scoring form for oral-motor
assessment scale, 207–8
screening phonological accuracy,
202–3
self-evaluation of speech, 215
Speech Situation Checklist,
226–28
Attention, 35, 118
concentration and, 57–58
types, 144
Attention deficit hyperactivity
disorder (ADHD), 61
differential diagnosis, 90, 97,
108–9
Attitude(s), 39–41, 120
Audio-visual feedback, 157, 171

prevalence of cluttering in family
members, 20
speech or language problems, 7
Fast rate. *See* Rate
Fear
of communication, 39
of sounds, 39
of speech, 95
of words, 95
Feedback loop, 160–70
auditory and syllable structure
awareness, 170–71
communication pragmatics,
181–82
goals of, 152
levels of language complexity,
178–81
melody and prosody, 177–78
pauses, 175–77
role of environment in
identification, 161–62
speech rate reduction, 171–74
speech rhythm, 175
word structure and syllable
awareness, 171
Feelings, 25, 40, 77, 88, 117, 119,
121, 125, 218
FFS. *See* Flexible Fluency Search
Flexible Fluency Search (FFS), 151
Fluency, 3, 73
protocol for differential
diagnosis of, 204–5
Fluency Assessment Battery, 5, 65–
66, 71, 76–80, 125, 135
analysis of disfluencies, 79–80
analysis of recordings and
questionnaires, 76–77
forms, 82
mean articulatory rate, 77–79

Fluency disorder(s), xiii. *See also*
Cluttering; Stuttering
language-based, xvi
Formulator, 36–37
Four-component model, 37–39
cluttering therapy, 117–26
cognitive component, 117–19
communicative component,
123–24
emotional component, 119–21
exercise hierarchy, 124–25
intensity of the treatment,
125–26
therapeutic considerations, 124
verbal-motor component, 121–23
Fragile X syndrome (FXS), 61
differential diagnosis, 106–7
Frequency Altered Auditory Feedback
(FAF), 173
Frequency of disfluencies, 12, 51, 52,
79, 93, 100, 108, 193
Frontal cortex, 21
Fun photo, 179
FXS. *See* Fragile X syndrome

G

Gilles de la Tourette syndrome (TS),
differential diagnosis, 107
Grammatical
construction, 103, 143
encoding, xvi
errors, 98–100

H

Habituation, 118–19
HAF. *See* Heightened auditory
feedback

L

Language, 7. *See also* Linguistic
  disfluency model; Linguistics
  complexity, levels of, 178-81
  development, 7-8, 50
  developmental disorder, 123
  differential diagnosis of specific
    impairment, 102-3
  dissociation between rate and
    language formulation, 69
  family history of problems with, 7
  formulation, 12, 21, 31, 33-36,
    57, 73, 83, 102, 167
  levels of complexity, 178-81
  production, 31-33, 35-37, 66, 160
  words for cluttering, 11
Language automatization
  deficit model, 31-32
  dissynchrony, 33-35
Language planning disturbances, 4-5
Language production, 4
  monitoring, 36
Learning
  difficulties
  disabilities
    differential diagnosis for, 97,
      98-100
    speech and, xv
  effect, 81
Levelt's model of language
  production, 33, 36, 136
Levodopa, 68
Linguistic
  complexity, 15, 92, 102, 148, 191
  disfluency model, 30, 31
  factors, 59
  word form, 78

Linguistics. *See also* Language
  skills, 75
  speech rate and, 59
Listening, 55-56
Locus of control, 126, 132, 138-39, 155

M

Main issues, 100
Maintenance of skills, 146-47, 182
Manic depression, 61
MAR. *See* Mean articulatory rate
Math-related exercises, 142-44
Mean articulatory rate (MAR), 77-79
  example, 195-97
Measurable, 130
Medications, 68-69
Melodic
  intonation therapy, 177
  patterns, 52-54
  monotony, 166
Melody, 166, 177-78
Memory, retelling a memorized story,
  83-84, 198-200
Model of language production, 31, 33
Models
  Explanatory, 29
  four-component, 37-39, 117-26
  International Classification of
    Functioning model, 29
  language automatization deficit
    model, 31-32
  language production, 31, 33
  Levelt's, 33, 36, 136
  linguistic disfluency, 30, 31
  Stourneras' four component,
    37-39
Modification, 115, 122, 150
Monotony, 53

THE AUTHORS

About the authors

Dr. Yvonne van Zaalen is a researcher, clinician and in-demand speaker, whose ideas about the nature of cluttering, its differential diagnosis and treatment have made her one of the world's leading experts in fluency disorders. As associate professor and the Chair of Health Innovations and Technologies at Fontys University, Eindhoven, Netherlands, she is responsible for scientific research and education regarding the production of speech and language processes in (dis)fluent speech of normal speakers and people with intellectual disability. As a senior fluency specialist, Dr. van Zaalen has more than 25 years of experience working with people with cluttering and stuttering. She is the president of the International Cluttering Association. Dr. van Zaalen was presented with the Deso Weiss Award, sponsored by the Stuttering Foundation of America.

Dr. Isabella Reichel is an associate professor at the Graduate Program in Speech and Language Pathology, Touro College, New York, USA. She has specialized in the treatment of stuttering and cluttering for over three decades. In her capacity as the chair of the Committee of the International Representatives of the International Cluttering Association, Dr. Reichel coordinates multinational collaborative initiatives in research, publications, and seminars at conferences. She is one of the few educators in North America who routinely teaches a graduate course in cluttering.